New German Film

New German Film | The Displaced Image

Revised Edition

T I M O T H Y   C O R R I G A N

Indiana University Press   Bloomington and Indianapolis

First published by the University of Texas Press, 1983

The paper used in this publication meets the minimum requirements of American National
Standard for Information Sciences—Permanence of Paper for Printed Library Materials,
ANSI Z39.48-1984.

Manufactured in the United States of America

Library of Congress Cataloging-in-Publication Data

Corrigan, Timothy.
    New German film : the displaced image / Timothy Corrigan. — Rev.
ed.
       p. cm.
    Includes bibliographical references, filmography, and index.
    ISBN 0-253-31439-9. — ISBN 0-253-20841-6 (pbk.)
      1. Motion pictures—Germany (West)   2. Motion picture plays—
History and criticism.   I. Title.
PN1993.5.G3C67   1994
791.43'75'0943—dc20

                                                           93-4971

1 2 3 4 5   99 98 97 96 95 94

For Marcia Ferguson

Und wir: Zuschauer, immer, überall,

. . . .

Wer hat uns also umgedreht, daß wir,
was wir auch tun, in jener Haltung sind
von einem, welcher fortgeht?

Rainer Maria Rilke

And we, spectators always, everywhere,

. . . .

Who's turned us round like this, so that we always,
do what we may, retain the attitude
of someone who's departing?

Rainer Maria Rilke

Contents

NOTE TO THE REVISED EDITION   xi

ACKNOWLEDGMENTS   xiii

INTRODUCTION: MANIFESTOS AND METHODS   xv

1. A History, a Cinema: Hollywood, Audience Codes, and the
   New German Cinema   I

2. Wenders's *Kings of the Road*: The Voyage from Desire to Language   19

3. Transformations in Fassbinder's *Bitter Tears of Petra von Kant*   33

4. Types of History: Schlöndorff's *Coup de Grâce*   55

5. The Charge of Translation: Handke's *The Left-Handed Woman*   75

6. The Semantics of Security in Kluge's *Strongman Ferdinand*   89

7. Sander's *The All Round Reduced Personality—Redupers*: A Depth
   of Differences   III

8. The Original Tradition: Hypnotic Space in Herzog's *The Mystery
   of Kaspar Hauser*   127

9. The Exorcism of the Image: Syberberg's *Hitler, A Film from Germany*   147

10. Schroeter's *Willow Springs* and the Excesses of History   169

CONCLUSION: OTHER COURSES IN TIME   185

NOTES   193

FILMOGRAPHY   207

BIBLIOGRAPHY   213

INDEX   221

"Postwar Germany: a divided image" (*The American Friend*).

Note to the Revised Edition

The problems and advantages of any study of contemporary culture, such as this one, are that to give itself definition it must take shape within a fairly demarcated critical field and that, because its materials are still very much in flux, it subsequently risks missing developments and questions that are outside its necessarily limited historical perspective.

With the first edition of this work, the problems were most especially ones of omission and of a still-developing critical and historical assessment. Important films and filmmakers are, unfortunately, always missed when writing to the moment; and more recent research and writing has highlighted trends and positions whose full significance was not fully visible in the late 1970s. To the extent a revision allows, this expanded edition attempts to take advantage of the expanding perspective on the New German Cinema and to fill some of those gaps with three new chapters and a revised introduction and conclusion. In this regard, I wish to thank the editors of *Film Quarterly* and *Discourse* for permission to use material I published in those journals after the first publication of this book. I am also grateful to Eric Rentschler and Routledge for allowing me to adapt an essay which first appeared in *German Literature and Film: Adaptations and Transformations*.

There remain, however, productive advantages in the original approach of this study: its basic premise, about the dialogic engagement of the New German Cinema and Hollywood, seems more clearly fundamental to this group of films than ever before, even if it now often serves as a background to highlight the various resistances, the different strategies, and the inevitable failures it promoted. I also stand by my concentration on specific texts and canonical directors, even while I am fully aware of its tendency to pass over (for example) more experimental figures such as Herbert Achternbusch and many of the extraordinary women filmmakers in Germany. This framework was never intended to be representative of a particular hierarchy or a full assessment of possibilities within contemporary German cinema. Despite its de-emphasis of some historical and cultural detail, its textual focus underlines that cultural and personal meanings, as they are communicated through the cinema and through different social institutions, are also a highly commercial and materially particular affair. Certain filmmakers are able to create and market themselves and their talents as a constellation of meanings; certain films have generated images, sounds, and meanings that work and provoke a spectator in precise ways that need detailed expositions. As viewers and cultural critics, we may rightly attend to the larger institutional and historical pressures that lend movies meaning, yet, even acknowledging the complexity of a varied historical period such as contemporary Germany's, this book—usefully, I believe—stresses the productive value and pleasure of looking at individual films as a distillation and processing of those complexities.

Acknowledgments

The real reward in writing this book has been the many encounters and conversations it has made possible. In this way, all of the following individuals have become — perhaps unwittingly — an important part of this study: Jordan Arenson, Bertrand Augst, Raymond Bellour, Charles Burkhart, Robert Buttel, Terrence Corrigan, and our always interested parents, Bernard Eisenschitz, Laura Ferguson, Dalia Judovitz, Jeannette Karaska, Thomas Kavanagh, Thierry Kuntzel, Claudia Lenssen, Monica Letzring, Judith Mayne, Tim O'Malley, Ruth Perlmutter, Nora Pomerantz, Don Rackin, Ingrid Scheib-Rothbart, Anne Schotter, Kay Smith, Robert Storey, Mary Sweeney, William Van Wert, Marc Vernet, Alan Wilde, and Steve Zelnick.

More particularly, David Cook first introduced me to film studies and had been an advisor and friend throughout the many years since then. Temple University provided crucial assistance in two ways: through two Summer Research Fellowships and through the intelligent and patient participation of my students in several German film courses. The great majority of this manuscript was written at the Connecticut home of Carr and Marian Ferguson, where they, their wildly extended family, and the irrepressible Gog created "a gay tournamonde as of a single world," a climate for imaginative thought. Susan Stewart and Alan Singer will always, I hope, be my touchstones as critical readers, pals, and colleagues in the confusion of the stars; and Suzanne Comer has been a rare kind of editor, combining rigor with a real appreciation of German films. I doubtless owe my largest debt, however, to Eric Rentschler and Miriam Hansen. Both have willingly shared so much of their broad knowledge of modern German cinema that it is difficult to imagine this book without their advice; they have been generous, demanding, and humane scholars in every sense.

Finally, I wish to thank Marcia Ferguson not just for our many dialogues and arguments about film (and this book specifically) — but mostly for a sense that these dialogues will continue.

Several sections of this study originally appeared in journals whose editors I gratefully acknowledge here: part of chapter 1 in *Quarterly Review of Film Studies* (Spring 1980); chapter 2 in *New German Critique* (Fall/Winter 1981–82); part of the conclusion in *Discourse* (1981). I am also grateful to the following distributors for help in acquiring stills and for making these films available to the American public: Grey City Inc. (*Kings of the Road*), New Yorker Films (*The Bitter Tears of Petra von Kant*, *The American Friend*), Almi Cinema 5 (*Coup de Grâce*, *The Mystery of Kaspar Hauser*), Liberty Films (*Strongman Ferdinand*), Zoetrope Studios (*Hitler, A Film from Germany*), Pacific Film Archive (*Willow Springs*), and New Line Cinema (*Germany in Autumn*).

Introduction: Manifestos and Methods

The parameters of this study are two collective statements made by West German filmmakers within a period of fifteen years of each other: the celebrated manifesto issued at Oberhausen in February 1962 and the extraordinary *Germany in Autumn*, a film made by multiple teams of directors and technicians in late 1977.[1] That these two documents together describe symbolic poles for the central years of what is commonly called the New German Cinema is obviously significant.[2] In terms of my investigation here, several other aesthetic and cultural indicators implicit in the two gestures are equally important.

(1) They are both *collective* reactions to an established system, and as such they dramatize a cultural process especially true of the cinema: that artistic change and revolution must be collective if they are to be in any degree effective. Contrary to popular opinion, the New German Cinema is not a critically fabricated unity made up of a number of scattered individuals, coincidentally German, making exceptional films at the same time.[3] If this were the case, their presence would probably be negligible and, whatever the value of individual films, these films would make a singularly ephemeral mark on the film industry and its circuits—especially in the United States.[4] Commercial cinema practices an aesthetic based not only in mass entertainment but in mass production; it depends fundamentally on repetition and scale to generate its significance, and only by reacting against this system as a co-ordinated power structure in which differences share at least some common ground can individual films become fully significant works (in the complete social and cultural sense). That many in the German film community perceive the "New German Cinema" as a foreign label that sometimes misses the diversity of issues and problems that contextualize contemporary German cinema is part of the paradox that motivates my perspective: however reductive, until this perceived organizational grouping became a (internationally) communicative trope, contemporary German cinema remained without a significant bargaining chip.

(2) The two statements represent, respectively, a demand for the tools to produce a new discourse and a demand for an open communications network that would approximate a true dialogue. The fifteen years that intervene between the two demands are clearly a learning period of the utmost importance for these German filmmakers; perhaps the most important lesson learned during this time is that the practical means with which to fashion a vitalized film language are useless without an audience to speak this language with. The shift in aims between Oberhausen and *Germany in Autumn* thus highlights a problematic at the heart of particularly those films made when the movement reached its maturity in the seventies, a problematic according to which the struggle to produce a new language remains tensely balanced by the need to communicate it.

(3) Paralleling this struggle between expression and communication is the conflict between relative independence and relative dependence in the actual production and distribution of films. If in those early years and first stages of the New German

Cinema the filmmakers projected a rather idealistic vision of artistic freedom and experimentation, more recent years have sobered even the most radical of innovators (such as Werner Schroeter) so that, for most, the art of compromise has become a necessary function of artistic creation.[5] All of West German cinema has, in fact, passed through several stages and manifestations: Young German Film (designating the original movement and valid until about 1970), New German Cinema (feature-length directors since about 1971), and New German Film (feature films that achieved international recognition beginning in the late sixties). The different phases, moreover, describe different adjustments: while Oberhausen represented filmmakers who made mostly short, independently produced films, *Germany in Autumn* received the majority of its funding from Rudolph Augstein, a successful businessman, publisher of *Der Spiegel*, a chief stockholder in the Filmverlag der Autoren. In various degrees, this kind of compromise with the financial forces of television and film informs most of the successful films made since the mid-sixties.

(4) Finally and less obviously, just as the Oberhausen manifesto presents a sketchy theoretical position, *Germany in Autumn* represents an implementation and actualization developing out of that stance. Each of the filmmakers and films examined in this study enacts a similar dialectic between theory and practice. This dialectic has less to do with their Teutonic origins than with the nature of their position as artists attempting to both redefine and create the aesthetic tradition out of which those works appear. Whether explicitly (like Kluge) or implicitly (like Herzog), these filmmakers must work between the concrete enunciation of a revised film language and a more abstract retheorizing of its inherent grammar.

Within these parameters, the major force of contemporary German cinema thus takes the form of a historical dialogue whose base structure is conflict. Indeed, one of these conflicts is the very concept of an auteur cinema. While this investigation somewhat reluctantly embraces this notion as a hermeneutical device, it must be emphasized that it is both a contradictory and troubled category within this film movement and, at the same time, an entirely appropriate one, which the filmmakers themselves often exploit.[6] As Thomas Elsaesser neatly points out:

> Without Fassbinder, Herzog, Wenders, Syberberg, Schlöndorff or Kluge there would have been no New German Cinema. Each of these directors has had a crucial role to play; they were influential, however, not only through the films they made, but through their ability to define a stance, a dogma, a theory or myth about the New German Cinema. In other words, they are more than film-makers, they are icons. . . . The New German Cinema became a reality at the level of discourse, by the interplay and intertextuality of different media, multiplying and mutually amplifying their effects. Yet as soon as the New German Cinema had been launched as a label, it was part of a range of commodities, a diverse accumulation of values, not unlike those associated with tourism, through which a country markets its national heritage and past, indeed even its present, if it can be presented as a spectacle.[7]

Additionally, while this commercial engagement moves in several directions, I have focused on certain films mostly because they lucidly and fruitfully direct this dialogue toward the Hollywood spectator who dominates nearly every Western film culture. This does not mean, of course, that these films do not also speak a specific German idiom and of specific German concerns; nor does it suppose that Hollywood is a monolithic and unchanging system. But, as chapter I makes clear, an important factor in the achievement of these films on American film circuits (within both Germany and the United States) and the central reason for including certain films in this study is their proven ability to manipulate, challenge, and displace the codes of the established circuits, each film sharing this common ground while presenting various successful ways of working it. While I have marked specific differences and similarities along the way, in short, each film examined here manifests in the work of its text a historical conflict and exchange that describes its defining context.

In a more or less explicit fashion, each of these films—all made between 1972 and 1977—addresses the problem of opening alternative avenues of communication while still operating within the usually closed system established by and generally associated with Hollywood. In the same way, individual directors discussed here have all, in different ways, become significant presences on the American film circuits they have historically been forced to challenge. The choice, grouping, and ordering of these films and filmmakers according to this double status—as familiar yet displaced—should, I believe, explain strategies such as the exclusion of militantly singular directors like Jean-Marie Straub/Danièle Hulliet and the inclusion of Kluge's anomalous and unusually commercial *Strongman Ferdinand*. While the selections and limitations of this work adhere notoriously to the perspective of the American market, the crucial functioning of this perspective within contemporary German cinema is precisely the point.

Much has occurred in German culture since 1977—and in the scholarship about it—to complicate this point of view. The powerfully symbolic action of Ronald Reagan's visit to the graves of SS soldiers at Bitburg in May 1985 and the fall of the Berlin wall in November of 1989 (anticipating the subsequent unification of Germany) appeared as cultural and historical restructurings with profound implications. On the one hand, they suggested the resolution of tensions that had propelled German culture since 1945 and, on the other, they seemed to offer the return, soon after, in frighteningly concrete forms, of the specters of fascism. Indeed, however one views these and the many other turns and crises which describe German culture in the eighties—as apocalyptic or regressive—what they make dramatically clear is that contemporary German culture has, perhaps more than at any other time, had to confront, construct, and reconceptualize itself as a history contending with itself, as a function of not one, but several historical trajectories.[8] In this crisis, German cinema has been no exception: as its most resonant single event in the eighties, R. W. Fassbinder's death in 1982 marked, for some, the collapse (or at least dispersal) of the old New German Cinema but signaled, for others, an opening up of that cinema for new visions and voices. Like German society at large, contemporary German cinema has evolved during the last fifteen years into an open and contested field whose boundaries have needed to be continually resurveyed. This study is a map of one critical stage in that evolution.

This is not, strictly speaking, a history. Happily, there are already several excellent histories of contemporary German film, documenting in detail the facts and figures that make up its different generations.[9] Nor, for that matter, is this argument comprehensive of the varieties and different strategies of filmmaking that other approaches might make available. These chapters, rather, are readings of specific, emblematic texts (referable in many ways to the directors' other work); each discusses a separate text whose bond with the other chapters is the decisive functioning of a historical context. Most importantly, each attempts to locate in the movement between text and context the individual and various strategies of a collective dialogue between two cultures, between an established aesthetic and filmic representations marked by their displaced differences. In this action, filmic texts are sites of a particular historical order: they have a unique ability to question the historical play of authority and meaning across their own material, their cultural history, and the positions and actions of subjective and communal interpretations. The textual "displacements" that this study follows are both historically circumscribed and historically continuous but, as Trinh Minh-Ha has argued so well, the most eloquent achievement of their textual particularities may be their ability to play themselves out well beyond their own cultural predicament:

> displacing established values does not simply consist of moving them around, but rather of *outplaying* them, producing a different hearing and, therefore, rendering them impotent by their own criteria. To listen, to see like a stranger in one's own land: to fare like a foreigner across one's own language. . . .[10]

New German Film

"Reframing Hollywood" (*The American Friend*).

ONE

A History, a Cinema

Hollywood, Audience Codes, and the
New German Cinema

I always had to think and write down the same old
thing, again and again, even if I woke up out of
the dream every once in a while . . . until I had
the idea in the dream to use another kind of ink,
the new kind. . . . And with the new kind I could
suddenly think and see something new.
Im Lauf der Zeit (Kings of the Road)

The originality of creative artists consists, here as
elsewhere, in tricking the code, or at least in *using*
it ingeniously, rather than attacking it directly or
in violating it—and still less in ignoring it.
Christian Metz

Discussing the cultural schizophrenia that overwhelmed Germany after the Second
World War, Wim Wenders explains in a 1976 interview that "the need to forget 20
years created a hole, and people tried to cover this . . . in both senses . . . by as-
similating American culture."[1] The same year Wenders refocuses this theme in his
film *Kings of the Road* in terms of the specific problems of filmmaking in contemporary Germany, as he constructs literally around the diegetic material of that film a
framework to delineate its sociohistorical underpinning. Through interviews with
two German cinema owners, Wenders recounts the Golden Age of German film, its
fall under Hitler, and the contradictory role that Hollywood played in rebuilding that
film industry after the war. By means of this frame he sketches the complex and
often opposed historical energies that so dramatically inform not only *Kings of the
Road* but a large number of other contemporary German films as well.

That Hollywood and the America of Hollywood are the reason and symbol for
much of this confusion and ambivalence is not surprising. For, although other, more
indigenous, historical pressures clearly play a large role in these films (the legacy of
the Third Reich, the general media policy of the government, etc.),[2] Hollywood has
been a primary focus for a double perspective in Germany: on the one hand, as an
image of redemption and unparalleled technical proficiency and, on the other, as the
propagator of ideological and economic imperialism. The double bind in this double

perspective on America is the sociohistorical situation that underlies a large number of New German films. A double and contradictory movement, it is the impasse out of which German cinema has been able to emerge only by confronting it and making it an advantage. The conflict has not been, moreover, a simple ideological struggle between the predominantly leftist filmmakers and capitalistic entrepreneurs. It has become, rather, a fundamentally socio-industrial showdown fraught with compromises and contradictions as German filmmakers have tried to build a solid home industry while discovering with every step that all the best machinery and building materials are American-made.

To clarify this crisis and illustrate how the German filmmakers dealt with it, I will briefly review the postwar conditions that led up to it, and then suggest how this sociohistorical predicament has produced certain cinematic codes.[3] Through a brief examination of the contemporary German film industry—particularly as it manifests itself in the Filmverlag der Autoren, two Wenders films, and, most significantly, *Germany in Autumn*—I will argue here that what is said in many German films and how it is said are often the result of a history and industry whose contradictory machinery has become the formative means for articulating any single filmmaker's personal perspective. For these filmmakers, in short, articulation has become a function of their contradictory relationship with the industry that makes communication possible, and artistic creation and statement have accordingly become ambivalently dependent on the commercial reception and audience interaction that support that industry.

The trouble began in 1945, when a divided Germany became the main arena for a cold war in which German films naturally became a powerful tool that the U.S. government carefully controlled. As several film historians have pointed out, German cinemas still bear the burden of these policies, whose immediate effects were two. First, since the cinemas and distribution of films were in the hands of the allied powers, the films shown to the Germans were largely American. Second, because of the shortage of funds and the watchful eye of American political censors, when German producers appealed to the government for funds, the government would encourage only the most politically innocuous and cheaply made films, thus creating a "Bavarian cottage industry" that could never compete with the lavish American cinema.

From 1953 to the mid-sixties little changed for the better, as the West German government's position toward filmmakers grew increasingly ambiguous and frustrating. Their home industry was a disaster—cinemas were closing at the rate of one a day, and 80 million more spectators stayed at home watching television each year. In an effort to rectify this, the government arranged guaranteed bank credits (*Ausfallbürgschaften*) through the distributors to the producers; various tax breaks such as those awarded by the FBW (Filmbewertungstelle Wiesbaden) that exempted films with a quality rating from an entertainment tax; a Film Subsidies Bill; and state film prizes. Unfortunately, all these apparent blessings proved curses, as they invariably brought with them a bureaucratic control inimical to experimental and political artists. At the Oberhausen Festival in 1962, twenty-six filmmakers, writers, and artists formally protested this situation with a celebrated manifesto that signaled the first appearance of what was to become the New German cinema. The first significant accomplishment of this group was the formation in 1965 of the Kuratorium Deutscher Film, an institution that gave a start to some of Germany's finest directors. But in the general euphoria of finding a means for serious, authentic production, the Oberhausen group neglected distribution strategies, and this oversight was to prove disastrous. For, if the regular distributors were at first happy to support the new spirit in German cinema, within a few years they realized that it was still more profitable to distribute porno films or American films that import laws made very attractive, or, better yet, American porno films, the favorite item on almost every German distribution circuit.

Government money began going to "good" films which were supposed to be synonymous with crowd-drawing films, and this was clearly a type of film that young German directors were incapable of making. Separated by massive distances between themselves and the literacy level of their audience, the young German producer-directors were in the exasperating position of trying to teach their German audiences a language they didn't know or enjoy in order that they *might* enjoy German films the way they enjoyed American films: in short, they were attempting to build a home industry that their national home didn't seem to want. For the regular distributors the risk in this position was too great, if not ridiculous: people came to the cinema to be entertained, and the New German films were just not entertaining. For many of the young German directors, moreover, the efforts and problems were finally too much, and some (such as the Schamonis, Roger Fritz, and Klaus Lemke) chose the simpler route of the standard commercial cinema.

One attempt to reopen the cinemas and to create a different kind of audience did, however, succeed. This was the founding in 1971 of the Filmverlag der Autoren, a loose-knit collective structured around a number of independent directors, including both Wenders and Fassbinder. The Filmverlag appeared on the horizon as the long-awaited solution to their problems: namely, an effective distribution machinery. Yet those historical tensions that lay latent in its structure began to appear more troublesome as success made the Filmverlag what it had always wanted to be: competitive with large American distributors. Thus in 1975, just when the Filmverlag was turning out some of its most radically original and German films, Laurens Straub, the managing director, returned from a trip to California ready to put the Filmverlag "on an American scale" not only with higher production budgets and the making of popular stars but with flashier distribution campaigns.[4]

One year later Straub resigned, but his policies were enthusiastically continued by Mathias Ginsberg, a sharp, experienced economist who knew little about cinema, yet who did know how to market a product, so that Straub's "American program" was endorsed with more commitment than its originator probably ever intended. The next logical move came in February of the same year when the previously small cooperative, the Filmverlag der Autoren, announced a new structure in which fifty-five percent controlling interest went to businessman-publisher Rudolf Augstein, while the leftist cinéastes—Wenders, Brandner, and the recently returned Fassbinder—accepted rather incongruous titles as minority shareholders.

This completed what Jan Dawson has called "the shotgun marriage of radical sub-culture and established capital."[5]

Sketched through the seventies, this brief history of the New German cinema corresponds roughly to the double movement that I suggested earlier as the structural underpinning for the postwar German film culture. For the New German cinéastes, the America of Hollywood became a pivot for this double movement, the object of both an imaginative hate and an imaginative love — hated for its postwar invasion of German film culture, yet loved and respected for its proficiency. For most of the German filmmakers it very quickly became very clear that while it was imperative to resist ideological and economic exploitation by the American system, cinematic fluency entailed economic solvency. This fluency and solvency would converge, moreover, only in production and distribution strategies that could retrieve some of those German audiences who, while figuratively stolen by the Americans, would paradoxically be enticed back only through the methods of the American studios.[6]

Turning back to Wenders's two films, we see these conflicts translated and argued on nearly every level. *Kings of the Road* is the story of two men, who, after rejecting their pasts, attempt to find some mode of communication in the present. Both are exiles, one a projectionist-repairman, and the journey follows his itinerary from one small-town cinema to another. Central to this journey, their more personal problems with the apparatuses of communication are paralleled by the more specific problem of communicating with cinema in Germany, that is, of finding good German films and good audiences to support them. From beginning to end, *Kings of the Road* is permeated by Americana. "The Yankees have even colonized our subconscious," says one of the characters; and the signs of this colonization especially mark the many cinemas in *Kings of the Road*, where the result of U.S. policy toward the German film industry is best summarized in Bruno's hypnotic loop film which shows again and again the breasts of a panting woman, a house burning, and a woman being raped in the mud, while the soundtrack drones, "Sex, Action, Violence."

This metaphor of pornography appears again in *The American Friend*, here particularly in the person of Minôt, the French organized-crime chief who is apparently fighting the American Mafia for control of the German porno film market. It is indeed significant that in Highsmith's *Ripley's Game* Minôt is a gambler rather than a pornography king, since the change thus quietly indicates that crucial sociohistorical dimension that I have delineated.[7] Wenders, moreover, underlines this dimension throughout the film: for example, Ripley's gift to Jonathan of a pornographic optic toy and the use of two American directors as unwitting antagonists (Samuel Fuller as a Mafia leader in the pornography business and Nicholas Ray as a supposedly dead painter whose art is making forgeries of his own works). Like Hollywood's early relation to the young German directors, the characters played by Fuller and Ray have no knowledge or interest in Jonathan, yet they as much as Minôt or Ripley function as antagonists to Jonathan simply by serving their own professional inter-

"The vanishing points of identity" (*The American Friend*).

ests. In Ripley and Jonathan's first encounter, for instance, Derwatt's (Ray's) presence in America is both a conspicuous backdrop and a catalyst.

Yet more so than in *Kings of the Road*, *The American Friend* presents the many levels of this German-American conflict as a common choice and mutual commitment. American exploitation may indeed be a strong refrain in both films, but it becomes more and more obvious in *The American Friend* that this exploitation is, much like the recent history of the German film industry, more accurately described as a series of shared twists, contradictions, and compromises in which one's responses encourage the other's actions. In both the film and the industry, the friendship develops around mutual need, admiration, and resentment; in both the film and the industry, the friendship is inherently, to borrow Jean Narboni's phrase, "a malady of love."[8]

This malady of love, moreover, goes well beyond the thematic level, and it becomes in its most interesting manifestation a formal problematic that Wenders's films share with many other New German films.[9] This connection between what is basically a sociohistorical conflict and the formal makeup of his films is suggested by Wenders himself when he notes that *The American Friend* is "really dialectical in its attitude to the American cinema: it's full of love and full of hatred, but it has not found a way out of this antagonism."[10] Yet it is Christian Metz who has provided a way to talk about it in some suggestive, if undeveloped, remarks on the tradition of the filmic plausible or *vraisemblable*. According to Metz, besides the economic censorship and censorship proper that are so obviously a part of every studio system, every filmmaker must confront an ideological censorship that springs from an industry's history and economic structures and which forces a filmmaker to interpret material in a particular manner, according to certain historically and ideologically determined codes. "Thus," says Metz, "behind the institutional censorship of a film, around it, beside it . . . the censorship of the *vraisemblable* functions as a second barrier, as a filter, that is invisible but is more insidious than the openly acknowledged censorships: it bears on all subjects . . . not exactly the subjects themselves, but the way the subjects are handled."[11] Under the influence of this kind of censorship, a director is always to some extent shooting someone else's film, with somebody else's eye. And for a German director in the sixties and seventies, this ideological censorship of the *vraisemblable* would mean that the roots of his or her style and filmic structures would always be more or less American and always to some extent in tension with his or her own filmic, cultural, and political history. Samuel Fuller and Nicholas Ray, in other words, would always be more than just characters in a German film.

"To tear oneself away, even partially," Metz notes, "from an attraction so profoundly rooted in the fact of culture, in the shapes of its *fields*, requires unusual strength of mind."[12] This strength of mind, I believe, is what so forcefully asserts itself in Wenders's films, as well as in the films of other prominent German directors. The tensions and contradictions noted at the center of the contemporary German film industry are now found in a special compositional confrontation with the American image itself and its tyranny over the *vraisemblable*. Another double movement, this confrontation manifests itself in *The American Friend* on the one hand through a rigorous decomposition of shots throughout the film, a kind of dissecting and emptying (not unlike the examination that Jonathan submits to in order to discover the nature of his disease) whereby the visual excess of so many deep-focus, Hollywood films becomes a flat Wendersian exactitude. One obvious example of this visual decomposition is the first encounter with Ripley in Jonathan's shop, where the exchange between the two men evolves around a number of internal frames (door frames, picture frames, window frames, etc.) which inevitably divide the action, foreground, and background into separate and abstracted surfaces which describe the joints and planes across which the men interact. On the other hand, though, many shots in this same film regularly create a textual brilliance that intentionally echoes and reproduces the texture of so many American films: the backgrounds of scintillating signboards and flashing, primary-colored neons express this brilliance no less than the glaring expressions of faces internally reflected with so much precision.[13] Aligned with the movement to negate these false images of its recent past, the decomposition is perhaps most dramatically present in the scene in *The American Friend* in which, immediately after his first murder, Jonathan is visually deconstructed by the impersonal regard of the different metro video-screens: as he dashes away from the scene of the crime, his flight is represented not only by Wenders's camera but within the first frame by several video monitors which double the representation on surfaces of different sizes and from different angles. Yet, concomitantly, these same shots and this same film create a Hollywood brilliance that cites and strangely moves beyond the images common to Hitchcock, Fuller, and Ford. In this particular sequence, the montage is rapid and sparkles with the play of the bright lights within the dark metro; at other points in the film, there are a Hitchcock train sequence, a spectacular metallic sunrise that closes the film, and a scene in which Ripley sits in his room engulfed in the synthetic glow of the plastic materials that surround him (while fittingly showering himself with a redundance of Polaroid images of himself). In nearly every scene and shot, there is, in Peter Handke's words, "an attention without curiosity" that is at once homage to the precise technical attention of the American cinema and rejection of its curious, explanatory eye.

Equally ambivalent with its radiantly empty landscapes, *Kings of the Road* offers both a series of shots and a verbal text that can serve as explicit metaphors for this antagonistic compositional structure in Wenders's films. The series of shots are aptly the opening sequence of the diegetic material of the film (following just after the first interview). Here, after four traditional establishing long-shots of Robert's VW speeding across the countryside, the camera cuts to a close-up of Robert, whose first action is to hold up a snapshot of a handsome middle-class home which, when the camera refocuses on it, he tears in two. After giving us the reality of the traditional image (a home, a history), that photograph's reality is destroyed; whatever the relative value of the image, in short, the camera suddenly testifies to a dramatic lack undercutting its own authenticity. Later, speaking in terms of a written text, Robert explains this gesture, the malaise that informs it, and the hope that counterpoints it: "I always had to think and write down the same old thing, again and again, even if I woke up out of the dream once in a while. . . . Abstract recurrences, lapses, directions, that I . . . experienced and wrote down at the same time. Dreaming was writing in a circle . . . till I had the idea in the dream to use another kind of ink, the new kind . . . and with the new kind I could suddenly think and see something new . . . and write."

As the semiologists of cinema are the first to admit, there are massive problems in taking too far the comparison between Robert's dream for a new verbal text and Wenders's struggle to break away from the vicious circle of the Hollywood idiom (although one might note here the pertinent connection that Metz makes between the dream, the figure of the circle, and filmic language in *Le signifiant imaginaire*). Yet the metaphor remains extremely valuable and illustrative as it describes the conflict found on various levels from the narrative form to the composition of each shot, where the writing is at once a deconstruction of the old idiom and an approximation of its fluency. Wenders himself has reinforced this metaphoric comparison several times, making it quite apparent that his famous love affair with the American cinema is neither simple nor superficial but rather a paradoxical product of having been weaned on a filmic language and culture which remain foreign despite their deep attraction. Speaking specifically about cinematic language and the obvious comparisons between *The American Friend* and *Strangers on a Train*, for instance, he says: "Writing the script . . . for *Ripley's Game*, I realized that this kind of story always tends to be done the way Hitchcock did it. . . . Of course I'm trying to avoid cre-

"Strangers on a train" (*The American Friend*).

ating the same emotions in the audience, but it's the techniques that are intruding."[14] There are clearly numerous examples of this conflict throughout *The American Friend*, such as the way the classical reverse-angle exchange of looks is broken or defracted. And finally it extends to Wenders's entire handling of a narrative built on its ambiguous characters and plot lines, both visually devoid of the psychological explanations that are the foundation of the American thriller. In this light, Michael Covino's mild objection to the film should consequently be recognized as in fact one of the main aims of *The American Friend*: "it perhaps was to be expected that trying to satisfy his own requirements while fulfilling those of the genre, he would not carry off this complicated thriller with total success. Loose ends abound everywhere."[15]

Despite many fundamental differences, the films of other New German directors reflect this same practical and theoretical problem. Fassbinder's celebrated (and hardly simplistic) infatuation with Sirk's Hollywood films is the obvious example, while, more surprisingly, Kluge has described his own far less accessible efforts in a manner that strikingly parallels the problematic I have been outlining here: "Because I like the chance film offers," he says, "I try to reinvent its possibilities. The difficult thing is to succeed. Because film is not produced by auteurs alone, but by a dialogue between spectators and authors."[16]

As Wenders's films demonstrate and Kluge states so explicitly here, a perspective on recent German filmmakers and their films must therefore begin with an understanding of these films as part of a dialogue, of a communicative exchange based in a particular conflict with an image established largely (but not wholly) by Hollywood. To be sure, a large portion of film criticism and theory has been based on the opposite premise, one which Metz's early work helped promulgate in terms of a unilateral coding process: "the cinema," he has said, "as opposed to a language-system is not a method of *communication*. It does not permit immediately bilateral exchange between a sender and receiver: one does not respond to a film with another film produced at that instant. The domain of *signification* is not confused with what is called communication. . . . The cinema signifies, but it does so as a means of expression rather than communication."[17] Yet particularly in light of Metz's own early essay on the *vraisemblable* and his recent concern with the psychoanalytic positioning of the filmic subject, a theory of cinematic signification and coding must now move nearer to a more dynamic understanding of how the institution of cinema communicates and how the circuit of that communicative process controls signification. This process doubtless does not take the shape of a bilateral exchange within the movie house itself. But particularly in recent German cinema, film does initiate a dialogue that moves dialectically across sometimes large historical and cultural borders, and it is these movements which define the areas where the spectator's desire for meaning can operate successfully.

Of the many branches of reception aesthetics that inform my attempt here to expand Metz's notion of a filmic *vraisemblable*, the literary work of Hans Robert Jauss seems to me to be the richest source for an investigation of the nature of filmic communication, first, because he sees the dialogue of aesthetic communication as multidimensional and, second, because his notion of a "horizon of expectation" allows one to take into account that desiring action at the base of film's relation to an audience.[18] Writing about literary history specifically, Jauss states:

> The historicity of literature as well as its communicative character presupposes a relation of work, audience and new work which takes the form of a dialogue as well as a process, and which can be understood in the relationship of message and receiver as well as in the relationship of question and answer, problem and solution. The circular system of production and representation within which the methodology of literary criticism has mainly moved in the past must therefore be widened to include an aesthetics of reception and impact if the problem of understanding the historical sequence of literary works as a continuity of literary history is to find a new solution.[19]

Part of what has become known as the Constance school of reception aesthetics, Jauss's program has not, it seems to me, been given proper attention in the United States (either in film studies or in literary studies), having been generally overshadowed by the work of his colleague Wolfgang Iser. While their work differs decisively in many important ways, both these writers offer, in brief, an important reorientation away from a focus on the putative objective status of an artistic text, instead situating the significance of that text in the dynamic exchange between the work and the audience from which it elicits its meaning.[20] Unlike some other reception theorists and precursors like Roman Ingarden, however, Jauss distinguishes his own perspective with a more critical emphasis on the historical nature of the interaction between text and audience. "The historical life of a literary work," he says, "is unthinkable without the active participation of its audience. For it is only through the process of communication that the work reaches the changing horizon of experience in a continuity in which the continual change occurs from simple reception to critical understanding, from passive to active reception, from recognized aesthetic norms to a new production that surpasses them."[21]

In establishing guidelines for this type of investigation, Jauss makes very conscious and careful attempts to steer clear of the random subjectivism that frequently threatens a phenomenological theory of the audience. He consequently offers concrete criteria with which to delineate the expectation horizon which is the hub of a work's significance. These criteria are defined by three paradigmatic categories: "first, by the familiar standards . . . of the genre; second, by the implicit relationships to familiar works of the literary-historical context; and third, by the contrast between fiction and reality . . . which the reflective reader can always realize while he is reading. The third factor includes the possibility that the reader of a new work has to perceive it not only within the narrow horizon of his literary expectations but also within the wider horizon of his experience of life."[22] For Jauss, these three dimensions situate an art work at the intersection of diachronic and synchronic planes, as the work's engagement with its audience's expectations organizes itself (1) according to the historical development of the art form of a genre, (2) with reference to other art forms within the same temporal frame, and (3) "in the relationship of the immanent literary development to the general process of history."[23]

Used in film analysis, these categories can be crucial tools for deciphering the filmic text as part of a question-answer structure evolving through film history. Most notably, Jauss's model provides a theoretical mechanism for describing the multiple diachronic and synchronic forces that make up a work's intertextuality, and this is especially important to film studies, where the special challenge of the text is precisely its unusual plurality of codes.[24] Regarding contemporary German cinema specifically, for instance, Eric Rentschler has described a significant phase of its development precisely in terms of these multiple networks that link audience expectations and filmic codes. Concentrating on the politics of subsidies and the penchant for literary adaptations, Rentschler outlines the political and aesthetic complexities that produced an artistic rut for many filmmakers in 1976 and nearly destroyed the advances these filmmakers had made toward broadening cinematic communication. "Make no mistake about it," he explains, "*der junge deutsche Film* and its more mature counterpart New German Cinema were from the very outset, and remain today, a subsidized enterprise. For a period during 1976 and 1977, these support systems showed a less benevolent face and demonstrated little generosity toward projects with controversial subjects or ambitious thematics. A virtual paralysis set in, and the undertakings that got public backing were literature adaptations, so-called *Literatur-verfilmungen*. Within a short period of time, film versions of works by Schiller, E. T. A. Hoffmann, Kleist, Eichendorff, Anzengruber, Ibsen, Fontane,

Storm, and Gorki adorned cinema marquees and occupied television screens.''[25] The conflict that resulted from this situation clearly parallels that of many recent German directors since the early sixties, a conflict in which various cinematic, literary, political, and economic factors dictate codes at odds with many kinds of information and perspectives. In addition, the off-centered dialogue that subsequently takes place between the new filmmakers and the figuratively entrenched spectator moves in other directions, such as the one described by television's pervasive financial and aesthetic influence on contemporary films. And these various planes of textuality can only be adequately acknowledged, it seems to me, with a model, like Jauss's, that offers a method for envisioning and discussing a plurality of codes as manifested in a single artistic system.[26]

As important as this question of a filmic text's plurality, Jauss's model further indicates an interface (what Metz calls a juxtastructure) where these more visible categories of history and artform entwine with the more subjective experience of reception. As I suggested, this possibility of integrating both levels of reception is particularly crucial to the cinematic experience, where the figuration of personal dreams becomes the property of a giant economic and social machinery. And this is where Jauss's model overlaps the concerns of modern psychoanalysis with its focus on how a societal language constitutes the subject. The conjunction can, in fact, be described in complementary terms: since the objects of psychoanalytic study are considered as languages, "unconscious motivation, which is the product of a vertical and historical process, presents itself in a horizontal discursive situation: the relation between patient and analyst. This relation recalls what Lacan holds to be true of the signifying process in general: all discourse is destined to another, and constructed in this relation with another.''[27] As an interface between history and the subject, an expectation horizon established in terms of a symbolic language and located through a question-answer process thus takes into account the mutual action of both the psychoanalytic and the social, of the conscious as well as the unconscious desires put in place by a movie industry. Providing for that crucial psychological dimension of the cinema, Jauss's model "does not exclude the standpoint and the activity of the subject, but rather includes him as the condition of knowledge, and this concept is to that extent specific to all sciences which would understand meaning, which would proceed from the assumption that meaning is a yielded truth — not a given one.''[28] One can go further, in fact, (especially when dealing with the cinema): the transsubjective patterns that are Jauss's primary material are more exactly intersubjective patterns of perception clearly discernible and describable through a psychoanalytic apparatus attuned to ideology.[29] Film particularly is very much what Deleuze and Guattari call a desiring machine, whose cultural and industrial makeup mirrors the play of the individual's unconscious. And it is at this point that the economics of an individual's psychic energies meet with a social, industrial history to mark a specific artistic horizon.

A thorough application of Jauss's theory to film (or to literature for that matter) would be a large and arduous task. It would involve first not only locating, through a look at the context of film history, the particular horizon and audience at which a film is targeted but also cross-sectioning that film and audience in terms of the mul-

tiple (social, psychological, political) planes which inform it. Second, a faithful application of Jauss's reception aesthetic would require a cultural and historical positioning of the critic/reader in order to account for the historicity of his or her own
understanding. (In this study, this second requirement is more or less built into my
position as an American viewer/critic examining a dialectic that mirrors my own: my
look at some of the developments in recent German cinema is to a large extent in
response to the look that many of these films have cast on the tradition of representation of which I am a part; my particular perspective and responses follow from the
questions that these filmmakers have directed this way.)

Although following Jauss's program in this entirely complete fashion would no
doubt prove extraordinarily fruitful, the immediate rewards, I believe, are from the
general reorientation that it asks for. Above all else, this kind of historically based
and audience-related perspective initiates what Miriam Hansen calls "a deviation
from modernist, deconstructive modes of cinema and the theoretical apparatus sup-
porting them."[30] It is obviously more than coincidental, moreover, that in many
instances the important analytical work moving in this direction today is devoted to
contemporary German cinema: besides Hansen's work on Kluge, Eric Rentschler
has recently called for an actual history of German film exactly along these lines;
and Thomas Elsaesser's most current essays on Fassbinder and Syberberg specifically address these problems of adjusting Baudry's and Metz's psychoanalytic models of the specular subject in terms of the practical social and historical exigencies
that position that subject.[31]

These studies often include a wider range of historical conditions than I propose
to detail here, as they relate the strategies of certain contemporary German directors
to such historical motivations as the nostalgic presence of German cinema's Golden
Age, the social imaginary of the Third Reich (in its fantastic spectacle of private life
as public life), the alienation of Adenauer's fifties, and the former state of a politically divided Germany. Clearly my work here does not pretend to involve compre-
hensively the multifaceted variety of these other historical factors. Yet, with the
same emphasis, it attempts to refine and detail a particular and central circuit in this
exchange between audience and screen, between social history and the cinematic
subject. While I privilege the filmic text as the center of the process, here that text
remains an intertextual surface infiltrated by specific extra-filmic dimensions—
historical, ideological, and psychoanalytic.

Given the necessarily self-reflexive nature of the New German Cinema, it is not
surprising that the filmmakers themselves, at a crisis point in their development,
provide a film that stands as a demonstration, description, and argument for the theoretical viewpoint on their films presented here. The film, *Germany in Autumn*
(1978), is aptly a diversely collaborative effort, featuring the work of eleven German directors (including Fassbinder, Kluge, and Schlöndorff); it addresses formally
and thematically many of the historical and social vectors that locate contemporary
German cinema as a cultural dialogue between spectator and screen. A quintessential piece of *Gegeninformation* (alternative information), the film scrambles fact and
fiction in an intentionally uneven pastiche; it makes little attempt to identify the in-

dividuals responsible for the separate sections; and it thus willfully dislocates perceptual responsibility from standard aesthetic categories or authorial justifications in order that the spectator accept a new part in that perpetual action.[32]

The sides of the dialectic that the film initiates are obtrusively and continually visible. On a diegetic level the film directly addresses the bitter confrontation generated by terrorist action and the conservative government's reaction in West Germany. The film specifically focuses on the tensions precipitated by the kidnappings of Kappler and Schleyer, the Mogadischu hijacking, and the deaths of Baader, Ensslin, and Raspe in the Stammheim prison. Yet, in some ways, these events serve mainly to crystallize the more pertinent opposition in the film, between a closed, unilateral system of information and an open, historical dialogue. The film delineates, in brief, first, the various historical, political, and cultural planes which form the predicament of a contemporary German filmmaker, and, second, the pressing necessity for these filmmakers to make the dialogic structure of film more truly a dialogue among different points of view.

Crucial to this argument is the Fassbinder episode which appears immediately after Kluge and Schlöndorff's documentary-style exposure of Schleyer's funeral which opens the film. With Fassbinder in the central role, this section is introspective to a consciously self-indulgent extreme, as his camera interrogates Fassbinder the director at the core of his social and personal identity. The many internal frames and the thoroughly self-reflexive nature of this piece are of course typical of Fassbinder's films, but the use to which he puts this perspective here is more concerned with his own (and, by implication, his associates') position as an individual artist interpreting social reality. In *Germany in Autumn* Fassbinder depicts himself as an individual whose image as an auteur—presented in the interview about his film career which begins the sequence—dramatically contradicts his lived personality, just as the sexual liberalism that informs his many films clashes with his fascistic exploitation of his lover in this film.

The episode is fundamentally an exposure and deconstruction. Using himself as example, Fassbinder specifically reveals the contradictions and deceptions which underlie the place he must occupy as a commodity of commercial cinema. Midway through the section, Fassbinder sits naked before the camera, masturbating, and feverishly speaking on the phone about the political paranoia around him. His visual presence (as well as his dialogue) here belies the stability, power, and glamour of his public image (particularly as it appears for outside viewers of recent German cinema). And the claustrophobic setting of the sequence, shot entirely within Fassbinder's poorly lit apartment, parallels the extraordinarily solipsistic structure of the perspective of this filmmaker who speaks to himself in tape recorders and physically attacks a lover who opposes his own opinion. This double-edged irony culminates, moreover, in Fassbinder's interview with his mother about recent political events. In these shots, as in the closed discourse of an auteur, the *inter-view* as dialogue quickly deteriorates into a forced interrogation whose ultimate goal is the extortion of Fassbinder's own views and the suppression of his mother's unanswerable and distasteful questions.

Fassbinder's episode, like the whole film, is a reaction to the historical present.

"The politics of perspective" (*Germany in Autumn*).

But, whereas Fassbinder focuses from inside his position on the explicitly cinematic binds which contemporary events have revealed in the New German Cinema, the other sections of the film turn outward in a less self-conscious fashion on the historical realities which could return film to its dialogic structure and free it from the vicious circle of the auteur perspective. Like Fassbinder's film, the other sections are structured on an irony, but in these cases the irony works more clearly to provoke the viewer rather than to indict the filmmaker.[33]

Contemporary events again become the central problem. Yet what charges these events with their significance now is their relation to a political and artistic history. Reflecting the insights of Jauss's reception aesthetic, the directors of these other sections of *Germany in Autumn* are not concerned with a positivistic notion of historical events but with the historical meaning of these events as produced for a viewing public through media representation. (In one sequence, quite germane to this distinction, a history teacher wonders whether she is digging for prehistorical remains or building a bomb shelter for the next world war.) Of these other episodes, the Schlöndorff/Böll section is exemplary in its incisively ironic look at television's censorious command of the image.[34] The conception of the section is quite simple: a director and editor seek, from the board which directs a regional television network, the final approval on a video dramatization of Sophocles' *Antigone*. The board watches a number of versions of the opening disclaimer which they sequentially reject as being too politically volatile for the present day. At one point, a board member complains, "It's little compensation that there were women terrorists in the fifth century B.C." In the end, therefore, the director resorts to a final version of the play in which all the members of the cast face the camera and denounce any terrorist connotations that a viewer might attach to the play. The double irony here is unmistakable: on the one hand, despite its origin, *Antigone* does indeed resemble the situation of the terrorists' death and burial; second and perhaps more obviously, the sociopolitical pressures directed at the play and the images themselves ridiculously distort any sense of an original text. Put in these terms and seen through these twists, historical realities thus become socially produced and reproducible realities, and the powers that control the mechanisms of representation are seen to dictate, to a large degree, how those realities are perceived.

Placing the spectator at the conjunction of ironies such as those of the *Antigone* episode, *Germany in Autumn* thus reopens a filmic dialogue between the audience and the image, between the image and its historical referent, between the plasticity of the frame and its significance. This in part explains Kluge's pseudo-documentary coverage of the Schleyer funeral, which, in pinpointing its fascistic icons, orchestrations, and media control of the event, places the viewer at the disturbing intersection of two historical representations, one acceptable to the middle class, the other not. Throughout the film, moreover, this play with expectations and conventional perception shifts between the historical and psychological in a way that indicates their mutual dependence in a reception aesthetic. Later in the film, for instance, an episode recounts a routine inspection at a border guard post. The sequence is mundane in content and form, yet it develops into a tense embrace between the audience and image, primarily through the expectations which the political environment and filmic clichés have established. As the guard casually chats with the man and woman in the car and jokingly pretends to recognize one as a terrorist (from a photo-chart), a suspense builds which has little to do with the referential status of the image and more to do with an audience predisposition and a traditional editing technique that artificially creates those tensions which reciprocally infiltrate life and art. The sequence, however, falls flat; expectations are undercut; and the narrative suspense defuses when the car drives away undisturbed.

By inverting conventional tropes in this manner (and through the roughly sutured form of the whole film), *Germany in Autumn* illustrates the ability of a visual medium and a sociopolitical perspective to support each other according to a unilaterally produced picture of reality. Conventional films, even ambitious films made by conventionally celebrated auteurs, communicate according to a closed circuit of exchange between spectator and film; *Germany in Autumn* attempts to disrupt that circle in order to produce what Julia Kristeva calls an open text.[35] Climaxing this argument, the film counterpoints the opening funeral with a concluding funeral for the terrorists that features two sets of cameras squaring off from opposing ideological positions. The structural and thematic irony inherent in the symmetrical positioning of the two funerals is self-evident: the geometrical security of the Schleyer funeral misbalances sharply with the confusion that surrounds the terrorists' open-air burial. Yet the more pertinent irony is the one whereby the spectator is situated in

"Antigone the terrorist" (*Germany in Autumn*).

the cross-fire of camera angles, that of the police filming the funeral and that of the *Germany in Autumn* collective filming the police. In the disjunction that supplants what should be a closure here, the viewer becomes the third angle, the point of signification where meaning is made, and it is his or her acceptance of this opening in the fabric of filmic communication that becomes the very point of the text, its third meaning.

As I suggested earlier, this conflict of viewpoints that *Germany in Autumn* works through on so many levels is at the center of the recent history of the German cinema, a conflict which binds together sociopolitics and aesthetics and according to which an alternative perspective can only be defined in terms of the dominant, capitalistic perspective it opposes. The result, it should be clear, is neither a total rejection nor a resigned acceptance of the traditional communication equipment that aesthetics and economics have mutually established. Rather, the result is a manipulation of and interweaving through that equipment—just as at the conclusion of *Germany in Autumn* the camera steers gingerly through the maze of police vans and barricades that encircle the crowd leaving the terrorists' funeral, a tracking action that finally breaks into open ground.

Like Wenders's films, *Germany in Autumn* makes its story a formal and political argument against closure, for a more active viewer, and consciously in terms of a reception aesthetic. The public sphere that this film attempts at once to counter and to integrate is of course much greater and more complex than that informed by Hollywood; besides the political and social climate of the time, there are many other, specifically German, cultural forces that the film engages.[36] Yet, that these arguments about politics and the media must implicitly seek an audience in the context of an information network permeated by Hollywood codes and controlled by a more localized media hegemony indicates why, even in this remarkably diverse film and others like it, the confrontation with a *vraisemblable* inevitably becomes a subversive compromise, a malady of love.

Like *Germany in Autumn* (but perhaps not so structurally radical), many New German films are fully aware that their filmic codes are, and in fact should be, in so many ways codes of the plausible, furnished by a public sphere and censored by forty years of Hollywood industry. Acknowledging this, these films then insist on putting this tradition under a close examination of its powers and limitations and on integrating its audience as a crucial dimension in that investigation. Indeed, perhaps the best testimony to and metaphor for this ubiquitous dialogue is the sequence in *The American Friend* (a film in its own way about a kind of terrorism) in which Minôt telephones Jonathan from his apartment across the Seine from Jonathan's hotel. As Minôt stands on the balcony, he tells Jonathan (and thus the spectator) to look at him. But, when the camera slowly pans the sparkling façades of the modern buildings—almost a Hollywood stock shot of buildings of any city—the insistence of Minôt's command on the soundtrack is denied by the inability of the camera eye (and thus the spectator's eye) to locate him. Here the shot both attracts and dissolves under its own unconcern, and, through the failure of the medium itself, the tiny inadequacies that always topple the history of a cinematic *vraisemblable* are disturbingly asserted. Wenders metaphorically summarizes here much of the recent history of the New German Film industry—a history which has been guided and nourished by the splendor of Hollywood and its images and which concomitantly has become painfully aware of the lacks and deceptions at the center of those images.

"Buddies across history" (*Kings of the Road*). © 1982
Gray City, Inc.

TWO

███████

Wenders's *Kings of the Road*

The Voyage from Desire to Language

> Although it is true that, when either my train or
> the one next to it starts, first one, then the other
> may appear to be moving, one should note that
> the illusion is not arbitrary and that I cannot
> willfully induce it by the completely intellectual
> choice of a point of reference. If I am playing
> cards in my compartment, the other train will start
> moving; if, on the other hand, I am looking for
> someone in the adjacent train, then mine will
> begin to roll. In each instance the one which
> seems stationary is the one we have chosen as our
> abode and which, for the time being, is our
> environment. . . . . Perception is not a sort of
> beginning science, an elementary exercise of the
> intelligence; we must rediscover a commerce with
> the world and a presence to the world which is .
> older than intelligence.
>
> Merleau-Ponty,
> "The Film and the New Psychology"

The films of Wim Wenders certainly specify and concretize the confrontation with the American film industry and its culture to an extent other German filmmakers often only approximate. While other directors share, willingly or not, Wenders's obsession with the social, artistic, and psychological presence of the American cinema within the German consciousness and theaters, few locate it so effectively and so regularly as the center and persistent background for the argument of their films. Thematically, stylistically, and geographically, Wenders's cinema is dislocated between two cultures, between that of Goethe and Heidegger and that of Ray and Ford; the crisis of identity that the characters experience in his various films is the crisis of the films themselves, as they aim concomitantly to speak, learn, and reinvent a language whose traditional syntax now tends more and more toward insignificance. Like Handke's goalie awaiting the penalty kick, in Wenders's films an unarticulated signified remains unsteadily poised before a foreign—an American—signifier, and in this tension Wenders locates a semantic rift whose origin was a catastrophic attack on the fundamental value of the image, an attack at the very center of the social history of Germany. He explains:

I do not believe that any other people have experienced as great a loss of confidence in their own images, their own stories and myths, as ours. We, the directors of the New Cinema, have felt this loss most acutely in our work. The lack, the absence of an indigenous tradition has made us parentless. . . . There was good reason for this mistrust. Never before and in no other country have images and language been handled as unscrupulously as here, never before and in no other place have they been so debased as vehicles for lies.[1]

Faced with this collapse between an audience and its images, the movements of and in Wenders's films accordingly become figurative and literal journeys back toward the possibility of a communicative significance, hopeful linguistic journeys marked by nostalgia and an anxious need to rediscover a native tongue. Not surprisingly, Robert, the traveler in *Kings of the Road* who, in his words, "specializes in a field somewhere between linguistics and children's therapy," thus describes his patients in a manner that could easily refer to many of Wenders's travelers, themselves dislocated by the course of time. When a child is very young, Robert explains, "the letters and numbers are still an adventure." Later, as the routine of writing sets in ". . . the memory of these fantasies fades away. . . . And only the problems that were brought out by these fantasies remain." For both the characters and the films, in brief, what propels their drive toward the language and images of America (its pinball machines, rock music, etc.) is precisely this nostalgic fascination with the possibility of speech and the contingent hope of fulfilling that possibility with the only language available. That this driving need to tell their stories is, however, repeatedly offset by the failure of the langauge is of course the crisis of contemporary German cinema: like Philip in *Alice in the Cities*, whose story is derailed by the mass of Polaroid images he collects, Wenders and his voyagers continually confront the fact that the images that recount their stories "never show you what you've actually seen." "In the U.S.," Philip says, "something happens to you, through the pictures you see. . . . I lost my bearings. All I could imagine was things going on and on." This endless and self-perpetuating search for meaning consequently becomes an open voyage through images which often serve only to impede the quest: a quest whose best map is Wenders's extraordinary *Kings of the Road*.

As explicitly as any film ever made, *Kings of the Road* is the story of a journey, an American road film, a film as voyage, and a journey through itself as medium. It announces itself on two levels: (1) the travels of two men, Robert and Bruno, across the plains of Germany and all that involves on a thematic level; and (2) the voyage through the film itself, which involves both the spectator's experience of the film and an analysis of the film mechanism as means of communication. Like all voyages, the underlying motif for both levels is desire, and the play between desire and the absence of desire becomes the structuring law for the entire film. Like all voyages, that desire implies a goal, and in *Kings of the Road* that goal is described negatively as the desire for what is not there. Yet *Kings of the Road* differs significantly from its traditional American models: it dramatically turns on the desire that informs it and confronts that desire from an angle of vision that reverses both the direction and possibilities of the cinematic voyage. Positioning itself between the desire that it initiates and a discursive dissection of that desire, *Kings of the Road* thus becomes one of the central and most incisive documents in an understanding of the New German Cinema and the bind of its recent history.

Aptly, the story of Robert and Bruno itself begins not with the desire to be somewhere or the vision of a new direction, but with the desire not to be somewhere and the choice of no direction. After the prefatory material of the film (which I will return to), there are four, very traditional, establishing shots of a VW speeding across the countryside. The camera then cuts to four close-up shots of Robert, the driver, taking out a picture of his handsome, middle-class home and tearing it in two.[2] Shortly afterward, Robert accelerates off the highway and plunges directly into a river. In this rapid and rather cryptic series of shots, a journey is visually established, but at the same time its direction is quickly aborted and transformed into no direction as the VW sinks in the river. The motivation, moreover, becomes rejection, rejection of a past, a home, and, in one sense, of desire itself. The journey that is constructed in one movement is deconstructed in the next.

Directionless, a journey that repeatedly abrogates desire and motivation becomes a sort of contradiction, in fact the central contradiction of the film: from the beginning to the end of *Kings of the Road*, both men find themselves yearning for an undefined, for the suspected but hidden; yet at the very moment that action becomes seated in an object, this object becomes threatening and thus rejected. Desire turns from itself in the very action of being manifested, and thus is formed the film's base figure: the circle, the wheel, and the hole which is the center of both.

Most obviously and regularly, this action is seen in terms of Robert and Bruno's friendship, which starts at degree zero and tentatively forms and unforms itself through the course of the film. At one point, for instance, the two men arrive at a theater and discover that the sound equipment needs to be repaired. While they work behind the screen, their silhouettes are projected and amplified on the screen; they soon get involved in a kind of gigantic, Chaplinesque shadow mime which Wenders depicts by cutting back and forth between the men behind the screen and the audience of children that watches them. They swing on ropes, juggle, and pretend to batter each other with clubs. The game projected on the screen becomes a kind of intimacy, the first intimacy displayed by either of the two introverted men. Yet soon afterward Bruno resentfully berates Robert about the dance-like attention they show each other: "When I was up on that ladder, I got a real shock all of a sudden. I was looking at my shadow, and at the same time I noticed you were watching me. That was it. I wanted to stop then and there. I was furious, and helpless. And then I didn't even know how I got started. And you were fooling around and I didn't have any other choice but to keep it up. That made me even more furious." During this conversation, the two stand before a roadside food-stand which has been remade from an old truck. The conversation is a medium-long shot with the two men standing side by side before the painted-over windows of the truck. When Bruno finishes, Robert responds by saying, "That's how it was with me too"; indignant, the two men spin away in opposite directions. Cutting to a new position at the other end of the truck, the camera is able to capture the circle formed by the men as they walk in different directions around the stand. The segment then closes with a frontal shot of them again side by side in companion windows of a truck. Their mutual attraction and rejection thus creates a literal circle in space; metonymically the two poles of this circle become the ubiquitous image of the two men joined yet separated by the window frames of the truck.

This circuit of desire, as Freud first pointed out, is fundamentally an infantile figure, an image of longing through which the child deals with the loss and return of the mother.[3] Accordingly, the narrative most clearly represents its action when Robert and Bruno return to their childhood homes, temporally dividing from each other before rejoining again later. Robert's return is a reunion with his father that quickly becomes a confrontation when he accuses his father of mistreating his mother. Similarly, Bruno's return is to the summer home where he spent much of his youth: searching out the home in a spirit of playful nostalgia, Bruno quietly explores the darkened, overgrown home, but then suddenly erupts violently, breaking windows and chairs. The visit ends with Bruno refusing to sleep in the house and weeping by himself on the back steps. Driven by a nostalgia for the object lost, desire here becomes a circular return that can only end in bitterness and frustration. Bruno, like Robert, yearns for an undefined something which has been lost, and with the almost cathartic frustration of that yearning, the journey begins again.

Thus the circle of desire becomes at once the emblem of frustration and the emblem of an independent solitude, the action that powerfully moves the characters toward an object from which they powerfully react along an opposite curve. Profoundly private on one level, this desire and its implications are not, however, confined to an interpersonal dimension. For, in *Kings of the Road*, the desire of the individual necessarily becomes involved in a multitude of other experiences, and its force invariably becomes linked to a variety of other voyages, most predominantly the cinematic voyage.

The most direct example of this linkage is the episode in which Bruno meets a young woman, Pauline, who is temporarily managing a cinema. They arrange a rendezvous at the cinema where she works, but the tryst naturally does not follow Hollywood logic of love and consummation: although sexual expectations are created for the characters and the film's spectators, they are not fulfilled; although Bruno and Pauline spend the night together, it is without any real intimacy. While she works in the cashier's booth, Bruno watches the film; afterward they sit in two balcony boxes, paralleled but separated by the two frames of the boxes; later, when Pauline lies down on a small bed, Bruno retreats to a chair in the theater, where he dozes. When Bruno asks how she lives, Pauline replies, "Alone with my daughter, and it's going to stay that way." Later Bruno echoes her resolution when he tells Robert, "I've never felt anything except loneliness in a woman all the way down to my bones."

Around and intermeshed with this movement of attraction and retraction by Pauline and Bruno is the desire for the cinema itself, the eroticism of the image. Explicitly joining the two, the cinema where Pauline and Bruno meet shows pornographic films which draw a sparse crowd of viewer-voyeurs, indicating that however else the spectator at the cinema and the man on the road may be related, they here share the sexual urge that propels them. The connections pervade the entire episode: Pauline tells of a couple who had to be carried out of the cinema together after the woman suffered a vaginal cramp; when Bruno investigates a blurred spot in the middle of the film's image, he finds the projectionist masturbating; and left alone with Pauline, Bruno splices together footage from the porno film to make a loop film that shows again and again a house that burns and falls, the breasts of a panting woman, and a rape scene. As the culmination of the episode, Bruno's loop film thus unites the figure of the circle with an image of the sexual desire that informs the entire scene. The form of the loop film, as a summation of its content, thus describes the debilitating and redundant predicament of each of the characters.

The conjunction that Wenders makes here is a powerful and complex one, one which Christian Metz has examined closely through his discussion of a psychology of desire and a psychology of cinema in *Le signifiant imaginaire*. While the applicability of Metz's findings along the total spectrum of films may be suspect, his work does put an acute theoretical light on this central segment and, by extension, on all of *Kings of the Road*, since this crucial segment of the film acts as a kind of discursive, visual deconstruction of the spectatorial desire of the cinema which Metz has analyzed in terms of its sexual base and its two components of perception and hearing. In Metz's words, "cinema practice is only possible through the perceptual passions: the desire to see (scopic drive, scopophilia, voyeurism), acting alone in the art of the silent film, the desire to hear which has been added to it in the sound cinema. . . . These two sexual drives are distinguished from the others in that they are more dependent on a lack, or at least more dependent on it in a more precise, more unique manner, which marks them from the outset, even more than the others, as on the side of the imaginary."[4] Following Lacan and Freud, Metz's model frequently relies on the Oedipal triangle, which obviously relates to the desire of the two men in the film, who confront fathers and weep over the memory of a mother. But, beyond these anchoring points along the diegetic level, Metz's model is especially valuable for its use of the concepts of the lack and scopic desire, the key notions in binding the diegetic voyage and the cinematic voyage, that is, in presenting one as a reflection of the other. Just as the two characters circulate through a voyage bounded by desire and an unattainable object, the cinematic voyager moves between the same two poles, except that his or her journey belongs to the realm of the virtual. The two journeys are strikingly similar, and Metz's description of the desire of the spectator again retrieves the figure of the circle turning forever from itself in the quest for the undiscoverable. Watching the film, the spectator's visual drives

remain more or less unsatisfied, even when their object has been attained: desire is very quickly reborn after the brief vertigo of its apparent extinction, it is largely sustained by itself as desire, it has its own rhythms, often quite independent of those of the pleasure obtained (which seemed nonetheless its specific aim); the lack is what it wishes to fill, and at the same time what it is always careful to leave gaping, in order to survive as desire. In the end it has no object, at any rate no real object; through real objects which are all substitutes (and all the more multiple and interchangeable for that), it pursues an imaginary object (a "lost object") which is its truest object, an object that has always been lost and desired as such.[5]

"The freedom of rock 'n' roll" (*Kings of the Road*). ©
1982 Gray City, Inc.

A monocular vision that draws the look to an infinite vanishing point is of course
a primary factor in this action of scopic desire. But equally important is the nature
of the filmic text itself, which is structured on the play of the presence and absence
of the signifier. As Metz explains, a film necessarily presents an object whose existence is by definition anterior, an object that is only evanescently present through
the medium of a moving text. Thus, the film "represents both the negation of the
signifier (an attempt to have it forgotten) and a certain working regime of that signifier, to be quite precise the very regime required to get it forgotten."[6] This play of
presence-absence doubly installs the film in the realm of the virtual, where it is first
placed through the fiction which is its signified.[7] Through the operation of the film's
signifying system itself, the spectator's experience thus approximates the kind of
experience into which Robert is plunged as his VW sinks in the river: his desire trig-
gered, he begins a voyage whose course is a somewhat directionless flux and whose
central characteristic is the play between presence and absence. Once again, the first
images of the film index this play for the characters as well as the viewer, first in
presenting an object—notably a photographic object—whose presence is violently
annulled and second through the metaphor of the VW as a vehicle which is present
one minute and disappears the next into the current of the river.

A river, a film, a circle: all suggest the movement of desire—that of the characters and that of the spectators—as it releases itself on an imaginative level where

finally no object can be found to replace the object lost. The spectator of *Kings of the Road* accordingly reflects the predicament of the characters in that the longing to *see* is both excited and frustrated not only by the material *in* the film but by the material *of* the film. Here the shadow mime episode is perhaps the best metaphor for this fetishistic hiding-revealing power of the Wenders-Müller camera, for in this episode the two men appear only as the shadows of their real presence behind the screen, flickering, momentarily projected, and then disappearing as Wenders cuts from the antics behind the screen to the perspective of the children in the audience awaiting a film. Less metaphorically, shots throughout the film initiate the same action whereby the film teases the audience with the presence of two men and a reality that this audience is drawn toward but can never grasp: the long and unusual silences of this film which echo with so much potential significance, the stark landscapes which are regularly deflected off the mirrors and windshields, and the frontal shot of the truck in which the reflection off the window only allows momentary glimpses of the men in the front seat. The film, in brief, seems aggressively bent on proving the point which Metz makes specifically about framing and camera movement:

> the point is to gamble simultaneously on the excitation of desire and its retention . . . by the infinite variations made possible precisely by the studios' technique of the exact emplacement of the *boundary* that bars the look, that puts an end to the "seen," that inaugurates the more sinister crane-shot (or low-angle shot) toward the unseen, the guessed at. . . . They have an inner affinity with the mechanisms of desire, of its postponements, its new impetus. . . . The way the cinema, with its wandering framings (wandering like the look, like the caress), finds the means to reveal space has something to do with a kind of permanent undressing, a generalized striptease.[8]

In a film in which the movement across the land is so prominent a theme, this last phrase is particularly pertinent, since the movement of the film through the journey of the two characters along the border between East and West Germany is not so much a revelation of the land as a promise of revelation that never comes: the landscape and the towns remain the same throughout; shot mostly through the stationary window frames of the truck, the country passes but does not change.

Despite all of these affinities, though, *Kings of the Road* is significantly more than a duplication or accentuation of a psychoanalytic formula for films in general. Rather, it is an explicit confrontation with that formula and the spectatorial relationship that it implies, not in an attempt to overthrow that formula but in an attempt to assimilate, defract, and readjust it. Necessarily locked within the circle which is the law of all films, *Kings of the Road* nevertheless attempts to create new figures within that circle or at least to disturb the psychological complacency which it inspires in a spectator. In a fundamentally essayistic and metaphoric manner, *Kings of the Road* endeavors to rework and challenge the ideal spectator that Metz describes by introducing, within the figure of the cinematic voyage, other figures which significantly change the nature of that voyage.

Most prominently, Wenders goes to the figurative center of the image with his challenge: he dissects that center, and in that gesture he disrupts the circuit of desire between the moving image and the imaginative spectator who completes the circuit.

Metz explains this circuit (circle) this way: "There are two cones in the auditorium: one ending on the screen and starting both in the projection booth and in the spectator's vision insofar as it is introjective (on the retina, a second screen). When I say that 'I see' the film, I mean thereby a unique mixture of two contrary currents: the film is what I receive, and it is also what I release, since it does not pre-exist my entering the auditorium and I only need close my eyes to suppress it. Releasing it, I am the projector, receiving it, I am the screen; in both these figures together, I am the camera, pointed yet recording."[9] As I have indicated, this double action describes the single figure of the circle (between the screen and the spectator), which Wenders then attempts to disrupt by at least momentarily arresting the desire that creates it. The cinema sequence is again the key illustration of this strategy. Here Bruno notices a blurred spot at the center of the film's image which has remained unnoticed by the apparently entranced audience. He follows the circuit of the image back to the projection booth, where he finds a somewhat elaborate mirror construction which forms a second circle within the booth itself and which catches the image before it leaves the booth in order to project it a second time on the back wall of the booth. With his back to the screen the projectionist is then able to masturbate privately. In addition to retracing the doubly circular route of the cinematic image, this sequence delineates and deconstructs two other elements in a psychoanalytic model of the cinema: namely, the mirror and the phallus. As Metz points out, the mirror is the crucial mechanism of the camera and the machinery of the mind. The psychoanalytic notion of the phallus, however, is more crucial to my argument here, since its disavowal is the foundation for the voyeuristic (fetishistic) desire that initiates and maintains the cinematic voyage. And in this sequence the exposure of the penis as index or metaphor for the phallus becomes a discursive overturning or deconstruction not only of the circular route of the filmic experience but also of the psychoanalytic taboo that upholds that experience (the phallus of the mother). In a partly metaphoric manner (since the penis is not strictly speaking the phallus), Bruno's discovery is that the blurred spot at the center of the image is linked by a series of mirrors to the phallus-penis at the other end of the circuit. Fittingly, under the dissecting eye of Wenders's camera, that original blurred spot on the first screen is paralleled and contrasted by the highlighted image of the penis on the second screen. It is as if the repressive action which Thierry Kuntzel has pointed out as a feature of a film's *défilement* is suddenly stopped and the circuit of desire disrupted.[10] In one and the same shot, this statement is made as the film lies heaped motionless on the floor and the penis lies exposed.

The cinema sequence is doubtless the most self-reflexive mapping out of this strategy of disruption and deconstruction in the film, but this figure of the exposed center is repeated throughout the film in weaker or stronger terms. The sexual dimension is generally underplayed, but the confrontation with scopic desire remains recurrent. There is, for instance, the memorable scene in which Bruno stops the truck so that he can "pee." He in fact defecates; in this medium-long shot against a slope of white sand, the image is aggressively blunt on a number of levels. Besides directly controverting Bruno's own statment, the shot is a frank disclosure of one of the less titillating facts that traditional cinema hides. Just as vomiting substitutes in

"The veer of a crossless Jesus" (*Kings of the Road*). ©
1982 Gray City, Inc.

the film for the character's possibility of speech, the scopic desire of the spectator
here confronts excrement at the center of the image.

This figure of a disrupted center is further complemented by yet another figure
present in a number of single images and the structure of the whole film. Related to
that disrupting center, it can best be described as a swerve, a veering off, or a defraction, and its action is notably opposed to the returning action which creates the
figure of the circle. It represents, rather, a "breaking out" of that circle, a defraction
from it that forms a tangent pointing nowhere but away from the closed circular
form. Imagistically, it is suggested by a large number of shots: for instance, the shot
of Robert walking up a diagonal plank that ends in mid-air; his later imitation of a
crossless Jesus in its motionless trajectory upward, miniatured and paralleling Robert's own gestures in this low-angle shot; and the sequence in which Bruno defecates, where that act is immediately juxtaposed with Robert leaping out of the frame
in the next shot to create the same veering from the logic of the montage. While
there is absolutely no narrative logic or explanation for any of these shots, each one,
particularly the last, suggests a powerful connection between the disruption of
desire—either the character's or the spectator's—and the figure of a trajectory that
results and flies off from that movement.

The logic of these three figures—the circle, the disrupted center, and the
swerve—or more precisely, the logic whereby the first two generate the third, is
what defines the entire film. *Kings of the Road* is finally more accurately described
through this figure of a series of swerves or defractions rather than exclusively

through the circular model of desire that Metz proposes for the majority of narrative films. Even the characters' voyage is not finally circular (and certainly not linear) but rather a series of loosely connected trajectories and detours which conclude with their two paths veering off from each other. Indeed the voyage of the two men takes the shape of something between a circle and a number of directionless segments, thus paralleling a medium whose circular, unrolling motion is nonetheless a series of separate frames. More importantly, however, the spectator's journey undergoes the same redefinition so that, besides the circular exchange uniting the viewer and the screen, there is the deconstruction of that construction through a forced veering off of the trajectory of the spectator's vision—such as Wenders regularly does when he spins the same landscape once horizontally in the background and again diagonally through the truck's rear-view mirror in the same image.

These variations on the traditional cinematic voyage are the key marks in *Kings of the Road*, since they periodically rupture or buckle the smooth rhythms of the reciprocation of desire that are the foundation of the classical cinema. Through the strategies I have been describing, Wenders attempts to reposition or redirect the spectator along an imaginative channel that leaves him or her standing on the edge of his or her own journey in a position something like the spectacular detour that Robert illustrates when he walks to the end of that rising plank. What this means in terms of the spectator—just as what it means for the two characters—is the radical awareness of a context or field of action outside the route of the voyage. The short-circuiting results in the realization that the voyager is not just a participant in the voyage but a watcher outside and independent of the journey itself. In the film, this realization entails dissatisfaction, isolation, and finally the possibility of action—specifically the action of writing that figures so largely in *Wrong Move* and *Alice in the Cities*. More importantly, for the audience, this realization entails the possibility of a new relationship between the spectator and the screen, one where the enforced spectatorial silence gives way to a reflective, critical language.[11]

In "Histoire/Discours (Note sur deux voyeurismes)" Metz has noted that one of the most important conditions for the filmic voyager-voyeur is that he or she is not regarded and can remain absorbed within the flow of the story, in the anonymity of a voyage where the Me and the Other merge.[12] This is precisely what Wenders tries to challenge through his acts of deconstruction or, in what is probably the most recurrent shot in the film, by putting the two voyagers—the diegetic ones and the filmic ones—face to face in a situation of forced recognition. Put another way, this means that Wenders turns the spectator in his or her seat; he defracts the line of vision so that the spectator now looks backward into the projection booth where one face of desire meets the other. That Wenders punctuates the film with so many scenes inside the projection booth is only the most obvious effort to locate the viewer's vision at the source of filmic experience and outside the grip of the endlessly metonymic movement of desire. For the entire film moves in its lyrical but relentless manner toward the same awareness, toward the possibility of commentary on desire.[13]

The dynamics of this confrontation are sketched within the story itself when

Robert, the man of words and society, joins Bruno, the silent traveler. At first, Robert clearly surrenders to the journey in and of itself. Yet, even in the early stages of the trip, Bruno notices him breaking off and making contact with another level of experience. At one point, Robert returns to his father's newspaper office, and the showdown is aptly a battle of words: "You know, the whole time that I've been gone," Robert says, "whenever I think about or say anything I see it printed immediately. The last time I wanted to talk to you I had to listen the whole damn time. . . . You talk too much." This power of language is intimately bound up with the movement of the mind from the undifferentiated flux of experience to the differentiating consciousness of the individual. And Robert's deviations from the voyage of the truck here and at other points are clearly deviations into language and action, a connection dramatically underlined when Robert takes a newspaper he has found to the end of that striking diagonal platform. This is not to say that the voyage and mental reflection are incompatible, but instead that the voyage remains more or less indecipherable unless marked by the deviation of words. Another more subtle illustration of the same dialectic occurs during one of Robert's wanderings from Bruno: he walks toward a river where some boys are sailing boats made from newspapers. Picking one of the papers, he reads the headlines. The newspaper suddenly pulls Robert back to a different register of experience; the incident marks him and his journey just as the newspaper boat was the single sign to mark the current of the water. The allegory is completed, moreover, at the end of the film, when Robert trades his suitcase for a pad and pencil, and Bruno tears up his itinerary after thanking Robert for helping him "see himself as someone who's put some time behind him." In each of these cases, the unconscious participation in the voyage is assimilated to another register of experience, and this register is explicitly connected with language and the arena of comprehension.

The same change of register, I believe, is literally forced on the spectator of *Kings of the Road* when he or she is brought to the projection booth again and again in the film. Repeatedly, Bruno dismantles projectors and explains their mechanisms, their faulty parts, and their history in numerous scenes usually shot from behind the projector or closely focused on the exposed and sharply lit internal parts: he demystifies the machine whose greatest power is the mystification of the spectator through its hypnotic circuit of desire. At one point he takes a part to the workbench in his truck, where he points to the maltese cross mechanism and explains to the projectionist and the camera that "there wouldn't be a film industry without this little thing." In this way, Bruno turns the spectator, in a sense, from the film: he explains the base of the apparatus so that the viewer becomes a type of comprehending viewer who does not simply experience but is able to identify and differentiate the discrete elements of that experience. The spectator is thus able to "write" a perspective, and the voyage then has the capacity to have landmarks and defining points (such as the one that so loudly marks the river in the film). Before only nostalgic, the voyager is now equipped to analyze, to remember. Within the dream, the voyage, the film, the spectator now has the possibility of changing registers in the manner Robert describes. "Dreaming was writing in a circle," he says, "till I had the idea in the dream to use another kind of ink, the new kind . . . and with the new kind I could suddenly think and see something new . . . and write.'' The circle of the film, in short, can and should be written on its tangent.

What this change of register involves, and one of the discourses it entails, is clearly indicated by Wenders in the two segments that frame the film. Interviews in a projection booth, these frame sequences pointedly recall the masturbation sequence in a projection booth at the very center of the film (particularly since the frame sequences and the masturbation sequence are both demystifications or deconstructions, one on a psychoanalytic level and the other on a sociohistorical level). The masturbation sequence, as I have indicated, is a deconstruction of the cinematic play of presence/absence and an uncovering of the phallus/penis behind this play. The frame sequences, on the other hand, act as a translation of this central sequence (the exactly central sequence in the film) into another frame of reference, a German historical framework where the absence is just as powerfully present. As told by the two cinema owners, this sociohistorical absence is at once the absence of a home film industry, of good German films, and of a critical audience that might desire German films instead of the pornographic films and American films that it has been weaned on. And in a highly significant fashion, this sociohistorical absence is cryptically indicated within the film when, in an extreme close-up, Robert, without comment, cuts out the face of Fritz Lang from the center of a photograph. This gesture obviously parallels Robert tearing the photograph at the start of the film, Bruno tearing his itinerary at the end of the film, and Bruno figuratively tearing the veil of the projection booth in the masturbation sequence. It, too, becomes an acknowledgment of the absence behind the image, an absence which in this particular shot refers not so much to an object lost as to the loss of a German film audience that Lang had created. Punctuated by nostalgic references to Lang, the frame sequences suggest that there has been no German film industry since UFA and that the hole that has existed in postwar German film history has been covered by an illusion sustained more by the Hollywood industry than by the active participation of spectators.

As Metz has noted, the film industry today has so thoroughly usurped the critical spectator that in the conflux of the desire of the spectator and the feeding of that desire by the industry, the question of a ''good'' or ''bad'' film has become nearly irrelevant. Compared to the notion of a ''bad'' film,

> the ''good object'' relation is more basic from the standpoint of a sociohistorical critique of the cinema, for it is this relation and by no means the opposite one (which is a local failure of the former) that constitutes the aim of the cinematic institution and that the latter is constantly attempting to maintain or re-establish. . . . The cinematic institution is not just the cinema industry . . . it is also the mental machinery—another industry— which spectators ''accustomed'' to the cinema have internalized historically and which has adapted them to the consumption of films. The institution is outside us and inside us, indistinctly collective and intimate, sociological and psychoanalytic.[14]

A powerful industry can thus create a situation in which nearly all films are good films in a psychoanalytic sense, in which nearly all films are desirable films. And this is the notion that Wenders forefronts in the frame sequences when the two cinema owners discuss Hollywood's takeover of Germany: as long as desire remains the single controlling principle for the industry and its audience—and it must while the spectator keeps his or her mind solely on the screen—the Hollywood industry in Germany will self-perpetuate with the crucial aid of the indiscriminating metonymic desire of the spectator. The only way out of this bind is for the spectator to move from the mute level of the voyeur to the verbal level of the historian, where to discuss Hollywood's tight hold on scopic drives is to begin a liberation from it or at least the redirection of those drives. To see the absence which motivates the spectator on a psychoanalytic level in terms of the larger content of a historical absence is not the abolition of either. It is, however, the beginning of the possibility of a new filmic spectator and thus new films.

What *Kings of the Road* argues, therefore—particuarly by means of the symmetrical positioning of the masturbation sequence and the frame sequences—is that the cinematic voyage is indeed psychoanalytically propelled but, in many important ways, historically conditioned. Both are voyages in their own right, the second being a voyage through the course of historical time. But it is only by demystifying the first that the second can in its turn be properly deconstructed and elucidated. The second level of the voyage is indeed the ultimately important outer context where meaning is written and new questions are proposed. But it is at the first level, in the desire of the individual, that primary and fundamental questions are raised (questions that should inevitably lead back to the second context of the projection booth). What attracts Wenders so profoundly to the American cinema must be, in large part, the knowledge that nearly all modern spectators remain mesmerized in the circle that Hollywood, that great desiring machine, has so competently created. Only by recognizing that circle as a starting point, however, do he and the other German filmmakers have a chance to write themselves out of it. For, like Robert, the spectator and the filmmaker have the option of detours, self-imposed or forced. And like Bruno, they have the possibility of figuratively turning in their seats and of deconstructing their journey. But finally both are first and foremost voyagers, and what the parable of Robert tells us in its simplest form is that one must first be a good voyager if one hopes to be a good writer of history.

"Emotional giants: the mural and the seduction" (*Petra von Kant*).

THREE

Transformations in Fassbinder's *Bitter Tears* of *Petra von Kant*

The camera introduces us to unconscious optics as
does psychoanalysis to unconscious impulses.
Walter Benjamin

If a sexual reality is the condition of the symbolic,
that through which the signifier comes into the
world, then there is little to do, nature wins; if
sexuality is always a symbolic production, then
there is a place for a politics of the unconscious,
for, that is, a grasp of the unconscious not as
closed but as historically open, taken up in the
historical process of its realisations, existing in
transformation.
Stephen Heath

That Rainer Werner Fassbinder is at once the most prolific of the New German directors and the most controversial of the group has a significantly causal relationship: the very rate at which Fassbinder makes films, along with the rapid changes of subject and style, alone is enough to alienate and confound viewers who, at a more leisurely pace, might accustom themselves to perspectives and materials which are deceptively difficult to grasp. In his excellent essay on Fassbinder, Thomas Elsaesser describes this logic and takes it one step further in positing a bond between Fassbinder's rate of production and the despair of the films themselves:

> What his critics have been quick to spot as mystification, the endless litany of victimisation, accompanied by a lugubrious celebration of despair . . . is in another sense the craftsman's delight in creating ever more perfectly constructed vicious circles. In this case the films are autobiographical in a very straightforward manner: they translate into fictional terms and formal configurations the personal experience of film-making. Having to overproduce in order to produce at all suggests the vicious circle of capitalist logic. . . . A capitalist entrepreneur in an age of monopolies, Fassbinder wants to articulate a message of utopian liberation while being himself in chains.[1]

Generally some of the most vociferous critics of Fassbinder, certain kinds of Marxist viewers are the first to note the monotony of this left-wing melancholy, suggesting, moreover, the negative political implications of such a repeated stance.[2] This kind of criticism is often fully justified, as it focuses mostly on sexual relations, political economy, and the necessary merging of the two, all points which are Fassbinder's own. Writing about Fassbinder's recurrent dependence on a tradition of the beautiful and the ugly, for example, Richard Dyer argues: "I am not claiming that Fassbinder's films . . . are *simply* patriarchal or bourgeois. Rather, the propensity for victims, while it may be expressive of compassion or pity, is enmeshed in a visual and narrative rhetoric that bespeaks and tends to reinforce a bourgeois patriarchal way of seeing the oppressed."[3] Dyer's comments here and in the entire essay provide some of the most engaging and intelligent criticisms of Fassbinder's films, for he not only pinpoints the troublesome one-sidedness of their political perspective but additionally describes the virtue of that trouble, namely, its effectivity: "that political effectivity—limited though it may be—may be far more important than the film's own political despair. In the end, it is not so much what the films say that matters, but rather what people do with what they say."[4] Fassbinder's films, in short, provoke, and this provocation may be far more important to cinema's rapport with its audience today than at any other time.

The nature of this provocation is, however, the elusive question, again bringing to the forefront the problem of audience and the relationship that Fassbinder's films have with that audience. Most importantly this relationship can not be tied to an ideal conception of the spectator, nor to a similarly static notion of Fassbinder's films. For, unlike Godard, Fassbinder does not aim to return to a utopian zero ground in order to create a new cinematic viewer as he creates a new cinematic syntax. Rather, like many of his German colleagues, Fassbinder has a decided sense of the historicity of his audience, German and otherwise, and he develops the formal and thematic features of his film in accordance with that knowledge. From Fassbinder's position, the point is not to convince viewers of the sophistication and depth of his own mind and politics but to motivate the viewer's own emotions and thought along a syntactical path that is accessible to emotional comprehension. Filmic revolution is, for him, an insidious affair.

Obviously the much documented love affair that Fassbinder has had with the films of the German-bred Sirk and other American directors derives in large part from this notion of filmmaking and its demand to communicate with an audience that, in most Western countries, has been weaned on Hollywood tropes. As he says in a 1971 interview, "American cinema is the only one I can take really seriously, because it's the only one that has really reached an audience. German cinema used to do so, before 1933. . . . But American cinema has generally had the happiest relationship with its audience. . . . Our films have been based on our *understanding* of the American cinema."[5] In other words, as Fassbinder remarks in his celebrated article on Sirk, "the main thing to be learned from American films was the need to meet their entertainment factor halfway. The idea is to make films as beautiful as America's, but which at the same time shift the content to other areas."[6]

Fassbinder came gradually to this awareness that good politics are incidental without effective avenues of communication, his strategies moving through intellectual phases associated with Straub, the "anti-theater," and the French New Wave.[7] Yet ultimately, with the assistance of his extraordinary cameraman Michael Ballhaus, he allied himself with the American cinema so that they could use its highly developed and proficient syntax to subvert its ideologically unsuspecting perspective. Through his manipulation and intellectual transformation of the Hollywood idiom—from the early seventies to his latest commercial successes, such as *The Marriage of Maria Braun*, *Veronika Voss*, and *Berlin Alexanderplatz*, Fassbinder's efforts have been, as he claims, "to learn how to show viewers the things they don't want to see in such a way that they *will* watch because it's excitingly made."[8]

No Fassbinder film demonstrates these strategies and the problematic response that they have generated better than *The Bitter Tears of Petra von Kant*, a film which appears late in Fassbinder's Hollywood phase and which makes use of what becomes one of the defining marks of his films during this period: Sirkian melodrama transformed into critical kitsch or camp, use of popular entertainment formulas but with critical, self-conscious distance. Midway through the film, Fassbinder underlines this not at all facile use of basic emotional formulas when the relatively uncultured Karin says to Petra: "Oh yes, I love the cinema. Seeing pictures about love and suffering. Lovely." The phrase sparkles with a multifaceted irony, most particularly since this is exactly the kind of film *The Bitter Tears of Petra von Kant* is. Yet Fassbinder's film of course becomes more than this: his is also a film about the way individuals relate cinematically amidst those central experiences of love and suffering, and so the film doubles back on itself. Whereas Karin can respond enthusiastically to that fundamental pleasure of the filmic text, Fassbinder's film is an extremely disconcerting attempt to move the viewer to a point where he or she can not only respond on that level but can also examine the murky middle ground where cinema and social life confuse the clarity of each other's communications. "I don't believe that melodramatic feelings are laughable," Fassbinder has remarked;[9] from his semi-Brechtian perspective on those melodramatic formulas comes his critical camp, his mixture of surface art and real emotions.[10]

This confusion of the cinematic and the social that Fassbinder puts in play in this film accounts to a large degree for the outcries it has drawn from nearly every sexual group with enough political sensitivity to react to the volatile issues that Fassbinder raises. Fassbinder's films are not mimetic; nor are they examples of social realism or utopian politics. They are, rather, relational mergers of different surfaces which do their work along the circuit that makes social reality itself a product of the psychoanalytic identifications that cinema initiates. Missing this relationship, a viewer finds inaccurate distortions where Fassbinder would say there are only distortions. Or put another way: if Fassbinder regularly uses transparently bourgeois figures, it is because these are the figures and images that bourgeois and nonbourgeois audiences alike have been trained to understand and enjoy. To alter ideas structured on these images, moreover, a filmmaker does little good in refusing the mechanisms of his audience's understanding but instead must manipulate those mechanisms toward a new understanding. Hence, as Judith Mayne observes, the crucial import of Fassbinder's use of Hollywood melodrama is that it "invites a consideration of the social significance of popular culture and the extent to which the entertainment factor can function in a critical way."[11]

Like Wenders then, Fassbinder situates his films in an American tradition and employs a high degree of critical reflexivity to mark his distance from that tradition. Yet, whereas *Kings of the Road* uses a realistic surface to tell the tale of two men and their wandering encounter with their own identities, *Petra von Kant* is a film of claustrophobic pessimism in which a lesbian couple substitutes for the standard heterosexual drama. Both films confront the threadbare cliché of the happy or normal family of American films.[12] Yet, conversely, the two films appear as nearly inversions of each other not only in their contrasting use of sexes and space but, most notably, in the relations that the films establish between themselves and a pro-filmic reality: while *Kings of the Road* seeks to introduce new filmic relations by short-circuiting the closed circle that describes the perspective of classical cinema, *Petra von Kant* turns inward to trace the exploitative grip that cinematic posturing has on life. That *Petra von Kant* is so radically insular does not of course mean that it is any less engaged with a social and political audience than *Kings of the Road*: the exaggerated isolation of this drama is—as with all Fassbinder films and as much as with any film in this study—a function of a complex horizon of historical expectations which have their center in the Hollywood subject but which also include a number of social formulations of a specifically German kind. Of these, there is most particularly the crisis of a social self in Germany as it developed out of the mass spectacle of the Third Reich, through the economic miracle of Adenauer's laissez-faire fifties, to its present condition where it remains haunted and divided by those past constitutions of self.[13] Seen in this context, *Petra von Kant* consequently becomes, in the very irony of its negations and omissions, as much a social and historical statement as any other Fassbinder film: a *Lola* without an explicit description of the street politics, a *Maria Braun* without the larger history of her economic progress to the insulated and fragile home of the final scenes. While both *Kings of the Road* and *Petra von Kant* serve, in short, as historical critiques of film's tyrannical power over perception and descriptions of the problem of identity in modern Germany, *Petra von Kant* argues this point not so much in the discursive or essayistic fashion of *Kings of the Road* but through an exaggerated style and decor which delineate the internal mechanics of the problem while not textually opening it (as Wenders often attempts to do). In this way, Fassbinder's pessimism becomes a pessimism of base content only, his negations traces of historical positives: for, in presenting that negative content, Fassbinder's stylized irony works ultimately to deflect and reflect its emotional pessimism and social isolation to a level which allows an understanding of those emotions and a clear view of those missing historical landscapes.

In *The Bitter Tears of Petra von Kant*, this work begins with the content itself, where those common cinematic motifs of love and suffering are displaced from a heterosexual couple to a lesbian one. Beginning with this switch in a Hollywood formula, the story then proceeds in a quite unremarkable way. Petra von Kant, a successful designer of women's fashions, lives with her servant-lover Marlene.

Once married, Petra has rejected that way of life and men in general, because of the exploitation and oppression that marriage and capitalistic sexual relations engender. In the second of the six sections of the film, Petra meets Karin, with whom she falls passionately in love, only to be abandoned by her at the end of the fourth section when Karin returns to her husband. The final sections describe Petra's complete breakdown and her last attempt to reconcile with the hitherto ignored Marlene. At this point, Marlene leaves.

In terms of audience expectations, the story itself is formulaic, with the important exception that the players of the melodrama are lesbian, a minority group generally ignored by films. In addition to this ripple in the standard Hollywood situation, moreover, the film entwines within the love story several long and self-dramatizing conversations that abstract and underline the important role that political economy plays in the usually foregrounded loves and desires of the characters. Early in the film, for example, Sidonie visits Petra to console her about the collapse of her marriage. In a dialogue that could serve as a subtext for the entire film, Petra explains how the relationship deteriorated, beginning by dispelling Sidonie's conventional expectation that the husband asked for the divorce or that adultery was involved. When Sidonie reproaches her for lacking humility and failing to use feminine wile, Petra snaps back: "I had no time for conjuring tricks. It only makes you unfree. . . . It's all very well for you and Lester. Maybe this lack of freedom is just what you need. . . . Frank and I wanted a higher love. . . . We wanted to be free, awake, know what's going on at all times. . . . We wanted to be happy together. . . . You understand: *together*." This romantic ideal of clarity and understanding begins, however, to turn to disgust when male dominance asserts itself through its principal vehicle, economics. "Men and their vanity," Petra complains; "He wanted to molly-coddle me and see I lacked nothing. . . . He wanted to be the breadwinner. . . . That way lies oppression, that's clear." In a patriarchal society, she says, there are two sets of rules, and her own financial success made these painfully apparent: "at first, it was: all you earn, my girl, will be put on one side; later on we can use it to buy a house, a sportscar. . . . At first, it was funny seeing his ridiculous pride being pricked, especially when I thought for sure he realized how absurdly he behaved. . . . And later when I tried to tell him that it made no difference who was on top or not, it was too late."

Economic resentment becomes sexual resentment, her husband's failure to control her financially resulting in a desperate attempt to dominate her physically. Sexual and economic exploitation merge, and while glossing over the economic dimension, Petra reacts bitterly against the sexual exploitation and abuse:

> The last six months were excruciating. He obviously saw it was all over, felt it at least, but wouldn't accept it. . . . He tried to keep the wife, if not wholly, then in bed. I let him possess me, I bore it. . . . That man was filth to me. He stank, stank like a man. What had once its charms now turned my stomach, brought tears to my eyes. . . . The way he bestraddled me, he served me like a bull would a cow. Not the slightest respect, no feeling for a woman's pleasure. The pain, Sidonie, you can't imagine. . . .

The honesty of this description and the reality of the suffering behind it should not be doubted. Yet, at the same time, Fassbinder sets in motion around this verbal discourse a complex series of visual and narrative qualifiers, which clearly reestablish its significance. Much in the fashion of the majority of his films, *Petra von Kant* offers a rather fundamental premise about love, need, and exploitation in a capitalistic society, and so exposes itself to the often facile criticism that the film itself is facile. Yet, the film then goes on to achieve its particular density by ironically layering that base theme again and again, in this way becoming an analysis and critical exposition of the surface predicament itself. Petra's long denunciation of men and description of the pain they have caused her is accordingly tangled through the course of the film in a larger visual and psychological drama which, in recontextualizing Petra and her dialogue, shows her (and all the other women in the film for that matter) exploiting and degrading women in the same manner that a male-dominated society and its cinema does.

Most explicitly, the film exposes the bombastic and indefatigable theatrics of Petra's personal and professional relationships. Elsaesser has rightly recognized these histrionics as a recurring element in Fassbinder's films, and notes that what results from Fassbinder's perspective on them is a "sometimes terrifying and often grotesque distance between the subjective *mise-en-scène* of the characters and the objective *mise-en-scène* of the camera." After 1970 especially, "the states of feeling are registered along a single dramatic and stylistic continuum: on the razor's edge, maybe, between risibility and tragedy, camp or kitsch, but what has disappeared is the ambivalence surrounding the characters' own role-playing, and with it the uneasy awareness of watching a documentary about people playing out a fiction."[14] The camera's first encounter with Petra begins on this note. After the credit sequence, during which the camera holds on the base of the darkened steps which lead down into the room, it tracks slowly across the wall-sized reproduction of mythically scaled nudes to the shadowy figure of the sleeping Petra. Light suddenly floods the body, and Petra awakes and quickly telephones her mother, saying, "Mother, I had no time yesterday. . . . No, I've been up for ages." She then turns, looks directly into the close-up angle, smiles, and insists, "It's true!" While this lie is ostensibly for the mother, the camera work and direction are clearly for the audience, turning to grotesque mockery the played reality that the audience observes, severing the theatrics of Petra from a perspective on them, yet concomitantly assuring the spectator's complicity in the act. The audience and Petra, in brief, have the advantage of their privileged positions.

The theatrics gain momentum from this point on. Petra's first act after she leaves the bed is to don one of her many wigs and elaborate dressing robes. Her second phone call (to the department store Karstadt) is another hypocritical ruse; during her long monologue with Sidonie, the camera focuses on the preciously tiresome process of making up her face as if for a performance. These painstakingly exaggerated warm-ups then culminate in the third section of the film when Petra and Karin confront each other in outlandish Wagnerian costumes and perform a dance-like ritual of seduction and melodramatic intimacy. It is here that Karin expresses her love of the cinema, and it is here that theatrics and cinema blend most effectively in stylized

"The planes of sexuality: Sidonie, Petra, and Marlene"
(*Petra von Kant*).

movements of emotion and manipulation, more like Brechtian "gests" than naturalistic gestures. In the final moments of this sequence, Petra tells Karin, "I can see
you now parading in public. . . . I'll make a first class model of you, Karin. . . .
You're beautiful, Karin." And as she convinces Karin to move in with her because
"it's cheaper," the statement coincides neatly with the climax of their mutual seduction through sex, theatrics, and economics. The scene as spectacle thus becomes, in Judith Mayne's words, a quintessential "guise through which the commodity form permeates social relationships," a theatrics of sexual reification.[15]
    The most salient sign of this reifying conjunction of theater, economics, and sex
is Petra's profession itself. As a fashion designer, she markets appearances, self-im-
ages made through clothing; the success of that marketing is appropriately the product of sexual appeal and financial interest. In short, she sells sexual images and does
it with a great deal of success. Visually the film is punctuated from beginning to end
by the tools of this trade—Marlene working with fabric, the mannequins, and so
forth—so that as Petra and Karin work in the foreground at their sexual relationship,
the business of desire superimposes on the business of design in the background.
Both occupations must purvey a more or less fantastic image to a client; both subsist
on the repeated and persistent cycle of production-consumption, the underpinning of
a capitalist culture. To emphasize this last point, eating and drinking (the elemental

and natural art of production and consumption) take place only on the bed, which is also the place where Petra makes her business calls, makes love, and gives work orders to Marlene.

While this business of theatrics has an obvious and neat correlation with the business of cinema, two other central motifs have a perhaps less obvious but equally significant connection with the film mechanism itself: nostalgia and dreams. Of these two, nostalgia interrupts the action regularly, and it thus contributes most strikingly to the confusion of temporal spheres in the film. Shortly after telephoning her mother, for instance, Petra plays the fifties recording of "Smoke Gets in Your Eyes" by the Platters, while she dances in a circle with Marlene. The reverie it inspires is repeated at the end of the film's second section when she plays the Walker Brothers' "In My Room" for Karin, and then comments: ". . . records from my past. They either make me very sad . . . or very happy." That these two instances (along with the Platters' song which ends the film) are American tunes from the postwar years is clearly not insignificant. But, more importantly, they and the parade of period costumes that the various characters wear signal an entrapment in memories which muddle and blur any sort of historical perspective which might lead to self-knowledge. After Petra's comment about her inconsistent emotional reaction to old records, she drifts into a memory of her former husband, and, with her new lover standing before her, she ironically remarks on the inescapable cruelty that emotions perpetrate and which she will soon become the victim of: "That was romance. . . . Pierre was killed in a car. He loved driving. He thought he was immortal, but wasn't. . . . Yet everything is predestined in life, I'm convinced. . . . People are terrible, Karin. They can bear anything . . . anything. People are hard and brutal. They don't need anyone. . . . That's the lesson." For Petra, however, these very words suggest it is a lesson unlearned again and again through the alternating periods of her life.

This tragicomic inability to distinguish time and experiences and thus to escape the bitter circle of love and suffering appears most dramatically in the second and third parts of the film. Stylistically and structurally the two parts parallel each other along anchoring points such as the elegant poses of Petra and Sidonie later reenacted by Petra and Karin. Likewise, there are the long monologues which form the core of each episode, in the first Petra telling of the collapse of her marriage, in the second Karin recounting her childhood and adolescence. Petra, moreover, delivers a small speech on humility in each of these sections, the second mirroring and reversing the first according to a pattern which describes the course of the entire film: first, she rebukes Sidonie's belief that humility is the key to a successful relationship; later she mildly urges that same humility on Karin. "You have to learn humility," she explains. "Everyone has his own theory of the world. . . . I believe you have to be humble to bear better what you comprehend. I'm humble before my work—and the money I earn. . . . In the face of things stronger than myself." These reversals outline the part-ludicrous, part-tragic pattern of the whole film through which Petra changes her stance to suit her desires: her nostalgic desire for what might have been (those "wonderful chances for that man and me" of her first marriage) forces her to switch her roles and her realities rapidly, and thus to become trapped again and again in the oppressor/victim cycle of sexual desires. This is most evident in Petra's chaotic movement through her sexual oppression by males, her dominating of Karin in part 3, Karin's exploitation of her in part 4, and finally Petra's offering of a new start to Marlene at the conclusion of the film, an offer which actually means a return to the state of the relationship at the beginning of the film. Stuck in a reality which is fundamentally nostalgic and hence utopian, Petra must act out her desire repeatedly in the bombastic terms of a grand soap opera, the artificial pomp of the gestures thus masking the flat redundance of the meaning. When Petra and Karin first meet, both comment that "nothing much can change in Germany." Similarly, while Petra views her history and future only from the perspective of her libidinal longings, her temporal reality stalls in nostalgia, the immobile voyage of cinema itself.

These longings and moments of nostalgia naturally manifest themselves as kinds of waking dreams in *Petra von Kant*, thus adding another layer to those central motifs of theatrics, nostalgia, and a film economics whose business is to manufacture dreams. Petra's first statement in the film is "Marlene, have some consideration. . . . I've had such awful dreams," which ironically signals her awakening into a world she will people with equally awful dreams. Later, after Karin arrives for her date with Petra, Petra begins her inquiry into Karin's past by saying, "tell me about yourself . . . what you dream of." Petra then sets out to fulfill those dreams of Karin, "to make something of [her] life" by transforming her into a "first-class model," the dream-image of both their desires. Finally, Petra's profession itself is a fairly transparent case of an occupation that sells dreams through appearances, and its obtrusive economic base begins to suggest more strongly the crucial connection between Petra, the designer, and Fassbinder, the filmmaker, whose business is likewise the purveying of dreams through appearances and images.[16]

The connection exists, in fact, at the film's center: just as the theatrical costumes that pervade the film as manifestations of the individual's dreams seem anarchically nostalgic (recalling without much order a mélange of different historical periods), the cinema itself relies on a manipulation of time apart from the actual present and makes its meaning through the reworking of filmic types and characters that originate in different historical eras.[17] Indeed, establishing this correlation between Petra's temporal and imagistic disorder and filmmaking is, on the one hand, Fassbinder's usual attempt at self-criticism, seen in many of his films from *Beware of a Holy Whore* to *Germany in Autumn*. Yet, on the other hand and more importantly, this correlation allows Fassbinder the distance needed to investigate and criticize at once the dynamics of a personality such as Petra's and the dynamics of a traditional cinema whose internal and external workings are the mirror reflection of that personality. In *Petra von Kant* the story of the loneliness and need that drive an individual to manipulate a personal history by means of artificial images becomes a descriptive figure and demonstration of a psychoanalytic and cinematic apparatus, which exploits desire with images, and especially images of women.

Besides the dislocation and deconstruction of Petra's anachronistic posturing, the single space of the film where those images flourish so randomly is equally striking and equally central to this self-reflexive status of *Petra von Kant*. Fassbinder has correctly noted that, although *Petra von Kant* was originally a play, he doesn't "find it a particularly theatrical film."[18] For, although the camera is confined to a single room through the film's duration, *Petra von Kant* appears less a product of its theatrical heritage than an attempt to create a world that has hermetically sealed itself into an arena where fantasy will have minimal interference from an external reality, a working space, in other words, much like the artificial set of a Hollywood film. Offscreen space has little weight here, except to suggest that this is not where life is usually lived; in this sense the single space of Fassbinder's film becomes more cinematic than a dynamically cut and edited film: the space of *Petra von Kant* becomes a kind of abstracted and isolated cinematic rectangle where the continuous transformation at the heart of all movies takes place. There are of course numerous references to places outside Petra's room, such as her mother's trip to Miami or Karin's life in Australia. But through the overwhelming presence that the one room acquires, these extra-filmic places have less reality than the large wall mural of the set or the Trojan fantasy that the character's costumes create: here the power of the visual imagination to control its space minimizes the substantiality of any other geography on the edge of the film.

This dialectic between a time and space artificially produced and a historical time and space outside the filmic image describes the most general conflict in which the spectator becomes inscribed. Yet, within that single space of the film, there are other, more specific cinematic tensions which operate as similar kinds of analyses of the filmic medium itself. Foremost on the level of technique is the constant movement of the camera across space, either as tracks, zooms, or rack focuses which stand out in sharp contrast to the stasis of space and the flat tableau-like vignettes of the characters. Developed to an extreme in *Chinese Roulette*, these extraordinarily emphatic camera movements function most obviously as alienation strategies that situate the viewer at a variety of distances from the image-making processes within the film and of the film.[19] On the one hand, the dramatic differences of the camera movement make the lack of movement or progress in the characters painfully apparent; on the other, this shifting camera eye becomes an unsettling visual commentary and context for most of the film's action and dialogue. As Fassbinder himself notes, "when the camera moves a great deal around something that's dead, it's shown to be dead. Then you create a longing for something that's alive."[20] In *Petra von Kant*, that longing is clearly for an activity of open spaces, an interaction of bodies rather than poses, and a temporal process other than nostalgia.

Most often these camera-commentaries refer to Petra, usually in her relation to Marlene. A good example is Petra's conversation with Sidonie about her marriage with Frank. As Petra explains in the foreground that "it was funny seeing his ridiculous pride pricked, especially when I thought for sure he realized how absurdly he behaved," the camera refocuses on Marlene sketching in the background. Fassbinder then begins a track in on Marlene, while Petra remarks that Frank never saw what was happening to himself. The track ends with an extreme close-up of Marlene which suddenly zooms backward and racks Marlene out of focus. Meanwhile Petra complains to Sidonie: "when I tried to tell him that it made no difference whether a man was on top or not, it was too late. . . . Soon as I broached the matter . . . like a blank wall, Sidonie.'' At this point, the camera begins a slow pan across the un-focused foreground, where the reverse zoom had ended, to a close-up of Petra in the mirror finishing making up her face and sighing, ''then sincerity gradually began to die.'' Across and around Petra's rather vacuous summary of the end of her relation-ship, the camera thus complicates and visually embeds what is otherwise an exces-sively simple point: Marlene pays for the sins of Frank as a surrogate victim. As part of her role, she must witness the tyrannical and hypocritical spectacle of Petra, just as Petra witnessed Frank's; yet sight and awareness also require that she must serve and never be seen; she must literally be blurred out of focus in order that the spec-tacle as exhibition goes on. As the last comment and image emphasize, the oppres-sor is the point of focus, acting out with total sincerity the illusion of a self-made image; the victim, conversely, is an audience, immobile and noninterfering. In Pe-tra's words, ''Marlene sees all, hears all, knows all. Don't worry about Marlene.''

As the visual dramatics of this last sequence illustrate, this kind of exploitative relationship depends to an unusual extent on the abstraction and separation of sur-faces. Exposing these surfaces does not mean, however, that Fassbinder has some contrasting belief, like Bazin's, in the sincerity and integrity of spatial depth. On the contrary, depth of any kind is, for Fassbinder, primarily a question of planar inter-action. He seeks to identify how different planes of action empower each other with significance and thus, through this identification, to challenge any mystical notions about the spatial ambiguity of reality. As part of this effort, Fassbinder uses roughly three major planar surfaces in *Petra von Kant*: the work area usually occupied by Marlene and the mannequins, the slightly raised bed area where Petra eats, flirts, and conducts her business, and the vertical plane of the wall mural which stretches across one end of the room. As in the sequence just discussed, the camera always positions itself in relation to one of these planes and then redefines or contrasts a character or action in terms of one of the other planes. As Petra finishes the last touch of makeup and recalls the lost innocence with Frank, for instance, the cam-era's last movement is to pull back slightly so the mural appears. One of the more intrusive presences in the film, this Poussin reproduction represents a sort of bac-chanalian rite in which an over-scaled male nude is surrounded by equally mytho-logically grand female figures, naked and fawning. In this sequence, the mural be-comes most obviously a spurious correlative for the prelapsarian innocence that Petra misses, as well as an image of the grandiose dreams of self and love that propel her throughout the film. That the camera angle here neatly joins the reproduction and Petra regarding her newly madeup face in the mirror makes this statement al-most too explicit, suggesting both the unreality of her imaginings and the two-di-mensionality of their theatrical function. In the course of the film, this visual met-aphor is frequently repeated and culminates in the penultimate section when a low angle shot describes Petra's overblown, theatrical collapse in front of the overblown mural, thus exposing her apparent emotional depth as the product of the play of the two planes.

This mirror play between surfaces occurs in an equally striking fashion at two other, adjoining points in the film where the dramatic crossing of spatial planes be-comes a critical reading of the same kind and not merely a seeing of this reality. The action begins at the start of the third section of the film, which opens on a dimly lit Marlene typing in the corner of the work area. She rises, and the camera begins one of its many parallel tracks through the work area, following Marlene's legs through the beams and mannequins as the legs pass on the higher plane of the bed area. (As usual, this kind of track most noticeably breaks up the continuity of space and simultaneously frames the action internally so as to mark off cinematic behavior within this particular cinema product.) Marlene then stops at the bed, and silently initiates a dance of legs in which she wraps beads around Petra, to create one of the several circular metaphors in the film. Petra leaves the room and Karin arrives, walking across the room and seeming to look directly into the camera while actually regarding herself in a mirror positioned just in front of the camera. Cutting to a new position, the camera appears to maintain approximately the same angle on Karin, behind whom Petra suddenly appears in the doorway and compliments her on her extravagant dress. At precisely this point, the camera swings 180 degrees, pausing on Karin's profile and finally facing Petra, as it pans out of the mirror into which it had again been deceptively shooting. After some flirtation, the same maneuver is repeated, this time with Petra turning out of the mirror in conjunction with the camera's 180-degree pan from the same mirror so that the illusion of face to face conversation between the two women is disconcertingly shattered and then reestablished. During this second shot, the camera again pauses a moment on Petra's profile to coincide with the first of her many leading questions: "Tell me about yourself . . . what you dream of."

In both these shots, the camera quite effectively upsets the illusion of a tightly defined space by creating a counterillusion according to conventional planes of action which the camera movement then promptly undercuts. On one level, this visual game works simply as a signifier, indicating how each woman's absorption in her own self-image is the catalyst for the romance: each makes love with herself, and the dreams and identity of the one are ultimately important only as they manifest the desires of the other's ego. The figure of the circle that the two complementary shots combine to form indicates the direction of such interaction. On another level, however, these shots function as literal dislocators of space, first anchoring the spectator's perspective and then cutting it loose from all illusory surface. Like the very pace of the film and the intentionally long takes, the spectator's usually passive acknowledgment of patterns of visual coherence must give way at these points to a more active reflection. As Fassbinder says of his long takes, "stylistically, it is a kind of alienation" whereby "the audience can really see what's really happening between the characters involved."[21] What for the characters is merely seeing, with the self as the center of an imaginatively whole space,[22] becomes for the viewer a reading of spatial surfaces that normally work to disguise how they produce fantasies of self as meaning.

Inhabiting the central space, Petra and her drama thus evolve at the intersection of two planes: she is flanked on one side by the gigantic, mythological scene and on the other side by the eerie mannequins which stand here and there in the work area. In this dialectic, the two-dimensional giants obviously represent the realm of dreams and desires, while the lower plane is the place of Marlene and the mannequins, both denuded and both functioning as the surface on which desires and fantasies can be acted out. Marlene and the mannequins are in fact nearly interchangeable, just as Petra's work as a designer is closely linked to her sexual exploitation of Marlene. (It is quite appropriate, therefore, that Marlene creates many of the fashions on which Petra's reputation is made, since Marlene is literally without character, living only to serve Petra's desires as a blank mirror present only to bear witness.) Summing this up nicely, part 2 closes with Petra inviting Karin to return the next evening because she "has a nice figure." As Petra rises from her bed, the camera tracks backward to the work area, once again cutting across different planes and eventually containing all three: the reproduction looms in the background, the bed in the middle ground, and the easel with Marlene's latest sketch in the foreground. The first two planes, moreover, are reframed in this shot by the wooden beams that separate the work area from the rest of the room, thus isolating all three as if they were merely separate aesthetic frames of action. At this point, Petra walks slowly toward the beams and camera, staring and contemplating either the budding romance with Karin or the new design by the insignificant Marlene. As Marlene enters the background to remove the tray from the scene of Petra's recent tryst, Petra remarks from her reverie: "You've altered the sleeves . . . yes, that's good . . . they'll like that better." Marlene gazes blankly at her as she lifts the tray, aware of but unresponsive to her role as a functioning cipher. The camera then focuses on the intersecting point of the three planes: of Petra's sexual fantasies and business fantasies, her dreams for Karin and her abuse of Marlene, the imaginative fullness of one and the bare emptiness of the other, an intersection that creates a planar depth without ambiguity.

The film proceeds temporally according to the same dialectical pattern that the camera initiates on a spatial level. Like the spatial argument, the reversals that occur through the course of the film's story work mostly to suggest not an ambiguity or contradiction but the very visible bind of a capitalistic logic. Most obvious is the reversal whereby Petra changes from the exploited wife to the exploiting lover and then back to the groveling mistress. Aptly, the conclusion to these vacillations of role is marked by a bare, bedless room, low-angle shots of Petra drunk and prostrate on the floor, and a close-up of the mannequins wrenched grotesquely onto the bed now moved to the work area: reversing its terms to their negation, her fantastic love is thus finally stripped of its theatrical covering and returned to the workshop from which those coverings originate; the third mannequin that hovers over the bed and watches becomes that outside perspective, here ironically reduced, as the crucial ingredient that empowers Petra's version of exhibitionary love.

Part 5 presents this same pattern by focusing it specifically on the family structure, a structure that Fassbinder exposes most ferociously in *Jailbait* and one that pervades the film from Petra's first phone call to her mother to the mother's departure when Petra returns to bed at the conclusion. From the outset, this traditional family structure appears out of kilter, fascistic in its exploitation of emotional bonds, and generally disordered. A dislocation as well as an exaggeration, the film has Petra lecturing her mother in the first sequence about borrowing and spending too much money; later, during Karin's long talk about families, Petra quickly takes the role of the condescending parent who both knows more and has more economic leverage. While Petra defends sending her own daughter away to boarding school because "it's best for parents not to interfere," she nonetheless gradually begins to interfere as much as possible in the life of Karin, her surrogate daughter-lover. As Karin relates her tragic childhood—during which her father is grotesquely victimized by a capitalistic economy[23]—Petra's role as mother-lover likewise becomes the oppressive power associated with class distinction, money, and sexual dominance. Part 3 continues this strained and awry family game when the thoroughly spoiled Karin reverses the situation to command Petra from her bed, just as Petra had ordered Marlene. Petra begs and whines for love and recognition, like a rejected mother; when Karin demands money, Petra sarcastically rebukes her like the parent of an adolescent leaving home: "I'm good enough to pay!" Speaking of these parent-child relations in general, Fassbinder succinctly describes the distortions and manipulations that become the terms of the nuclear family which Petra and Karin mirror so oddly in their changing roles here: "Everyone who comes into the world," he says, "is not taken seriously as a human being. . . . As time passes, the parent becomes the figure which the child in one respect accepts as dominant, which means that all through their lives they will accept dominant figures while at the same time trying to destroy this dominance in order to exist. Actually a child develops a dual need for dominance and destruction, which is to say that one becomes sadistic and masochistic at the same time."[24]

This central concern with the psychological and ideological base of the family is, however, far more than just Fassbinder's hobbyhorse, for in this structure the ideological fixing of the subject finds the sociological counterpart for the constitutive power of the cinema that Fassbinder works so carefully to deconstruct. In *Language and Materialism*, Coward and Ellis indicate how the apparatuses of the family and the cinema function similarly in this material fixing of a subject according to an established discourse:

> Ideological practice is then doubly material: it works to fix the subject in relation to certain fixities of discourse, and it is concretised in certain apparatuses. Behind these lie repressive apparatuses, which can be used to ensure the continuance of existing power relations by force if ideological practice fails to do so. The notion of materiality of ideology consisting in its fixing the subject alters the status of the ideological apparatuses themselves: the family assumes a greater importance than accredited to it by Althusser and ceases to be an ideological state apparatus. It becomes the arena in which the subject is produced in a certain relation to discourse, and therefore meaning.[25]

With Karin's departure, the ideology and security of this tortured family structure vanish, and Petra, in a characteristic reversal, furiously attacks the very model on which her relationship with Karin was based. The day is appropriately her birthday, marking a passage of time that she has continually worked against and gathering about her the members of a family she has continually tried to to exploit. At first relations proceed as one would expect in a family hierarchy of this type: when her daughter, Gabriele, tells how she "is terribly unhappy" because her love for a boy is unrequited, Petra laughs, not seeing in Gabriele's longing for this Mick Jagger look-alike the mirror image of her own theatrical love. When Gabriele protests Petra's treatment of Marlene, Sidonie naturally rebukes Gabriele: "I don't think you're old enough to judge what your mother does." With Sidonie's arrival just previous to this remark, however, the patina of social order begins to crack, bombastically announced when the camera zooms to Petra shattering a glass in her hand on hearing Sidonie's name at the door. Straining appearances to an extreme, the two women kiss and welcome each other warmly, and Sidonie then gives Petra a present, a plastic doll which resembles Karin enough to elicit an expression of pained recognition from Petra. This doll-child, as the quintessentially possessable image, merges here into one parodic figure of the child Petra mothered in her relationship with Karin and the silent mannequins, symbols of the blank surface behind her many façades and fictions. The forced recognition of the dual nature of this loved image naturally triggers an explosive tirade from Petra, who then attacks the family myth that has supported all of them. "You all sicken me. You're a pack of liars. . . . A pack of bloody parasites," she cries while knocking Gabriele to the floor. Turning on her own mother, she screams: "You were kept by father and then by me. You're a whore, mother." Confronted with this outbreak and Petra's lesbian relationship, Gabriele goes into shock, and the mother wanders dazed toward the bed with the mannequins. Later, in the coda of the film, the mother sits next to Petra's bed, distractedly remembering that even her conventional marriage and dead husband had not been preserved from disillusionment and violation. As an analogue for the power of cinema itself, the family remains a fragile illusion held in place by desperation and melancholic faith in its sacrosanct image.

This familial cycle of exploitation and disillusionment finally comes full circle when Petra makes her offer of equality to Marlene. Prior to this, Petra admits to her mother that "love should be undemanding. . . . I learned my lesson and it hurt." Yet, Petra's stripped face, her position in bed, the lighting, and the camera angle all suggest that this is not the case, and that Petra has merely returned to the emotional point which opened the film. When the mother leaves, Petra approaches Marlene, who is busy sketching as always, and says, "I owe you an apology. . . . In the future we'll really work together. You shall have what you deserve: freedom and joy." Marlene bends over and kisses her hand. But Petra immediately rejects this gesture: "Not like that. Tell me about yourself." Knowledge and freedom, however, are impossible for Marlene, as Fassbinder explains:

> The servant accepts her own repression and exploitation, and is therefore afraid of the freedom she is offered. What goes with freedom is the responsibility of having to think about your own existence, and that is something she has never had to do. . . . When she leaves Petra she is not . . . heading for freedom but going in search of another slave-existence. . . . It would be wildly optimistic, even utopian, to imagine that someone who has done and thought nothing for thirty years except what others have thought for her would all of a sudden choose freedom.[26]

The double irony is of course that Petra would be as incapable of giving this freedom as Marlene would be of accepting it. Yet, even the idea of playing a manipulated role other than that of a passive observer is as frightening to Marlene as freedom is: Marlene can observe but not become part of the spectacle. Hence, as Petra starts another cycle of pretenses and nostalgic distortions, Marlene packs to leave. The closing frontal medium shot remains stationary as Marlene moves back and forth across the stage space of the bedroom, walking offscreen left and right, between the grand image on the wall and the work space of the mannequins, collecting belongings to toss in a suitcase in the middle of the floor. Meanwhile Petra sits mutely on the bed listening to "The Great Pretender," which plays on the record player for the entire shot. The last item that Marlene picks up and holds over the suitcase is the doll that resembles Karin, a mannequin child that neatly symbolizes the kind of exploitative existence that Marlene needs and Petra cannot escape, a diminutive figure which, following Marlene's repetitious moves back and forth across the room, is figuratively born of that recurring pattern — that is, out of the cycle generated by a perceptual alternation between those vicitimizing giants of the imagination and the bare forms they necessarily return to.

That these desires, exploitations, and delusions are so explicitly bound here to that cinematic figure of the circle and the specular giants associated with the filmic screen is the specific center of the film's argument about a perceptual figuration, a particular figuration of the body traditionally fostered and supported by a Hollywood ideology.[27] Besides the many obvious connections in *Petra von Kant* between Hollywood representation and the drama of the characters themselves, Fassbinder's use and critique of this aesthetic, in other words, has focused most importantly on the motif of the human figure as object of desire, a motif which since its historical inception has been film's central subject and the cultural base of its representation. Theoretically, Metz, Baudry, and others have persuasively discussed this cinematic figure in terms of a psychoanalytic model in which scopic desire inscribes itself onto the body as text.[28] And as a material and communication model, this figure as trope has been the dominant presence in film from the time of Méliès's erotic conjuring of dancing girls and polar giants to Pasolini's studies in film as sado-eroticism, the body consistently being the mystery to be resolved and the source of audience fascination. In the middle of this tradition and exemplary of it, moreover, is *Citizen Kane*, a film in every sense about the jigsaw-puzzle pursuit of a figure and lost body across a space whose notoriety is its flamboyant physical depth and different representations of that lost body. More so than in any other medium, as Fassbinder's film makes clear, on the cinema screen the body has been, in Foucault's words, "the inscribed surface of events (traced by language and dissolved by ideas), the locus of a dissociated Self (adopting the illusion of a substantial unity), and a volume in perpetual disintegration."[29]

Petra von Kant engages the representational base of this pervasively established cinematic figure on several levels. As I have indicated, the story itself depicts Petra's sexual desire as fundamentally a producer of two-dimensional postures which are the mirror-image of her inflated ego; underlining this point, the camera presents and examines the depth of the film's single space *not* in order to generate an erotic surface (across which scopic desire can play off the ambiguity of depth) but to delineate the separate planes of action which when demystified indicate precisely the emotional mechanics of imagistic desire. What the film describes in this manner is a predicament (that of Petra and of classical cinema) in which scopic desire fluctuates between the utter absence of an object and its exaggerated presence, between the body as an unmarked surface and the body as resplendent giant. The economy of finances of this predicament are, moreover, a crucial element in the dialectic since, in both cinema and social life, the power to seduce a perspective is often a function of the quantitative value attached to the image, a value frequently indexed by size, texture, and material investment. In *Petra von Kant*, in short, Petra's exploitation of her lovers parallels the exploitation of the spectator by the cinematic image, and Fassbinder's technical deconstruction in this film becomes a bi-level project in which the financial erotics of social life share a space with the desiring machine which is the film industry.

In this effort, *Petra von Kant* pinpoints its target even more precisely as the cinematic representation of women and woman's body, doubtless the most exploited object of cinematic representation. Indeed Fassbinder has cavalierly tried to explain his continual use of women as the centers of his films in some rather superficial ways.[30] Yet, in *Petra von Kant* the choice of women as the objects of representation is central in Fassbinder's exposure of cinematic representation, since the power of cinema as an oppressor in its own right has been traditionally dependent on maintaining the status of woman's body as an erotically controlled image.

In one of the first rigorous essays to deal with sexism as a basic underpinning of the classical cinema, Stephen Heath examines this issue and in doing so touches on many of the tenets about desire and vision that Fassbinder works through more concretely in his film. Operating from a Lacanian framework, Heath argues that, except for radical efforts like Chantal Akerman's films, most conventional films subject women to the reifying gaze of the male as signifier. This dominance of the male point of view, he notes, has always been part of the patriarchal culture described and to some extent propagated by Freud and Lacan:

> Given the perspective of visibility established, it is the sex of the woman that is taken as the very instance of the unseeable, the hidden: Freud records his belief that "probably no male being is spared the fright of castration at the sight of a female genital"; Lacan talks of "the pre-eminently original object, the abyss of the female organ from which all life comes forth. . . ."
>
> The function of castration as the articulation of the subject in difference is brought down to a matter of sight, the articulation of the symbolic to a vision. Where the conception of the symbolic as movement and production of difference, as chain of signifiers in which the subject is effected in division, should forbid the notion of some presence from which difference is then derived, Lacan instates the visible as the condition of symbolic functioning, with the phallus the standard of visibility required; seeing is from the male organ.[31]

Pornography being a crudely transparent example, the discourse of classical film has always perpetuated this formula of vision whereby the woman attains significance through the sight of the male. Her very definition is as the body displayed, and the narrative structure of conventional cinema works explicitly to naturalize this erotic image of woman while still maintaining it as that possessable object of desire: "It is as though the fiction film of the dominant cinema knows the imaginary of its image of the woman at the same time that it seeks to reconfirm it, with the narrative the arena of that knowledge and the tactic of its containment . . . the woman's body is displayed . . . and the narrative allows a certain action of a woman in order to keep her in image, the same image."[32] Recalling Metz's use of the psychoanalytic lack as the motivating force for the spectator's scopic desire, Heath summarizes:

> The woman is not the ruin of representation but its veritable support in the patriarchal order, the assigned point at-on-which representation holds and makes up lack, the vanishing point on which the subject that representation represents fixes. . . . The difference of woman is the visibility of man, the assured perspective, the form of exchange; with woman's representing as *the* lack, *the* difference, her projection as image and screen, the point—the erotic return—of a *certain* mystery, the veil of truth.[33]

Heath's dense description here almost patently fits the dilemma of Petra von Kant: as a designer of appearances, Petra is a mistress of representations, whose tragedy is in large part that her representations, of herself and her lovers, are based in male structures of perception. As Moustapha Safouan notes in *Sexualité féminine*, "the woman finds her being not as a woman but as phallus," and thus becomes a reflective spectacle of male perception in which the self and vision of self are postured and defined by the male gaze: "if the woman looks, the spectacle provokes" and so "she must not look, is absorbed herself on the side of the seen, seeing herself seeing herself."[34] In this light, Petra's climactic and hysterical collapse in part 3 becomes more than a response to the rejection by and loss of Karin. Entirely dislocated from her sexual and familial identity, it becomes additionally an opening onto the chaos of self-imaging, a desperate reaction to her self-representation within a masculine model of signification: "the hysteric is unsure as to being woman or man . . . hers is a body in trouble with language, that forcing of the signifying matter, resisting and accepting simultaneously the given signs, the given order."[35]

As the emblem of a Quattrocento perspective, the large Renaissance mural that forms that two-dimensional plane in the film both depicts and dramatizes unmistakably the domination of this masculine point of view whereby the phallus is the ultimate signifier. Besides the representation itself (females languishing slavishly before a nude male), this mural emphasizes the informing presence of the male signifier several times in the film when the camera positions the penis of the nude precisely behind or above Petra during her conversations or theatrical manipulations. Here again the camera interlocks planes in order to show that the total absence of men in the film is only a surface illusion; in terms of the psychoanalytic reality of the images in the film, the male as signifier is constantly present, just as Petra's expelling men from her life is true only in terms of her biological behavior, not in terms of her psychological or social behavior. While Petra claims to have created sexual parity among women, her images belie her, just as the spate of dialogue in the film indicates the constant and controlling presence of a patriarchal discourse and the sexual difference it represents.[36]

What *The Bitter Tears of Petra von Kant* accomplishes, consequently, is, first, a garishly lucid examination of how individuals, regardless of sex, accept hopelessly redundant patterns of exploitation put in place by a patriarchal society and, second, a visual dissection of how this society maintains these sexual and corporeal patterns through the tyranny of an image whose mechanisms of production it must hide in order that they succeed. Regarding the second, Fassbinder's camera exposes and deconstructs these mechanisms as separate fields of activity so that the power of the established film image, like the power of the established sex, appears not as the product of some mysterious link with nature but as a symbolic act generated by an economics of presence and absence, as a business of covering lack with the inflated dreams of giant images. The single room of the film becomes both the pro-filmic and filmic space for this argument, the suturing point of the two poles of production within which a possessable image and symbolic meaning are fabricated for the subject. Flanked by a bombastic image of desire and the blank figures of lack, the rectangle of the room critically represents the conjunction of these two poles as a spectacle normally meant to absorb the spectator and so disguise the artificial terms of its production. As Heath explains:

> Any social formation depends for its existence not simply on the economic and political instances but also on a reasoning of the individual as subject, reproduced in images, identities of meaning, finding his or her delegation there. The term of this process is suture, suture as representing: . . . the achievement in representation of the bind of the spectator as subject-construction, as in possession (the representation of "for me," as "mine"). Cinema is an institution of representing, a machine for the fabrication-maintenance of representation; it is as such that it is a crucial ideological investment.[37]

Through the mystification of the mechanics of representation, cinema enforces a difference and division that it mistakenly purports to be grounded in a biological sexuality, in a physical body, while in fact this difference is mainly ideological. Replacing the reverse-angle cut with lavish tracks and zooms, Fassbinder quite graphically moves the spectator outside the logic of this suturing action as he describes the spatial illusions which function according to that logic. Undercutting the sympathetic identification of tragedy with the distance of an uneasy laughter, the film thus exposes the imagistic constructions that control both conventional cinema and conventional sexual relations as specifically symbolic productions whose suturing point encapsulates the history of the patriarchal subject always under construction and whose summary metaphor is the risible plastic doll that appears out of Marlene's last dialectical walk back and forth across filmic space itself.

Focusing on the ideological base that conjoins sexuality and the cinema, Fassbinder's *Petra von Kant* consequently operates something like Hellmuth Costard's *The Oppression of Women Is Primarily Evident in the Behavior of Women Themselves*, a film whose painfully drawn-out time scheme and use of a male as the housewife disturbs *on the level of representation* the passivity of the patriarchal spectator, a passivity which relies in social life and in the cinema on the complacent acceptance of an oppressive representational difference located in terms of the body.

Despite its theatrical look, *Petra von Kant* fundamentally and specifically attacks cinematic representation, not in order to dismiss the emotional force of the filmic experience but to subvert, like Costard, the passive structure that this experience imposes on the spectator. "The only kind of realism that interests me," Fassbinder points out, "is that which happens in the head of the spectator, not the realism on the screen."[38] Here, the imaginative and emotional needs which the cinema dramatizes are not at fault. What is at fault, rather, is the spectatorial passivity that conventional cinema has traditionally fostered and the subsequent ability of this cinema to disguise the productive and symbolic nature of sexual politics and representations.

I am not suggesting that *Petra von Kant* is an ideologically faultless film. Of Fassbinder's many films, this hermetically sealed work in particular has problems with its political aesthetics — not the least of which concerns that left-wing melancholy which can easily make a theoretical Marxist in Germany into a mindless third-generation terrorist. Additionally, there is the bombastic aestheticism itself which, while it may be intended as a Brechtian maneuver, becomes in this film especially such a studied and convoluted beauty that its point can often be lost in the glare. Yet, Fassbinder himself would hardly claim that *Petra von Kant* or any of his films, for that matter, are either faultless products or completed achievements: often they are intentionally rapid sketches made by an incredibly active intelligence and directed at very specific political and emotional concerns; again, it is less the film's political and emotional scope that is at stake than its ability to provoke a viewer's emotional intelligence actively to consider itself in relation to the world of representations that it inhabits.

Early in the film, Petra notes that "people need one another, are built that way. But they haven't learned to live together." Perhaps no German filmmaker has understood this emotional need and its dependence on symbolic images of self better than Fassbinder. Perhaps no German filmmaker has understood better than Fassbinder the sexual and political complications that frustrate this need. Indeed, for Fassbinder, communicating this understanding necessitates a certain amount of despair, since activating the need in a positive way initially demands a disturbing exposition of the cinematic mechanics that have traditionally controlled not only how one behaves but how and what one understands. For Fassbinder, a vision that can act according to its full symbolic potential begins only when the spectator sees his or her actions in terms of the representational structures that construct these actions. In his words,

> People often criticise my films for being pessimistic. There are certainly plenty of reasons for being pessimistic, but I don't see my films that way. They are founded in the belief that revolution doesn't belong on the cinema screen, but outside, in the world. When I show people, on the screen, the ways that things can go wrong, my aim is to warn them that that is the way things *will* go if they don't change their lives. Never mind if a film ends pessimistically; if it exposes certain mechanisms clearly enough to show people how exactly they work, then the ultimate effect is not pessimistic. I never try to reproduce reality in a film. My goal is to reveal such mechanisms in a way that makes people realise the necessity of changing their own reality.[39]

"The strain of love before the movement of time" (*Coup de Grâce*).

FOUR

‎█████

Types of History

Schlöndorff's Coup de Grâce

> The basis and possibility of an art of the film is
> that everyone and everything looks what it is.
> Béla Balázs

Quite unlike the self-reflexive cameras of Wenders and Fassbinder, the films of
Volker Schlöndorff situate themselves much more ingenuously in a realist tradition
that seems to put a kind of honest faith in the camera's ability to interpret facts accurately. Compared to the cinema of many of the other German filmmakers of his
generation, Schlöndorff's films have a strikingly conventional look to them, stylistically unextravagant and narratively bound to a clear, novelistic development that
employs traditional strategies of suspense and climax.[1] If this tendency toward con-
vention makes Schlöndorff's films less interesting to the followers of Herzog or
Syberberg, it should not detract from their often unobtrusive rigor and craft. For the
comparative ease and accessibility of Schlöndorff's style are, it seems to me, intentionally and seriously both of these: while his tactics spring from a notion of political realism that directors such as Fassbinder would clearly not share, these tactics,
much like the motives behind Fassbinder's aesthetic, remain based in a functional
understanding of film production/distribution and the need to communicate issues
and positions mostly outside the ken of the common spectator. As Jack Zipes notes
about *The Lost Honor of Katharina Blum*:

> The purpose in making *Katharina Blum* then was to reach a wide audience through an
> American distributor and to raise the consciousness of this audience so that it would be-
> come more critical of political repression. In other words, Schlöndorff saw in the mate-
> rial of Böll's novel a vehicle to delineate the political reality of the Bundesrepublik more
> clearly for a popular audience which might be moved to think more critically about its
> situation *vis-à-vis* violence and repression. His starting point was the political reality and
> the problem of spreading word about this reality more efficaciously—a problem of pro-
> duction and distribution.[2]

Put another way: however one might damn with faint praise *The Tin Drum* when
viewed next to Syberberg's monumental examination of the Third Reich, the
Schlöndorff film can claim, unlike many German films, a mass reception and

ground-breaking recognition from the Hollywood academy, meaningless perhaps as an aesthetic or political standard of inherent value but crucial as an index in a reception aesthetic where audience rapport dictates so much of textual practice.

This clear success, defined and motivated according to a reception aesthetic, may however also serve as an indicator of the shortcomings of Schlöndorff's films. Of all the films examined in this study, his are doubtless the most accessibly moderate along the horizon of a contemporary viewer's expectations. This would seem to indicate that, in the conflict between a spectatorial passivity aligned with traditional films and the uncomfortable activity of reading alternative films like Fassbinder's, an adherence to a classical realism today succeeds in finding an audience only at the expense of neutralizing that audience's participation in the medium. As part of a dialogic process, Schlöndorff's films may ask the right questions, yet, as literary and film theorists attuned to the problem of political form have pointed out, these questions may be posed in a manner not sufficiently geared to provoke a spectatorial reply. As a realism engaged with history, these films may indeed have little trouble finding an audience, yet the final question remains whether this kind of aesthetic moves an audience merely to accept history as a reality or to engage it as a horizon that can and should be changed.

Early in his career, Schlöndorff obviously began to define his aesthetic precisely around these notions of reception and distribution, problems which he shares equally with his colleagues but which he discusses much more readily and more vociferously than most of them. "Now I see," he has said, "that the few people who make films are not only able to bring a child into the world but must also look after its growth. Filmmaking today also includes the responsibility of production and distribution, and because of this, almost two-thirds of the attention is being focused on these other fields."[3] Doubtless Schlöndorff's apprenticeship in France contributed a great deal to his awareness of the importance of a distribution network outside the one imposed by the established powers. But, because of the unusual control that the American distributors maintain in Germany, Schlöndorff sees his present bind as distinct, generating odd alliances with the forces he originally battled. Especially in recent successful years,

> our allies are the American distributors, because they push our films, with the rest of their merchandise, the American films—even in the cinemas that we don't want. . . . It's obviously contradictory to see Herzog working with Fox, Fassbinder and me with United Artists, and me with CIC, that is, Paramount. It's paradoxical that it's these who must be our saviors since, on the other hand, it's these who made the market what it is, knowing that the German cinema—ours—holds a place there of less than 5%, maybe 8% with recent receipts, and that the American cinema alone has more than 60%.[4]

The economics and politics of this predicament, moreover, are hardly difficult to decipher. By 1979 Schlöndorff could say:

> At this moment, the whole world wants us and makes bridges of gold for us. But two years from now, this craze for the German cinema, in which there is also a good deal of

snobbism, will pass as was the case for the Czech, Canadian, and Swedish cinema. . . . The world's interest in the German films is first of all an interest in a Germany whose influence it begins to feel. This is why it must be our objective, during the fat years, to construct machinery for production and distribution which will permit us to continue when the fashion changes and to consolidate our power in our own country.[5]

What further complicates this situation—especially for directors like Schlöndorff, Fassbinder, and Kluge—is that their leftist politics, however politically various they may be, are flagrantly at odds with the multinational film corporations with whom they must deal if they hope to have a commercial audience. In an interview with *Libération*, Schlöndorff notes how the anti-establishment politics of certain films from Germany unmistakably run counter to their financial and stylish attractiveness, so that while the German cinema gains some international notoriety and makes some headway with government agencies and production sources, these films must continue to bargain for their own audiences, must continue in fact to create an audience which would be more responsive to political perspectives contrary to the established ideology.[6] Schlöndorff writes,

> Our little company for the distribution of auteurs, the Filmverlag, doesn't touch more than 400 cinemas out of 3,800 which is absolutely minimal; and most of the others refuse purely and simply to do business with the Filmverlag. . . . The professional journal of the commercial cinemas, *Filmecho* . . . can only malign the German cinema each week, that is, the films we make; and, although these films have prestige, they don't want them. And even when they are successful, they regret it. . . . When *Katharina Blum* was very successful, they wrote: Excellent receipts, suspicious public! Their great hope is precisely to crush the cinema that we are making.[7]

Along with Kluge, Schlöndorff has perhaps confronted this problem more directly and with more energy than most other New German directors. Claiming to spend more than half of his time with bureaucratic and political officials, he has remarked on occasion how one must necessarily adapt to some extent to the established opposition in order to accomplish even the most minimal changes.[8] While his views remain liberally left, consequently, Schlöndorff's strategies have become something far different from the radical ideals he frequently espouses, as he has discovered the necessity of implementing these views with formulas and avenues of communication, such as the SPD, that the establishment has made available to him.[9] The same problematic, moreover, applies to his films, where his putative confidence in cinematic realism and its conventional discourse becomes a kind of political plea-bargaining, the accessible look of the representation being the acceptable vehicle for a more subversive tenor.

Both *Katharina Blum* and Schlöndorff's contribution to *Germany in Autumn* are lucid examples and descriptions of this stance and the dilemmas it provokes. In the latter, the ludicrous showdown between a network board and the auteurs climaxes in the board dismissing the adaptation of *Antigone* because of the terrorist connotations, the triumph of the media here thus reinforcing their own ideology and abetting the paranoia that serves their position. Similarly, *Katharina Blum* (co-directed by Margarethe von Trotta) is the story of a woman persecuted and eventually destroyed not so much by the pseudo-fascist police squad that harasses her but by a media coverage that in purveying sensationalism becomes the right arm of the conservative right-wing. In the opening sequence of the film, an undercover agent for the police secretly films the terrorist who eventually compromises Katharina, and these first subjective shots through the agent's camera identify the first of many media tools in the film used to exploit a reality. For Schlöndorff these tools are certainly the most pertinent issue in this and other films, since he consistently attempts to break down and open the closed and repressive framework that reactionary forces put in place with these tools, as they bind facts and resist the dynamics of exchange. Achieving the alternative is, however, for Schlöndorff always an indirect process whereby he must describe the same social reality but as a historical dialectic; continue to use the camera as a seemingly unreflecting window on the world but also as a window with two directions and sharp borders; and finally employ the standard conventions of realism but primarily as conventions of communication. Whereas Wenders emphasizes the existential and psychological problems of cinematic perception and Fassbinder the political and sexual, Schlöndorff's concerns are the historical, social dimensions of perception which traditional cinema intentionally mutes or disguises in serving the interests of its established position.

Not as politically obvious or as artistically self-conscious as *Katharina Blum*, *The Tin Drum*, or *Circle of Deceit*, *Coup de Grâce* may be the best example of the unobtrusive way that Schlöndorff packages his liberal politics in a conventional form. Additionally, more clearly than his later films, it demonstrates his important aesthetic connection with the French New Wave and especially with Jean-Pierre Melville, to whom *Coup de Grâce* is dedicated. Since Schlöndorff worked with Melville on several films, the French director naturally influenced him greatly, Melville considering Schlöndorff his "spiritual son" from the moment of their first acquaintance.[10] Of the several points of contact between the two filmmakers, there are two which seem particularly significant here. The first is the realist tradition of cinema, which for Melville is a function of the invisibility of the director: "whenever the spectator becomes aware of a director's intentions," he says, "the rhythm of the film is inevitably broken."[11] The second is a dislocated engagement with Hollywood cinema, a kind of engagement that aligns Schlöndorff with many other New German directors who practice what is basically an aesthetic of conflict.

Unlike the films of Fassbinder or Wenders, however, this dislocated engagement with Hollywood is for Schlöndorff less a direct confrontation with the American industry than a detour through the French tradition found in Melville and frequently in Renoir. What Schlöndorff discovers via this detour is most importantly a tradition of transposition whereby the formulas of cinematic realism can serve both as realistic illusions and as historically visible types put in place as social actors (types like those so prevalent in Renoir's films). This disjunctive recuperation of Hollywood formulas is obviously behind Melville's observation that "All my original scripts, without exception, are transposed Westerns," as well as his remark that his character-types "are all *double*."[12] Indeed, Melville does not appreciably change the nature of the filmic type or the Hollywood formula with his transpositions, even when irony informs them, and his characters ultimately adhere to and support Stanley Cavell's useful definition: "types are exactly what carry the forms movies have relied upon. These media created new types, or combinations and ironic reversals of types; but there they were, and stayed. Does this mean that movies can never create individuals, only types? What it means is that this is the movies' way of creating *individualities*. For what makes someone a type is not his similarity with other members of that type but his striking separateness from other people."[13] Perhaps best exemplified by a Bogart character, this notion of the individuality of a type certainly applies to a large number of American films and also to many of Melville's, yet it is Schlöndorff's redefinition of this figure that valorizes his particular use of it: for Schlöndorff, the filmic type accedes to an identity larger than individuality, mostly because he purposely forefronts the historical and social dimensions of that classic figure. Cavell may claim that "the individuality captured on film naturally takes precedence over the social role in which the individuality gets expressed. Because on film social role appears arbitrary or incidental, movies have an inherent tendency toward the democratic, or anyway the idea of human equality."[14] But, for Schlöndorff, the dynamics of a filmic type have a crucial social dimension which he consciously abstracts from cinematic and political history: in Schlöndorff's films, the democratic humanist is only a type whose place is becoming increasingly less viable.

In *Coup de Grâce* this redefinition of the filmic type within the formal context of a cinematic realism provides Schlöndorff, above all else, with a vehicle for partially expanding the ideologically static reality that classical cinema imposes on its audience: it allows him to represent realism as a genre in its own right that must be continually revised to accommodate an ever-growing historical reality and to delineate the types of history as likewise constantly undergoing transformation. Yet, even with this redefinition and flexibility, Schlöndorff's notion of types and their relation to historical reality focuses a central and crucial limitation in his aesthetic, recalling explicitly Lukács's concept of *typicality* and implicitly the criticism of Lukács by Brecht and Bloch. Based in a kind of Hegelianism, Lukács's *typicality*—and by implication Schlöndorff's types—tends, according to Brecht, to fetishize one particular formal relation with history (one rooted in nineteenth-century literature), and it regularly appears to replace the historical dynamics of representational forms *as productive forms* with a calculus that seems naively to relate infrastructure and superstructure.[15] A "concept of realism must be wide and political," Brecht says in revising this position; "we must not derive realism as such from particular existing works, but . . . use every means, old and new, tried and untried, derived from art and derived elsewhere, to render reality to men in a form they can master."[16] As opposed to Fassbinder, Kluge, or Syberberg's more Brechtian emphasis on the productive relationship between history and the representations that organize it, in short, Schlöndorff chooses to work, however expansively and critically, within the more traditional Lukácsian formulas of historical realism: while his films certainly dramatize the historical dynamics of types and representational forms, they clearly choose to limit the possible kinds and numbers of those forms in order to be more accessible to an audience.

Containing many of these tensions between tradition and history in the adapted story itself but foregrounding them in a significant departure from the Yourcenar novel,[17] *Coup de Grâce* is thus essentially a historical film whose subject is the intense fighting between Bolshevik forces inspired by the Russian revolution and a White Russian aristocracy attempting to preserve its traditions in the wake of that revolution. The action takes place in the Baltic region of Eastern Europe, the chaotic meeting ground for the advancing leftist forces and the well-entrenched upper class—"lost areas," in the narrator's words, "where German and Russian names mean nothing." The first shots of the film clearly announce this conflict: after a prefatory text that describes the historical background of the film, an extremely low-angle shot follows the feet of two soldiers running across a bridge, through a field where shells explode, until they arrive on the outskirts of a darkened villa. As they shoot a flare to illuminate the mansion, the film's title appears and a voice-over comments, not in native German but in dislocated French: "It was only after that darkest night that we reached Kratovice. The darkened house stood out like an abandoned ship's hull. . . . It is said that the dead ride quickly. The living do too." This narrator is eventually identified as Erick, and his comrade is Conrad, the young master of the house and brother of Sophie. Together, these three form the center of a film in which their home and what it represents are relentlessly besieged by forces of change that drive them from the stasis of their old order. The rapid movement in the first shots accordingly couples with and opposes the corpse-like house appearing "like an abandoned ship's hull." For, resisting the rapid movement of time and history and thus becoming its victim, the house and its inhabitants are already figuratively dead. Highlighted momentarily by Erick's flare, this house remains precariously balanced between the fleeting light of archaic ideals and its extinction through the course of an appropriately black and white film.

Even more so than in *The Bitter Tears of Petra von Kant*, *Coup de Grâce* uses the family as the touchstone structure around which the story evolves. Sophie and Conrad are the last remnants of their family, which they desperately try to hold together, at least in appearance. Shortly after the arrival of the two men, Erick's voice-over remarks that "the presence of her brother restored Sophie as mistress of her house"; as the camera follows Sophie and Conrad around the grounds of the estate, he tells her of his dream of restoring the harmony the house once represented. "After the war," he says, "we'll turn this house into a place where writers and artists can meet." The next sequence of shots then shows Sophie flipping through a family photo album as an introduction to one of the film's several drawing-room scenes permeated by eighteenth-century manners and mores. The fragility of both these sequences, however, becomes obvious through the violence that punctuates them. In the first, Conrad's remarks follow this graphic awareness of the present with its "smell of the fields after the battle," its "indelible mark of death," and "mangled bodies." In the second the polite gathering around the piano is shattered when a bomb explodes outside the window. Both the traces of this traditional family structure and its grotesque relation to an unaccommodating present then crystallize in Aunt Prascovia, the mad gnome-like ruin of the old aristocracy, who, according to Sophie, "once looked human."

This effort to retrieve and restore the family order of another time is focused most specifically in the relationships of Erick, Conrad, and Sophie. In another historical era, Sophie's love for Erick would have a mechanical logic to it, and her perception of him as a likely mate is both natural and expected in the context of the villa of Kratovice. Erick, in turn, responds to Sophie again and again according to formulas which would suggest that he too feels the social appropriateness of their being lovers: there are, for instance, several scenes of intimacy between the two, and Erick is properly jealous and protective of Sophie at numerous points. Yet, Erick resists all of Sophie's advances, and the peculiar paradox of this yet unexplained resistance becomes the center for much of the illogical tension within the makeshift family at Kratovice. When Sophie declares her love, Erick replies, "I couldn't offer you a worthy existence. . . . You don't even know me." But, counters Sophie, "we spent our childhood together!" Their love and proper union thus hangs ambiguously between what should be (in terms of their past) and its failure to occur (as they move into a new future).

This ambivalent tension builds throughout the film, but it is eventually resolved when Sophie discovers Erick's homosexuality, a discovery which dismisses any desire to recover the family order of Kratovice. As Erick prepares to leave on a military mission, Sophie whispers her repeated plea through a closed door, "I love you"; and he replies, "Wait until I return"—the physical structure of this scene, with the shot alternating between the two separated by the door, thus becoming a metaphoric summary of an attraction that has been continuously frustrated by barriers of one sort or another. Immediately following the departure, Volkmar, Sophie's most recent lover, returns wounded from the mission; when his frantic offer of marriage is refused by Sophie, he bitterly reveals Erick and Conrad's homosexual relationship. Dazed and angry, Sophie then walks to the top of the foyer stairway, where she tells the aunt that "it's the end." Returning down the same steps she meets Erick, who has just returned himself. "I've had enough," she cries, "your war, your virile friendships, your honor. The war is a pretext for your pleasure." And, now stripped of the pretenses of an honorable resolution to their sexual chaos, Erick responds in kind: "Streetwalkers shouldn't enroll in the vice squad." Shot from a high-angle, this final breakdown aptly occurs on a staircase, which, as Lotte Eisner has pointed out, is often the traditional scene and symbol for the aspirations and idealism found in classical German cinema. In this film, however, chaos erupts on the stairway after the house has been bombed; Sophie vomits there after a drunken evening with the soldiers; and in the sequence just described, the last hope of regaining the aristocratic family collapses in an acknowledgment of radical sexual deviation from the aristocratic norm. As Sophie leaves the grounds of Kratovice to join the communist fighters and live illegitimately with Gregory, she stops to ask the guard about his family, a wistful and ironic reminder of how clearly the traditions of Kratovice have failed to survive.

The toying and wavering that Erick and Sophie engage in throughout the film cannot be dismissed as simply hypocrisy and self-deception, for a major motif of the film is that these characters have learned to live according to certain appearances or codes which even the concomitant knowledge of their inadequacy cannot justify altering or forsaking: rejecting these codes would be tantamount to rejecting reality itself. Even after their climactic confrontation, Erick goes to search for and retrieve Sophie; just before he must order her execution, he interrogates her not to obtain military information but to be sure of her marital status. "Gregory's mother said you were married," he says; when Sophie denies it, he retorts with an entirely inappropriate concern, ". . . but you slept together." This sort of ironic entrapment occurs at several points in the film (some of which have been indicated). Usually the ambivalence and irony arise from the characters' inability to distinguish between an appearance naturalized as honorable and the emotional significance that has been dissociated from it. Erick's tender care for Sophie after her drunken bout with the soldiers, for example, borders on sincere and particular affection for her until cruelly abstracted by his final comment: "what I'm doing, I'd do for Conrad or any of my friends."

Each of the characters deals with this split between static forms of behavior and an opposing reality. Conrad is probably the least tragic of the three main characters since he is clearly the least aware of the situation. Like Oskar in *The Tin Drum*, he is a man-child, surrounded by a rocking horse and other mementos from his youth, translating the harsh facts of his life into "a foxhunt that will last until the end of the war." This nostalgia is of course shared by the other characters, yet Conrad's results in a blindness that the others rarely approach. After Sophie leaves, Conrad petulantly tries to blame her for their defeats, despite Erick's much more sober counter-remark that "she's no Mata Hari." In the next sequence, Conrad is killed almost offhandedly by an exploding shell, a significantly short and brightly lit sequence emptied of soldiers and signs of war and thus an ironically anonymous death for one who so adamantly retained the glittering illusions of his class throughout his life.

Erick and Sophie, on the other hand, are acutely aware of the rift between historical reality and the appearances that they cling to, and differ only in their response to that awareness. In one of their first conversations, Sophie asks Erick, "Why did you come to Kratovice? What are you defending here? Your mother lost everything before the war." "Perhaps I like lost causes," he answers with calculated candor. Insisting on a more active response to change, Sophie then offers a historical insight of her own: that "the new has no use for our traditions." For Erick, though, this may be true of public history, but he has enlisted himself in a closed, private history where, in his words, "no one chooses his own story," since one is bound and determined by the inflexible codes of a particular class. While Erick may, as Sophie remarks, "have none of Conrad's illusions," still he continues to argue that, compared to Sophie's progressive notions, "Conrad's beliefs are truer" since "they don't come out of books."

Erick's unbending insistence on remaining enclosed in "his own story," despite his awareness of a much larger context, ultimately makes his tragedy a more horrific version of the tragedy of his class. Like Sophie's, his personal story has two sides, one social and one sexual, and his struggle to preserve both sides is what tangles him so inextricably in a suicide pact with himself. Within the world of Kratovice, there is only the military problem of maintaining the values of the ruling class against the wave of revolutionaries and social outcasts. Yet, according to the standards of the very world he defends, Erick's homosexuality becomes as unacceptably perverse and anarchistic as the behavior of the Bolsheviks outside the house. As he knows too well, he has no consistent position: either way he is ruined, by the historical forces that will destroy his class sanctuary or by his own sexuality which will undermine his place in a family tradition. That his homosexual relationship with Conrad subsists on his military defense of Kratovice, moreover, only further complicates an already contradictory stance. (Very near an unhappy cliché here, Schlöndorff seems to suggest a conjunction between homosexuality and a fascist aristocracy.)

Erick, however, maintains his course and façade, the logic of which becomes dramatically apparent in an early prefigurement of his final break with Sophie. In this particular sequence, Erick charges into Sophie's room to close the shutters that she has intentionally left open during a plane attack on the house. When he berates her, she in turn rebukes him: "Responsibility, duty. All the rest is dead. You're incapable of feeling. . . . You cling to life, Erick." This life he clings to is of course the life inside Kratovice, a world defined by effete forms of responsibility and duty and one he knows is collapsing. After a sharp exchange of glances, therefore, Erick picks up a lamp, opens a shutter, and walks out on a balcony into the night, where he appears in the long shot as a beacon in the darkness. As in the opening sequence, the villa is momentarily lit and exposed, and the plane promptly explodes a shell on the roof. Here Erick's position is not difficult to decipher: if he protects Kratovice, it is not because he believes he can save it. When he and Sophie reenter, they fall on the floor in a passionate embrace, his brief abandonment of Kratovice being a type of sexual abandonment as well. Erick quickly runs from the embrace, however. As the house burns and the shriveled aunt screams, he wanders dazed on the staircase, the camera angle spinning and turning with him, while strained, dissonant violin music mounts on the soundtrack. Despite the chaos and confusion that underscore it, Erick thus chooses here the ruled path. This path clearly leads to a violent dead end, as the conclusion of the film indicates even more clearly than this sequence; but for Erick the logic of appearances and its codes for reality are—no matter how they contradict history—the mainstay of life.

For Sophie, these codes have little value: an iconoclast through self-education, she threatens Erick's stability in large part because she rejects the logic of appearances that is the foundation for both his sexual and social life. Shortly after informing Erick that "the new has no use for our traditions," Erick's narrative voice-over remarks that "Sophie barely hid her sympathy for the Reds. . . . She met Gregory, who gave her Marxist literature." Gregory hence becomes the male counterpart to Erick, the leftist intellectual and activist who represents the world outside Kratovice and evidently inspires Sophie to seek alternatives to her traditional role as aristocratic mistress of the villa. Before leaving to join his comrades, Gregory gives her a volume of Georg Trakl poems with the inscription "Always follow the voice of your heart." As she follows this advice, she becomes increasingly unsuited for life at Kratovice and the role model expected of her, both being products of formal perspectives, not emotionally active ones. She smokes a pipe, dresses like a man, propositions Erick, seduces other men, and grows generally more independent of the mores of her class. She so completely subverts appearances, in fact, that a new officer mistakes her for a servant.

The context of Kratovice makes it impossible, however, for Sophie fully to escape definition by its patriarchal, aristocratic codes. Always seen and put in view by these codes, Sophie, as a woman, will invariably appear as a product of its lexicon: either as the mistress of the house or as its servant, as a virgin-wife or as a whore. The terms of the former opposition account for the officer mistaking her for a servant. The latter helps explain her behavior when, deprived of legitimate lovers, she indiscriminately and frenetically couples with one soldier after another. In many ways, Sophie's manic prostituting of herself here springs from the same bind that turns Erick's determined adherence to certain appearances into a decision to self-destruct. For, according to the rules of this game, aristocratic appearances and codes dictate an either-or logic whereby one accepts or rejects them—and to accept at Kratovice is to choose dissolution and death. As Sophie openly becomes more sexually promiscuous, therefore, she intentionally and logically exposes herself more and more to the typhus epidemic in the hospital. At the end of the film, likewise, her request that Erick shoot her himself and his unflinching fulfillment of it is the *coup de grâce* of a logic which, with searing irony, unites the two throughout the film.

With some important qualifications, the structure of this logic is surprisingly close to that found in Fassbinder's films: for both filmmakers the ruling class creates the spectacle yet avoids at all cost the intrusion of a critical eye from outside the circle of its appearances. For both filmmakers, these spectacles within the film operate according to certain codes for interpreting reality. Schlöndorff's films differ, however, in that part of the codification process behind these spectacles involves the character's naturalization of the codes themselves (as in nineteenth-century literature), so that the power of the scene derives much of its force from an individual's disguising its status as a viewpoint and embedding itself in other codes. In *Coup de Grâce*, in short, the creator of the spectacle becomes the writer of realism, much like the one Roland Barthes describes in *S/Z*, where the speaker is the privileged viewer and thus maker of reality:

> It could be said that the speaker, before describing, stands at the window, not so much to see, but to establish what he sees by its very frame: the window frame creates the scene. . . . In order to speak about it, the writer, through this initial rite, first transforms the "real" into a depicted (framed) object; having done this, he can take down this object, *remove* it from his picture: in short: de-depict it (to depict is to unroll the carpet of codes, to refer not from a language to a referent but from one code to another). Thus, realism . . . consists not in copying the real but in copying a (de-picted) copy of the real: this famous *reality*, as through suffering from a fearfulness which keeps it from being touched directly, is *set farther away*, postponed, or at least captured through the pictorial matrix in which it has been steeped. . . : code upon code, known as realism.[18]

Indeed the reality of Kratovice is in every sense this spectacle of postponement (of history), and it is maintained to the extent that the character's viewpoint as writer of reality remains inviolable. The type through which reality is interpreted absorbs its position into the reality it describes, and only by ironically contextualizing this perspective within the voice-over narration and the audience's privileged point of view does Schlöndorff significantly develop his traditional realism of typicality: in Fredric Jameson's words about Lukács, "the notion of the *typical*, no longer quite appropriate for this more general formal point of view, gives way to another kind of terminology. Here, the principal characteristic of . . . realism is seen to be its anti-symbolic quality; realism itself comes to be distinguished by its movement, its storytelling and dramatization of its content; comes, following the title of one of Lukács's finest essays, to be characterized by narration rather than description."[19]

In *Coup de Grâce*, the viewpoints from which those spectacles of types and realisms develop derive first and foremost from a character's social power and the distinctions of class. When Sophie finds Erick flirting with the cook in the kitchen, for instance, she lashes out at him for exposing their emotional imbroglio to a lower-class eye. The rest of the social dance inside Kratovice is similarly strict and exclusive, as the characters work to sustain an etiquette of appearances, according to which they are there to be seen and to be seen specifically as authoritative models of propriety. When a captured Bolshevik is shot in the courtyard (fittingly, offscreen), Erick quickly apologizes to Sophie for the unseemly fact; early in the film, a servant-spokesman stiffly reads a pompously worded mandate calling for the slaughter of the Bolsheviks, a specular parody of the aristocrats' posturing in which the servant beats his drum and looks directly into the close-up.

The visual strain of these and other shots is analogous to and ultimately a product of the dichotomy that tears through so many of the characters' personal lives, which the camera critically exhibits as formal types that have become inadequate to the realities they live. As Cavell has pointed out, the type is a specifically cinematic figure because, unlike a dramatic or novelistic caricature, it is solidly rooted in the world's reality, a perceptual reality which, whether a particular film engages it or not, is film's special province. Working with this problem up to and including that horrific carnival of types in *The Tin Drum*, Schlöndorff's camera aims not to deny this type-figure of cinema but to illustrate the dangerous failings of types which do not remain responsive to the exigencies of a historical reality. Like Oskar and the world he reflects in *The Tin Drum*, Erick Lhomond refuses to grow with history—he fights to make the world fit his character rather than change his character to fit the changing world: in Gregory's words, "what could Lhomond do in Berlin, an out of work officer?" Yet, even with a war, the historical and private inadequacies and contradictions in Erick's type gradually appear, if not to the inhabitants of Kratovice, then to Schlöndorff's viewer. At the first social gathering at Kratovice, for instance, the scene presents all the signs of a standard aristocratic spectacle: music, photographs, posed groups, and banter. Yet, through a deft exchange of looks and responses between Erick, Conrad, Sophie, and the aunt—orchestrated by camera close-ups and reaction shots—an imbalance infiltrates the scene, a disharmony in

"Aunt Prascovia—the horrific center of the Christmas
spectacle" (*Coup de Grâce*).

the seeming harmony of the party: as the camera almost casually picks up an excess
of meaning in the exchange of glances between Erick and Conrad, a thin and disturbing crack begins to spread across the stereotype that Erick projects, a small surface explosion that just precedes the one that shatters the window to end the party.

This drama of types is most consistently and ironically enacted around the reverse-angle shot model with which classical cinema creates and maintains filmic
types (most evident in films such as *The Big Sleep* or *Grand Illusion*).[20] Especially
through the eyes of the iconoclast Sophie, this formal pattern, according to which a
personality usually is projected and verified through mutually supportive recognition, now becomes the means of challenging the type and the social network that
contextualizes it. Bruised by Erick's lack of interest in her, for example, Sophie intentionally draws the attention of Erick and the other officers when she calls her new
lover, Franz, to leave the room with her and then unabashedly turns and poses herself as a violation of social code before her audience's disconcerted gaze. Similarly,
when Erick accidentally interrupts Sophie and Volkmar, another lover, in her room,
the exchange of significant looks by the two men in the foreground is matched by a
close-up of Sophie's shifting eyes evaluating the effect of this disruptive *mise-en-
scène* that so powerfully ripples the surface formalities. The silent buckle generated
in this sequence breaks, moreover, in a summary showdown between Sophie and

Erick in which the stability of the classical shot/counter-shot becomes a volatile collision of different ways of seeing. The setting is a Christmas party where the stylized glamour of a putative family union reaches its peak, the climax of this evening taking place when the officers gather around the mistletoe for a kiss from Sophie. Here each embrace becomes a humorous performance, Sophie playfully doling out each kiss as a separate drama. Just as Erick enters the room, though, Volkmar comes forward for his kiss. There is a pause as the camera carefully notes Sophie watching Erick watching her; with the proprietary eye of Erick on her, she changes the playful drama to a passionately untoward embrace. Erick charges at her, slaps her, and is in turn challenged by Volkmar. The party then collapses into chaos as the aunt pounds madly on the piano, the soundtrack merging this diegetic cacophony with the recurring dissonance of violins.

These instances of internal chaos within Kratovice result, in most cases, from the clash of opposing points of view, from the resistance of a look to the typing that another perspective imposes on it, and, most significantly, from the disruption of the homogeneous and ideologically ubiquitous space that the interaction of shared views establishes. Somewhat as for Fassbinder, space for Schlöndorff is the screen on which images are made and their politics enforced; but in Schlöndorff's film space adheres to two basic definitions: one that is static, sealed, and controlled, such as that through which the types inside Kratovice move, and one that is dynamic and relatively undifferentiated, like the shifting, misty landscape that surrounds Kratovice.[21] Hence, just as the reverse-angle shot within the house often becomes a highly charged visual battlefield, the dialectic between the world inside the villa and the space outside becomes the actual battlefield on which images of reality are determined. At one illustrative point, therefore, Sophie discusses marriage with her aunt and, as the camera follows her, she casually peers out the window to notice Erick and Conrad rolling and laughing in the snow. She does not of course grasp the irony and significance of the juxtaposition, but for the spectator the conversation about a (hypothetical) orthodox sexual life becomes a grotesque misunderstanding and misinterpretation of the image of the male lovers outside.

This distance and barrier between the inner context of Kratovice and the larger context encircling it punctuates the entire film. While under attack from the Bolsheviks, Sophie looks across the battlefield through a periscope that then subjectively frames and distances the retreating Gregory, depicting him literally as another image far from the images of Kratovice. Likewise, Schlöndorff's use of shock cuts emphasizes a spatial disjunction which generally contrasts a destructive violence with the ersatz constructs of the inside: at one point, as Erick and Sophie dry their clothes in the firelight while quietly talking of love, the camera remains at an erotic distance from their bodies, which flicker in the unsteady light; the next shot is of a harshly lit barrel of a machine gun firing rapidly. Indeed, what this radical distance between images and the characters' failure to bridge it signifies is neatly encapsulated in a short sequence in which Conrad futilely tries to repair a broken windowpane from inside a greenhouse: outside in the rain a servant finishes filling in a grave.

Unable to suture their internal drama with the images of a changing reality and fully dependent upon socially anachronistic character types for interaction, the inhabitants of Kratovice thus becomes figures of death and reification or, more precisely, characters infused with death because tied to figures of reification. A repeated index of this is the many animal heads hanging from walls inside the house, which, like the aristocrats themselves, are trophies of a better time. Additionally there is the typhus epidemic during which the only recourse is to open windows and jettison their belongings for burning; toward the conclusion of the film, Erick comments that throughout Kratovice there is "the calm of a monastery or tomb." From the first shots of the dark and cold interior, in fact, the images of Kratovice are those of a dead and barren society whose formulas and types have become stiff and repetitiously horrific, like the freakish Aunt Prascovia, who aptly cuts endless reams of toilet paper while recounting an affair between Volkmar's father and Rasputin.

In *Coup de Grâce*, activity degenerates into the repetition of a formulaic spectacle, since any vital development is impossible within the claustrophobic space of Kratovice. Like the aunt's cuttings, the servants continuously rehearse dinner formalities and count place settings; in the same way the characters desperately reproduce reflected images of themselves, as a specifically fetishistic action marking their transition from an effete aristocracy into a bourgeoisie. In Jean Baudrillard's words, this is an order of "symmetrical arrangements, where things are duplicated in order to be reflected. Here an object does not exist literally unless it is thus repeated in itself," so that the "sign no longer designates anything at all," but "approaches its true structural limit which is to refer back only to other signs."[22] Inside the house, mirrors multiply figures and settings to create a reality that is active only in its redundancy: Sophie's first encounter with Franz rebounds between two mirrors that the reverse-angle shots set in motion; Erick's discovery of Volkmar and Sophie in her room occurs within the space created by three different mirrors, one outside the door, one in the back of the room that reflects a bed, and one reproducing the angle of Sophie's vision as she watches the spectacle she has produced. This reproduction of images and spectacles manifests itself in its most perverse form, finally, in Sophie's sexual dance of death. After Franz's brutal death, she mindlessly prostitutes herself to any soldier, parodying again and again the intimate love she had longed for. Erick discovers this in an appropriately formal manner: he unintentionally passes before a window and, looking inside (the only time in the film that vision is directed that way), he sees Sophie framed by the window like a medium shot, spreading her legs while a partially clothed soldier mounts her. Rebelling against the role her society demands of her, Sophie can only become an anti-type: a repetitious whore rather than a repetitious virgin, a pornographic loop film rather than a sanctimonious litany.

Set against this lost world of Kratovice is the vaguely defined reality of the Bolsheviks. Although Schlöndorff's political Romanticism (so evident in *Katharina Blum*) only gets a partial chance in the film, this counter-reality of the Bolshevik peasants does allow him here to indulge his rather transparent sympathies. As in his other films, Schlöndorff's depiction of this other reality ultimately detracts from the stark effectiveness of the film as a whole. The communist characters are generally noble and sensitive, and Gregory's household is the one glimpse in the film of a healthy and happy family. Moreover, the sequence in which the soon-to-be-executed Bolsheviks share a single cigarette in a darkly lit freight car draws out a kind of rustic integrity and individuality—as the camera slowly pans from face to face—that the decadent aristocrats never attain. The contrast is further underlined when, during their last meeting, Sophie turns her back on Erick to stare through the window at her comrades outside in the background of the shot. When Erick puts his hand on her shoulder, she flatly rejects the imposture this time and leaves for her death outside.

Despite these tendencies to sentimentalize the left, the world outside Kratovice remains a crucial outer context within which the aristocratic house and its values are defined and through which description gives way to narration: it becomes, in one important sense, a greater realism or alternative image against which the spectacle of Kratovice must be measured. For Schlöndorff, what describes this greater realism is above all else a historical dynamics and a social dialectic whose principal law is change. At several points in the film, transitions are made from one sequence to another with a bridge shot of the house, from an exterior perspective as it appears during different seasons, and this punctuation serves mainly to emphasize the inexorable passage of time as it contrasts both the unbending structure of the house and the rigid framing of the shot itself. In the abstract, the Bolsheviks of course represent the force of social change, and the narrative structure of the film reflects the pattern of this force as it meets and eventually engulfs its resistance: the film, that is, develops as a series of vignettes in which the temporal stasis of these isolated scenes accumulates as a kind of narrative montage that becomes the film's development.

To distinguish the authenticity of these two realities in *Coup de Grâce* presupposes an ideological position which would significantly differentiate Schlöndorff's brand of realism from Renoir's or the Italian Neo-Realists'. One sequence midway through the film makes this difference unmistakable—with a gesture of enunciation as dramatic as it is singular. One morning while Sophie and her lover Franz lounge in bed, he says, "Do you know what I saw in a dream last night? . . . Me with my throat cut . . . by the family tomb. I'm going to die soon." Sophie comforts him by reminding him that "it was a dream," an implied distinction that is the foundation of most realist aesthetics. In this case and in this film, however, the distinction dissolves, just as Kratovice gradually becomes absorbed into the world it opposes. After Sophie's words of consolation, there is a cut to the hallway as Franz is brought in, his throat slit open. The logic of this shock cut is disturbingly surreal, almost completely at odds with the naturalistic decor and form of the film. Yet, conversely, this sequence becomes a brutal reminder of the film's logic and argument throughout: namely, whereas both the individuals at Kratovice and the film itself rely fully on a realist's perception of the world, its types, its divisions, and its formulas, the film's narrative labors from beginning to end to demonstrate at the same time how insular and hence inadequate that conception of reality is. Cut off from a larger context and more dynamic sense of history, the people of Kratovice tragically live images of reality no less oneiric than their dreams. The mainstay of their existence becomes, horrifically, the ability to package experiences and divide acceptable realities from those that are not: the war becomes a "foxhunt"; Erick becomes a potential husband; and, in the context of Kratovice, Franz's dream becomes simply a dream.

In *Coup de Grâce*, therefore, the discourse of the film itself functions as a third context where the first two engage each other, where realistic expectations look increasingly like bizarre dreams, and where nightmares become fully realized realities, what Schlöndorff (writing about *The Tin Drum*) calls "Realism: grotesque and irrational, unfettered by the constraints of Naturalism."[23] For Schlöndorff, the dividing line between what one admits into a world view and what one dismisses as fantasy must constantly adjust to the demands made by history and the pressure of social alternatives, so that an individual's images of reality are regularly decentered from their position of power. Franz's dream and death are thus a sort of socialistic parody of Adam's dream, from which he awoke to find it had become reality. And just as the confusion of realms in Milton's poem is, in one simple sense, a sign of a much greater perspective than the individual's, Franz's dream-death in *Coup de Grâce* signals a dislocation of one set of images in terms of another with an entirely different motivation. Here the imagistic medium of reality comes into question not for its quality but for its lack of scope and variety, and by means of this inquiry Schlöndorff establishes a realistic discourse in which the mundane and the horrific are less a question of fact than of perspective.

Here contexts of vision are continually being put into place around narrower contexts in order to suggest that this is how realism should be defined. For Schlöndorff, realism is not a mass of experiences, a conglomerate of data, or even an inclusive recognition of social variety and classes. Rather, it is a social and historical evolution within which the character types of a society and their social formulas must advance.

Failure to do so results in the mock tragedy of Erick, a character type that mechanically performs its decided responsibilities and coldly embraces the destruction which that entails. When Erick assesses Sophie's request that he kill her, the irony of his words is the special privilege of the spectator, who as always sees and hears within the third context of the film's own discourse: "At first," Erick's voice-over relates, "by asking me to be her executioner, I thought she believed she was giving me a final and definite proof of her love. Since then I've realized that she only wanted to take revenge and leave me with regrets. Her calculations were correct, sometimes I have regrets. One is always caught in a trap with such women." Here, as throughout the film, Erick's commentary on the soundtrack becomes the counterpoint and inversion of the strident musical score that ruptures the naturalistic surface of the entire film: his description and evaluation of events, at first so innocuously flat, ultimately appear as the strained and distorted interpretation of a man battling the harsh reality of history. Erick's last statement is, of course, an ironically accurate analysis of Sophie's actions: her request is in part a reaction to his repulsing her love, and her rebellious death fittingly completes what Schlöndorff himself calls a "story of a humiliation that ends with a revolt."[24] But, more importantly, Erick's final comment, as a distillation of the voice-over throughout the film, represents the strained attempt to counter and contain the uncomfortable facts of historical change.

"Outside Kratovice: Sophie's averted gaze" (*Coup de Grâce*).

Erick's novelistic narration is thus much more than the literary residue of Yource-nar's novel; like the worn literary perceptions that infuse Kratovice, the narration is rather the ironic contraction of the actual significance of events within a self-serving and static confine. Regarding this final sequence specifically, Erick recuperates and defuses with his unemotional explanation the documentary horror of the mass exe-cution, just as, quickly between the two, he poses with his men for a photograph, the more modern and mechanical way to stop and record reality with the images one chooses. As he and his soldiers pull away on the train and the camera tracks back-ward from the scene, gravediggers arrive to bury the corpses in the background. Here the flat, repetitive automatism of the train tracks visually parallels the fleeing legs of the opening, and the retreating perspective of the camera angle correlates with the backward vision that the film so deliberately delineates.

Like Fassbinder, therefore, Schlöndorff's investigation of types, spectacles of realism, and the play of power through images is finally an attempt to introduce the spectator to that space where the lived images of reality are manufactured through a dialectic with history. Yet whereas Fassbinder's is an internal and more self-con-scious perspective through which the spectator participates in the emotional process of production itself, Schlöndorff moves the viewer to an external point of view, a third context as unlike Fassbinder's as the open gray spaces of *Coup de Grâce* are unlike the garish closet-drama of *Petra von Kant*, a context which puts an almost naive faith in the viewer's willingness to read the film carefully. For Schlöndorff, the significance of his own images derives not so much from a deconstruction of the dominant images but from an emplacement of those images within a greater historical reality, a reality defined by the evolution and plurality of alternative types and images. Most clearly and ironically displayed in *The Sudden Wealth of the Poor People of Kombach*, the realistic surface that is such a powerful attraction in Schlöndorff's films thus works together with a temporal or historical distancing, so that the visual facts of social reality become recontextualized as a process and cultural product. Quite significantly, this historical distancing usually works in two directions in Schlöndorff's films (the realities of *The Tin Drum* and *Young Törless* looking forward to *Katharina Blum*, which in turn looks back to the fascism which still exists today); and, while *Coup de Grâce* is most obviously a specifically dated historical drama, its conclusion leaves little doubt that this is in fact a historical stage rather than an isolated drama: the comportment, uniforms, and actions of Erick and his soldiers unmistakably forecast the reality of *The Tin Drum*, the logical development from the images of Kratovice. In *Coup de Grâce* history becomes the contextualizing of reality through the power of images, and, establishing itself and its spectator as a third context, the film becomes a forum or debate, in which the spectator participates about the facts of history, rather than a mere depiction or even analysis of these facts.

Whatever Schlöndorff might share with the realist aesthetics of Bazin or even Kracauer, it is therefore clear that the conventional realism of many of his films is intended to be primarily an ingredient and not a raw material, one of many signifiers or codes and not the signified or message itself. To pretend to some positivistic ideal for a filmic reality would be to stumble into the closed images which Kratovice epitomizes and which, as there, result in a repetitious automatism that mechanically repeats images as a means of verifying their reality. Since this same repetitious automatism accounts for the reality effect of most Hollywood cinema, moreover, Schlöndorff's recurrent attack on realities such as Kratovice and the perceptual illusion of automatistic ways of seeing clearly marks the distance of his aesthetic from the realism practiced by classical films.[25]

What Schlöndorff's aesthetic offers instead is a recontextualization of realism, which becomes in effect an avenue for information: as Jurij Lotman notes in his *Semiotics of Cinema*, "the quantity of potential information depends on the presence of alternative possibilities. Information is the opposite of automatism. . . . Therefore those properties of an object which result from their automatic ties with the material world become, in art, the result of free artistic choice and thus acquire the value of information."[26] Alternatives arrive with the recognition of an open context within which images remain perspectives in a dialogue rather than singular and hence only repeatable analogues of reality. Indeed, the inability of the characters at Kratovice to admit this outer context is what so limits their alternatives and ultimately prevents any knowledge of their own actions. In the same way, the automatic machinery of an established film industry and its audience quickly becomes a closed network of images that likewise resist alternatives and any knowledge of social realities, and this is the machinery of realism that Schlöndorff's films seek to engage and redefine.

In confronting the industry through his films, as well as through his work with production/distribution outlets, Schlöndorff aims, if not to deconstruct fully, at least to contextualize and thus to place in proper perspective the powerful codes and images that the established cinema purveys. Within the third context which is his films, aesthetic realism itself attempts to redefine its nature as alternative realities, to become a Lukácsian discourse that speaks the language of information about the social realities one lives.

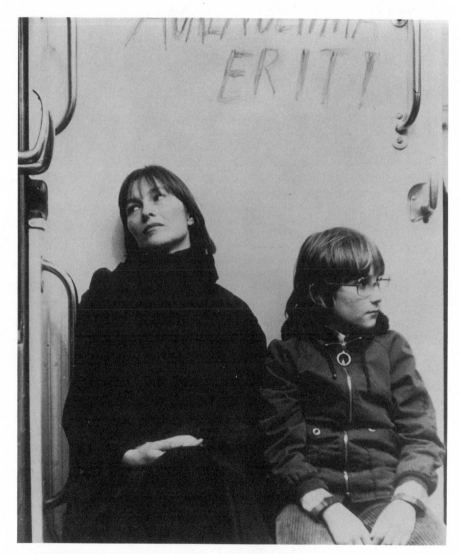

"The mother, the son, and the tension of public
communication" (*The Left-Handed Woman*). The Museum
of Modern Art/Film Stills Archive.

The Charge of Translation

Handke's The Left-Handed Woman

The mirror above my fireplace reflects the
  reflected
Room in my window; I look in the mirror at night
And see two rooms, the first where left is right
And the second, beyond the reflected window,
  corrected
But there I am standing back to my back. . . .
              . . . in both directions
I can see beyond and through the reflections the
  street lamps
At home outdoors where my indoors rooms lie
  stranded,
Where a taxi perhaps will drive in through the
  bookcase
Whose books are not for reading and past the fire
Which gives no warmth and pull up by my desk
At which I cannot write since I am not lefthanded.
              —Louis MacNeice, ''Reflections''

Left-handed woman, you've given yourself away!
Or did you mean to give me a sign?
              —*The Left-Handed Woman*

A movie seemingly about radical isolation and difference, Peter Handke's 1977 *The
Left-Handed Woman* has become a historical marker of one of the more turbulent
periods and issues within contemporary German cinema. Eric Rentschler explains:

> During a few months in 1977, much controversy ensued in the FRG over an alleged *Lit-
> eraturverfilmungskrise* (literature adaptation crisis). Perhaps no other single moment in
> the history of West German film has so dramatically exhibited the many problems inher-
> ent in a state-subsidized cinema in a country well-known for its strained relationship to
> the medium. It appeared for a few months as if the manifest destiny of West German
> filmmakers—for all their well-documented realist ambitions and progressive
> persuasions—lay in illustrating literary classics of the 19th century or in recycling best
> sellers.[1]

Promoted by a subsidy system that demanded the submission of completed scripts

whose literary merit would unavoidably become a determination of financial support for the cinematic project, this crisis often is seen as a historical flight from the
complexities and "immediacy" (related to the *sensibilisten* movement in West Germany) of contemporary German life and into the safer subject matter of canonized
literature—such as the stories of Theodor Fontane, the drama of Schiller, the life of
Heinrich Heine, or, as so viciously parodied by Schlöndorff and Böll in *Germany in
Autumn*, a classical play like *Antigone*. "Once again," says Niklaus Schilling in
1977, "we find among us a particularly fatal tendency not to trust the power of the
filmic medium, but rather to construct films from the most classical literary sources
possible in order to escape the danger of having to work with images and in that way
to tell our own stories."[2]

Despite these denunciations, this widespread dependence of German cinema on
literature and its classics can conversely be seen as a strategic attempt to enlist the
literary traditions that have frequently articulated successful films for German, as
well as foreign, audiences. "Literature is the backbone of German cinema," writes
Ronald Holloway; "Remove that backbone from the history of New German Cinema, and it appears to be a jelly-fish."[3] For contemporary German cinema, in
short, a central value of literary adaptation is its potent and tested ability to attract
many different kinds of spectators within the mainstream: it identifies and positions
an audience denominated in terms of a well-rehearsed literary history, yet one now
mobilized in terms of the cinematic possibilities of the present. In these conflicting
or compromising terms, the discourse of literary adaptation then dramatizes the conflict between a literary retreat and the attraction of a cinematic present; and, as the
two-tiered theme and representational project of *The Left-Handed Woman*, the crisis
of literary adaptation thus enacts the language of a contemporary German film culture apparently divided against the regressive/progressive understanding of its own
history and present identity.

This debate about the possibilities and problems of fiction-into-film will doubtless continue in as many directions and with as many conclusions as it has sustained
since Vachel Lindsay and Sergei Eisenstein addressed the question. Few filmmakers
or films, however, have focused that debate as explicitly and rigorously as Peter
Handke and his *The Left-Handed Woman*. Hailed as "that rare thing, a genuinely
poetic movie,"[4] *The Left-Handed Woman* is the second feature film by this drama-
tist, novelist, and poet, whose reputation has been based primarily on his literary
achievements[5] but whose entrance into filmmaking brought immediate comparisons
with the likes of Jean Cocteau and André Malraux.[6] Handke's success with this film
was not, though, unprepared. Together with Wim Wenders, he made *3 American LPs*
(1969). In 1970 he directed the TV-film *The Chronicle of Current Events*, a self-
styled allegory about two years of recent West German history. The next year he
provided the novel and the script for Wenders's film version of *The Goalie's Anxiety
at the Penalty Kick* (1972). In 1974 he collaborated with Wenders once again, this
time on *Wrong Move*, a loose adaptation of Goethe's classical Bildungsroman,
Wilhelm Meister's Apprenticeship.[7] Handke's literary texts have always been peo-
pled by notorious cinephiles and voyeurs, and, not surprisingly, in *The Left-Handed*

Woman, a film produced by Wenders, the novelist's vision is realized by the cine-matographer Robby Müller and the editor Peter Przygodda, important contributors to Wenders's lyrical tales of men seeking a language in a world of images.

In *The Left-Handed Woman*, however, the dialectic between the visual and the verbal, so dominant in Handke's career and literary work, becomes concentrated and emphasized as never before, both as a symptom of the larger *Literaturverfilm-ungskrise* and as a resistance to it. Unlike *The Goalie's Anxiety at the Penalty Kick*, this film was first conceived as a film and only then written as a novel. This reversal of the usual pattern of adaptation affects both the fiction and the film in crucial and telling ways—ways well beyond the obvious omissions, additions, and alterations that here and elsewhere often describe the main differences between a novel and its filmic adaptation. (In the film of *The Left-Handed Woman*, some of these simple changes include the moving of the setting from Germany to Paris and the inclusion of a scene from an Ozu film.) Specifically, because of its filmic conception, Hand-ke's literary version of the story contains an unusually cinematic grammar and prose in which the lack of adjectives and adverbs reduces the characters and their actions to unusually flat (even for Handke) representations. Little is attributed to the char-acters through the connotative force of language, and, throughout the novel, any emotional depth in or between the characters appears only as the indirect product of the static independence of the images. The strictly imagistic quality of the language and the literal significance of the words thus join in the novel across the image's resistance to any narrative or symbolic meaning and the word's insistence that that meaning be made. Ultimately one might argue that the inadequacy of this particular novel follows from just these austere limits that Handke chooses to impose on his language—for it seeks to convey an imagistic order that, by definition, can never really be made apparent in the novel and that, as a function of the work's concep-tion, has preceded it.

At one point in the novel, for instance, the text reads:

> That night the woman sat by the window with the curtains drawn, reading; a thick dic-tionary lay beside her. She put her book aside and opened the curtains. A car was just turning into one of the garages, and on the sidewalk an elderly lady was walking her dog. As though nothing escaped her, she looked up at the window and waved.[8]

As with much of the novel, the visual dynamics of this scene are its center: as she replaces her reading and dictionary with a gesture as simile, what does not escape the woman is precisely the discrete images which the window as frame makes avail-able to her; she reacts to and with gestures and images, and the prose of the text accordingly seems tensely abstracted from the real drama. The film, moreover, en-acts this same tension between an imagistic independence and the languages that seek to appropriate it. But, in the film, the reality of the images and their materially given and authentic status introduce the absent member of the novel's drama, and so make *actually* present the dramatic tension that is at the heart of this and most other works of literature/film adaptation: the dramatic tension of translation itself, of the impossible adaptation of language to image and image to language.

If in *Kings of the Road* and other films, Wenders works rigorously to return images to the writing of history, Handke's is a distinct variation on that argument. Richard McCormick has noted the persistence of a tension between imagistic and linguistic registers across the collaborative work of these two, and, in *Wrong Move* specifically, he demonstrates how Wenders filmically revises Handke's scripts of imagistic isolation to emphasize a return to language as history:

> It is in this context, perhaps, that Wenders's film can be best distinguished from Handke's screenplay. . . . Wenders's film suggests that, in a "postrevolutionary" era, it is important not to succumb to the conformism of the dominant social order, as Handke's adaptation of *Wilhelm Meister* stresses, but that it is also all the more important to learn from history rather than withdraw from it or attempt to eliminate it.[9]

However accurate this assessment may be of *Wilhelm Meister*, I will argue a different point about *The Left-Handed Woman*. Signaled first in the female protagonist who replaces the male buddies of Wenders's narratives, this Handke film is not a withdrawal or an elimination of historical or social discourse but a movement toward it that is far more tentative and suspicious of its inherited structures of power: to speak oneself as an "authentic" image in this film requires a creative insertion of that image which, like translation, always testifies both to what is lost in the process and to the possibility of renovating that historical discourse, through translation, as a new direction.

From the beginning of the film, the central image and measure of this authenticity are clearly the woman herself. In the book and film, she suddenly announces her break with her husband by saying that she has "had a strange idea. Well, not really an idea, more like an—illumination" (p. 13); and her distinction is especially appropriate since what she is claiming is herself as image, not her position as an abstraction in some larger discourse. In this announcement, there is none of the verbal explaining, none of the social and psychological rationale that generally define (in literature and film) this kind of decision to break with a husband and the social world he represents. Her crisis does not concern any search for identity but simply and plainly a claiming of an identity already possessed but unacknowledged. Like the home where she continues to live, her "leaving" is, more accurately, a staying. In this way, *The Left-Handed Woman* is both less than and more than a feminist film, involving little of the social and psychoanalytic work associated with a feminist position today and instead defining her mainly and quite idealistically in terms of her stoic resistance to *any* typing or social positioning.

The course of the film, in fact, could be described as a series of negations or resistances through which Marianne holds off different individuals and different discourses that attempt to coopt her (image) into their language. In the opening of the film, she picks up her husband, Bruno, at the airport and listens passively as he talks continuously about his trip to Finland where, ironically, he had been completely isolated by the language he could not speak. Later, speaking of "the mature beauty of master/servant relationships," he takes her to dinner in order that they may luxuriate in being served by others. After being confronted with her decision to live alone, he explains it with a terminology that has no real bearing on the act, calling her a "mystic." Finally, when Marianne and their son visit him in his office, Bruno acts out the "stare" with which he hopes to exercise enough power to become a member of the board, the stare through which one controls another's image. Several other men whom she encounters come to represent similar versions of this need to appropriate and dominate Marianne: the publisher who hires her uses the opportunity to court her, and, when she resists, he tries to coerce her by telling a tale of a lonely writer whose isolation eventually made it impossible for him to use words at all; her father visits her in a confused and half-hearted effort to reconcile her to a world that grows more hostile with old age; and even the strange unemployed actor she meets one day pursues her with a silent and romantic passion that, for all the two seem to have in common, is entirely inappropriate to a woman whose ultimate desire is not to get entangled with the objects and desires of the world.

Despite its usually masculine nature, this is not, however, only a patriarchal order that threatens her. Marianne's close friend Franziska, while allowing Bruno to live with her, urges Marianne to join her feminist group so that she may locate an image of herself outside the one forced on her by the dominant male culture. Yet, what Franziska does not realize is that for Marianne the feminist circle offers only another socially and subjectively made image, not one independently isolated in its own integrity. Marianne consistently and stoically remains apart from any discourse that attempts to encroach upon her; her placid expression and extraordinarily silent manner are peculiarly nonaggressive and undemanding, bearing witness to a claim for self-possession and nothing more. As Stanley Kauffmann has remarked, she is not violently mute like Elisabet in Bergman's *Persona* (1966) but verbally restrained and sparing in a manner that makes her separation a more confident and less dependent break with the social world around her.[10] If she is part of a woman's film tradition, it is not that of Paul Mazursky's *An Unmarried Woman* (1978) or Agnès Varda's *One Sings, the Other Doesn't* (1977), but that of Chantal Akerman's *Meetings with Anna* (1978). This is not a flamboyant assertion into or against another social order but a quiet departure from the abstracting terms of any social discourse.

In this resistance to discourse, Marianne becomes almost pure image, a negation of social languages.[11] It is more than twenty minutes into the film before this central character utters her first word, and for the remainder of the film she says extremely little, a passive listener in most of her conversations with others. After her husband accuses her of mysticism, she regards herself in the mirror and says, "Say whatever you want; the more you say the freer I'll be of you." This confrontation is, on the one hand, directed at her absent husband and his attempt to bully and manipulate her with language. On the other hand, it is aimed at her own divided self as an image produced by that patriarchal discourse and as an image independent of those words, more distinguished in its difference, the more those words atttempt and fail to claim that image. The scene becomes a metaphoric reversal of a Freudian mirror stage, a negation in every sense, as she identifies an image of herself present before that infantile mirror stage when social/linguistic transformations produced a socialized

"The negation of the other image" (*The Left-Handed
Woman*). The Museum of Modern Art/Film Stills Archive.

image of her. She identifies herself, in short, as a left-handed image: free of language and logic because she can see herself as an isolated and singular image. Here as throughout the film, she lives according to negation, not contraries; ultimately, her efforts are to claim herself not as an opposite discourse but as an entirely separate presence.

Formally, the film is most striking in its dramatization of just this imagistic isolation. Assisted here in large part by Müller and Przygodda, this use of the image as a discrete entity and value follows almost too patently Wenders's sensibility from his first student films to the more recent *The State of Things* (1982). But, as in the case of Wenders, and as Handke makes quite clear in this film, the first source of this sensibility is the Japanese filmmaker Yasujiro Ozu. Cited several times in *The Left-Handed Woman*, Ozu is most noticeably acknowledged when the camera pans from a dimly lit shot of the woman silently crouched against the wall to a poster of Ozu and then back to the woman. The importance of Ozu to Handke and Wenders is mainly the manner in which Ozu's films valorize the image in itself and formally isolate it from both human and diegetic significance. In Noël Burch's words about Ozu, images and objects as images often appear in his narratives as "pillow shots," and, like his mismatching, they reflect "a culturally and complexly determined sign of dissent from the world-view implicit in the Western mode. This mode, of course, is profoundly *anthropocentric*."[12] In Ozu's films these shots "intervene in a certain kind of discourse, and each de-centering effect possesses its own specificity. These shots cause a suspension of the diegesis. . . . The space from which these references are made is invariably presented as outside the diegesis, as a pictorial space on another place of 'reality.'"[13]

Despite these clear connections with Ozu and his compositional methods, there is a difference. The sequence with the poster of Ozu follows shortly after a sequence in which Marianne, seated between her son and his friend, watches an Ozu movie, *Tokyo Chorus* (1931). In the sequence from the Ozu film, a family is seated in a circle apparently playing a clapping game of some sort; but, while pretending to enjoy herself, the mother-wife is secretly crying. In one important sense, this sequence describes the tragic isolation of the woman from the familial and social circle around her, and it thus partially reflects the predicament of Handke's own woman. Yet, Handke's woman falls asleep during the sequence, and one way of reading this would be that the predicament of the insert film contains nothing filmically or fictionally interesting (or provoking) for Marianne because she has, at this point, moved outside the tragic pathos of that circle (just as Handke's film recontextualizes Ozu's). Significantly, this image of the mother asleep on the shoulder of her son is one of the two images that Handke says is the source of the film.[14] The image suggests a negation (eyes shut, asleep, and uninterested) of the social bind Ozu's mother represents and, at the same time, it enacts a perfectly passive overturning of the traditional gestures of support in a family hierarchy. Handke's perspective is not, therefore, merely a recreation or appropriation of Ozu's world; rather, his heroine and the discrete images about her describe a different drama, since Marianne has already achieved and now only works to maintain the internal authenticity and harmony that Ozu's characters constantly struggle toward. She inhabits the pillow shots that beckon from afar to Ozu's men and women.

The connection between Handke's woman and Ozu's film is therefore not between the characters of the two worlds but between the extrahuman images around Ozu's individuals and the human reality of Handke's woman. Quite systematically, *The Left-Handed Woman* establishes an equation between its protagonist and the extrahuman realm of the discrete objects and images that tragically evade Ozu's all-too-human characters. The film opens with a series of these shots: grass rustling as a train rushes by, newspapers blowing across an empty station platform, a motionless urbanscape, the woman's home depicted in a symmetrically flat frontal shot, and a still life of fruit. Throughout the film, these kinds of static images punctuate its course with a logic that, while breaking with the diegesis, establishes concomitantly a connection with the woman herself. The montage that develops around these shots paradoxically separates them from the realm of human discourse while linking them to Marianne's independent status as discrete image. Among the many examples of this action, perhaps the most explicit are the shots of tulips (at the restaurant meal, for instance) with trembling or falling petals, which, after being pictorially disconnected, are graphically linked to the woman herself. As Rentschler notes, these "pillow shots suggest a concrete world existing outside our everyday consciousness, a world waiting to be discovered, a living world beyond the compositional center of the film's narrative."[15] And the strange irony that permeates and controls this film is that this external consciousness is exactly what defines the new subjectivism that Marianne has claimed as her own and works to maintain through the course of the film. She is at once the compositional center of the film and an image at odds with that center.

The imagistic singularity of Marianne also helps explain her imperviousness to the temporal pressures directed at her. Several times in the film different characters attempt to remind her of how her retreat into a new subjectivism will be eroded and destroyed by time. In a speech that Marianne deflates as rehearsed posturing, an overdetermined social discourse, her husband taunts her with the fact that she will "grow older and older and then hang herself." The publisher tells her of the "ghastly old age" that awaits an author who has inexplicably stopped writing. The theme of her father's visit is primarily the pathos of growing old and the struggles of memory. Likewise, the narrative of the film itself is marked with titles announcing the changes in months from March through May—months of birth but, as T. S. Eliot has made famous, also months of cruel growth. Against these movements stands the woman in her imagistic isolation, resisting temporal patterning just as she resists social and patriarchal discourses. She retreats into herself against the pressures of time and, more importantly, against the action of a narrative temporality that necessarily threatens to inscribe her in its own conventional scheme.

In this dialectic with narrative itself, one sees the most significant connection between *The Left-Handed Woman* and other feminist films that, in their different ways, confront a patriarchal order in the very structure of narrative cinema, whose temporal ordering purportedly reflects a male mode of seeing and organizing experience.[16] Specifically, these films aim at a nonnarrative disengagement from the fetishizing action of the male perspective that has dominated filmmaking since its historical beginnings; and the resistance of Handke's pillow-shot woman to a temporal composition thus takes on a larger political character as it works to separate the image of the woman (and her image-making activity) from the formal temporality of another order.[17] For her, the fears of an old age must be incidental threats; for her, the imagistic stasis of an extrahuman perspective always detaches itself from the human (and male) dynamics of narrative film. Like the windows seen from the inside and the outside of the speeding trains in the film, the perspective of this woman and this film places such a radical emphasis on the frames of the image that its course through time becomes a truly secondary and separate context.

Where then is this woman's place in the public sphere? Does she in fact have such a place, and is it defined only by her separation from the other discourses (of men, of temporality, of any group consciousness) that surround her? Here lies the central tension in the film. For, if this woman defines and maintains herself through an imagistic isolation in the extrahuman, the second direction of the film is her translation of herself slowly and subtly back into the human realm, a translation of the image she has claimed into a language for its communication.

Appropriately, her first foray into the matters of the social world is to take a job as a translator, and much of the film evolves around this first assignment of translating Flaubert's *A Simple Heart*. The signs and significance of this movement from a state of singularity to that of human discourse appear again when she pulls her husband from the path of a truck after he has been pleading "I exist too"; and later in the film a shot of her in a café shows her face partially covered by a newspaper, the first she has read for some time and one aptly titled *Le Quotidien*.

The image of another woman and child that drifts now and then across Marianne's course is an equally crucial symbol of a potentially less enclosed relation with the world, and Marianne's own strange son comes to dramatize both the problems and possibilities of a social relationship that could preserve her own image while communicating it with others. As a natural bond that potentially both constricts and opens her, this son represents and crystallizes a dialectic with an outside order that she must separate herself from yet needs to respond to, which she moves toward but only in the tentative hope of establishing a new relationship with it. It is the intrusion and badgering of her son and his friend that make her toss her typewriter and translation off the table in anger and frustration. Often these two Kafkaesque children play strange communication games—with walkie-talkies or with vaudevillian gestures of violence—which at once mirror and stand in ironic contrast to the mother's strained efforts to establish her own idiom for communication. As a reversal of the conventional structure of family and society, individuality in this family must begin as an outside image and can only then start to work on a fresh language and restructured social relations.

With the full scope of its implications for film this crisis of translation means, for Handke and his characters, finding a language to speak an image not as a language but as an authentic image. It means in effect creating a language as a negation of all that conventional language implies. Like the unemployed actor whom Marianne and her father meet at the photo booth (Rüdiger Vogler, a regular in Wenders's films), this image would have to discover the impossible formula for communicating intimately and naturally while being controlled by conventional rules. As Marianne's father tells the actor, "You always seem embarrassed by your lines. . . . You're posing." To show that he has understood this message about making a filmic image speak a natural language, the father asks the actor to make the image communicate intimately: "In your next film signal me that you understood." He concludes by suggesting that with these changes an authentic image can harmoniously enter a temporal order: "I look forward," he says, "to watching you grow older on the screen." Here, as throughout the film, to become a viable language the image must aim at a radical and discrete movement back into the human world: a movement by which the singularity of imagistic identity would use yet resist the conventions of discourse, a strained and balanced movement such as this barely visible and relatively static narrative structure that nonetheless remains very much a narrative and temporal order.

More specifically, this effort to translate the image takes the form of a tension between identity and allegory. Throughout the film there are obtrusive marks of allegory, such as street names like "rue Terre Neuve" or "rue de la Raison" (on which the woman lives). And Handke has remarked that these allegorical planes are central to the film's project, as they appear alongside those striking moments of im-agistic identity to create a kind of friction. In his words: "The fact that names of this kind, completely casually, appear in the story, was not used as a device to show symbolic constriction — but rather served as a kind of distortion correcting pleasant-ness through the gestures of allegory."[18] As a specific semantic play, this tension and dialectic thus recalls the tension of translation. Its unconstricted balance is clar-ified further when, in describing the image of the suburban houses that inspired the film, Handke uses the term "a separate togetherness."[19]

On the one hand, this tension between allegory and identity involves the life of the image itself, which, for Handke, exists as a sort of pure and romantic identity, a self-sustaining pleasantness outside the abstractions and weight of any discourse or structure. On the other hand, there is the communal or social order, which repre-sents itself and its elements in terms of allegorical discourse, a language to be read and spoken through larger patterns of meaning, but one here without the stability and semantic unity of symbol. Unlike a symbolic discourse, with allegory there is no interpenetration of image and language; rather there is a slight distortion, which in a curious way fits together the language and the image it appropriates, so that meaning lies in the dramatic gap between the two and the image speaks only as a slight negation of the language that surrounds it.

At one point in the film, Marianne walks down rue Elise and from a neighboring house we hear Beethoven's "Für Elise." Earlier, just after she has told Bruno of her illumination, she rushes home and, without explanation, walks around her living room on stilts. In both cases, the image and action vibrate with a significance that comes from literal, allegorical props (romantic pathos, escape, etc.). Yet, in both cases, the singularity of the image and the artificiality of the allegory generate an attraction and repulsion that allow the image to speak through the allegory but as significantly more than it. In a way central to Handke's entire aesthetic, translation becomes a negation of its vehicular language (as allegory), since in appropriating the image the main service of this language is to create a friction (like balancing on stilts) between the allegorical props and the referent image, calling that image for-ward as meaningful while testifying to its own basic inability to claim that meaning. In *I Am an Inhabitant of the Ivory Tower* (1972) Handke explains this in different terms: "It is not only a question of unmasking clichés . . . but of entering into, with the help of clichés of reality, new conclusions concerning reality."[20] In translating the image, this negation therefore insinuates a positive meaning: like the shot of Marianne sitting in a small shed, looking defiantly up and shutting the door on the eye of the camera, the act of negation becomes a positive claim to the fundamental value of the image as self-contained meaning.

Stylistically and structurally, the most salient action with which Handke estab-lishes this dialectic of translation is an imagistic montage, what Rentschler has called a "collision" of elements.[21] Thematically, this collision is present in the central predicament of the film: a German woman in a French city, displaced in her place. But usually this montage or collision works through a narrative or visual jolt, a surprise or friction, whose immediate consequence is a static charge. Con-nected with the abrasive stasis of those pillow-shot images set against the narrative flow or the friction created by the tension between allegory and identity, the indirect purpose of this charge is to generate meaning. More specifically, it locates within its tension and along its surfaces either a character depth or a radical interaction between characters. As a dramatic illustration of this, there is again the sequence at the photo booth. The actor and Marianne move tentatively toward each other to shake hands as they prepare to part, but, just at that moment, a static electric shock anticipates their fingertips. They quickly look up at each other, smile uncomfortably, and, in this way, communicate silently beyond the formal gesture that initiated the contact.

The narrative of *The Left-Handed Woman* is, in fact, disrupted continually by these jolts and collisions. The two children leaping unexpectedly from the suitcases, the awkward and peculiar confrontation with the publisher's chauffeur at her door, the café scenes with their disparate figures and angular visual planes, and especially the final party scene at Marianne's house: all describe simple social or visual shocks and unexpected collisions within the diegesis, which make disturbingly apparent a world into which isolated characters and images must integrate themselves. The party scene is especially pertinent in this regard, for here one sees a gathering of all the character-images that have somewhat randomly gathered around Marianne through the course of the film. As alienated figures, these characters confront each other for the first time, and, in the clumsiness of their separate identities, they make an abrasive contact like the friction between the actor and Marianne. As summary of this contact and the communication it represents, the party ends with a fumbling fight between Bruno and the actor, which leads to the two men comforting each other as they leave. A more strictly visual version of these and other scenes is the striking shot of Marianne walking a path that parallels the path of a horse and rider, which, in turn, forms a parallel with a speeding train: each moves along its own imagistic lines, but in the contiguity of those lines there appear dramatic fissures that define both their differences and their shared space, their separate togetherness.

In *The Left-Handed Woman*, these moments of visual strain, friction, and confrontation become the film's center. They illustrate the action by which an identity (self and image) is distorted through the pressures of allegory (the discourse of society). They dramatize, above all else, how the pleasant integrity of the image — observed most readily in the stunning beauty of so many shots — becomes profitably distorted through the communal sense of allegory. In these distortions, the film and its images speak.

In *The Left-Handed Woman*, consequently, the singularity of the image continually and, at least from Handke's perspective, unavoidably translates itself through the force of its negations into a discourse of meaning. More accurately, the pure image in Handke's film always teeters with a visible friction on the edge of a larger allegorical sense that, even in the ironic inadequacy of that sense, redeems the image from isolation. Usually, in this drama of the visual and the verbal, the static charge that is at its center serves, through its speaking, to illuminate the different sides of the dialectic. But, at least once, the film introduces a strange merger of the subjective and the objective, of allegory and identity. Here one witnesses Handke's dream of translation, an impossible and utopian making of image into an integrated discourse, freed of friction.

Of the significantly few times this utopian translation actually appears in Handke's work, the most striking in *The Left-Handed Woman* is a medium-long shot of Marianne looking out of a second-story window below her son who is in a parallel window on the third floor. It is a night shot, and the windows are brightly illuminated as sharply defined images of the two characters. As with much of the film, the shot is dramatically silent. Suddenly, the son tumbles from the window, across the gaze of the mother, and lands miraculously on his feet. The shot is unsettling since, like many of the shots in the film, it has a very tangential relation to the diegesis, but, more importantly, because the unexpectedly surreal nature of the shot makes it extremely difficult to locate in terms of the film's studied realism. This narrative jolt is clearly part of the disturbing friction that surfaces throughout the film, but the exceptional status of the shot indicates that it is also a central anchoring point in the film—against which the tension between allegory and identity can be measured. The content of the shot suggests itself a kind of wish fulfillment: a vision of the son, Marianne's potential link with new social relationships, saved from the disaster and tragedy this son and society could represent.[22] Formally, moreover, the same type of salvation is represented: just as Marianne's vision here metaphorically gathers up the image of the son as it crosses hers, the tension between the two internal frames is ultimately diffused into a very different image with an obviously new (surreal) look, an image which teases with the human significance of a *natural* discourse. Across the tense juxtaposition of these frames-within-the-frame, the extrahuman vision of Marianne gives way to an imaginative interaction, a new kind of image that connects and integrates those previous oppositions. With this single shot, the collision between identity and allegory reconciles temporarily in a startling example of the utopian state that Marianne quietly seeks to translate herself into: where the self as singular image finds an opposite and *positive* idiom with which to speak that image to others, where image retains its identity while yet expressing itself in a social discourse. This, then, is a rare moment of true feeling.

Whether as a negative dialectic or a positive drama, this rigorous effort to translate an authentic image into a social discourse is the best indicator of Handke's distance from Bresson and Antonioni, two filmmakers to whom Handke is often compared. Despite resemblances between the work of Handke and that of these other filmmakers, Handke's style is not transcendent. As Rentschler has pointed out, observers who miss this point fail to recognize the sociohistorical dimension in Handke's powerful individualism.[23] If Handke regularly focuses on the extrahuman, it is only to return his characters and audience to a human integrity. Aptly, the publisher who gives Marianne work translating Flaubert is played by Bernhard Wicki, who once appeared in Antonioni's *La notte*. There Wicki plays a writer whose death early in the film introduces a dismally stark world of rigid images that overwhelm speech and any possibility of human society. Here, in Handke's film, Wicki is resurrected; and, fittingly, as a symbolic messenger of translation itself, he points the way to bringing those images of alienation back into human discourse. In brief, he brings the possibility of finding words to suit the radical difference of the image. Wicki, as the integrated presence of actor and man, thus indicates Handke's path through the alienation of Antonioni and Bresson (and, for that matter, Ozu) and toward a world where the individual subject isolated in images can translate himself or herself back into history and social discourse.

For Handke, this possibility is an extremely tenuous one, its appearance often as tentative and awkward as any attempt to move between images and language. Yet, at the end of the film, Marianne does, through patience and endurance, finish her translation of a novel about human transcendence won through suffering. Shortly before, she makes a first, a prosaic gesture of friendship toward Bruno by buying him shoes. The final shots recall the opening pillow shots: blossoms on the side-walk, Marianne watching her son swing, a train passing through an empty station, and commuters walking through a subway tunnel. But, in this ending, the images have begun to fill with a human and social content, not appropriate, strictly speak-ing, to a pillow shot. The final shot of the two children parting at the end of the tunnel to go their separate ways, moreover, is explicitly a summary image of prom-ise: figures of a future dividing in the middle of the frame yet joined by the sym-metrical tension of the otherwise static borders. The children move out of the frame, allegorizing a path for the spectator, and Handke underlines the direction of that path by closing the film with a written quotation from Vlado Kristl: "Have you noticed there's only room for those who make room for themselves?" Besides the telling irony of a verbal text having the last word in this film about imagistic identity, here is the central paradox and hope of *The Left-Handed Woman*: a definition of a social space only as it is produced by an individual's demand for a private space.

If *The Left-Handed Woman* has been (correctly I think) seen as a feminist film made by a man, it consequently can equally and perhaps more profitably be de-scribed as a story of images made by a celebrated writer of German. If it is a film of aggressive isolation and negation, it is also a social film precisely in the aggressive-ness with which it speaks those negations. In this purposely difficult adaptation, translation is achieved only by being adamantly and literally faithful to the original. Images are capable of joining the social allegory of language only by resisting as an identity apart. The chief, ironic revelation of the film then becomes that the left-handed eccentric of the title is, in fact and by nature, a right-handed everywoman and that, in the historical sense practiced (for instance) by Fassbinder in *Effi Briest* (1974) or *Berlin Alexanderplatz* (1980), the crisis of literary adaptation opens inci-sive, if displaced, perspectives on the present and future — both for native speakers and for their foreign interlocutors.

"Ferdinand: in search of information" (*Strongman Ferdinand*).

The Semantics of Security in Kluge's *Strongman Ferdinand*

All that sets men in motion has first to pass
through their minds; but the form it takes within
those minds depends mainly upon circumstance.
　　　　　　　　　　　　　　Friedrich Engels

Doubtless more committed to the left than most other successful German filmmakers, Alexander Kluge is not surprisingly the most Brechtian in his theoretical perspective on the cinema industry as a whole and in his particular practices as a filmmaker. This double attention to the theory and practice of cinema is in part a consequence of Kluge's intellectual heritage as a novelist, university professor, attorney, and Marxist philosopher. Yet his assiduous concern with where aesthetics and business join is likewise and significantly connected with one of his first encounters with the film art, in which he witnessed the shameful degradation of Fritz Lang (that symbolic center of German film history) in the hands of a postwar entrepreneur, Arthur Brauner. Kluge recalls:

> My first experience in cinema was very depressing: I was the assistant to Fritz Lang in 1958–59 while he was shooting *The Tiger from Eschnapur* and *The Indian Tomb* in Berlin. I watched a producer, made rich by the black market, come to give orders and take advice from his wife and his wife's sister, rather than the advice of his director. Fritz Lang didn't even have control of the cameramen, the electricians, etc. . . . At his hotel he would receive a case of champagne but the film slipped more and more from his control. It was then that I became aware of the necessity of a new politics for the cinema.[1]

Compounded by the general crisis in German cinema in the early sixties, this early lesson confirmed for Kluge the necessity of attending not simply to the integrity of ideas but to the actualization of these ideas. For Kluge, alternative images and alternative films are indeed crucial if social reality is to be understood as a concrete plurality. But without a physical machinery to implement these new perspectives, the potential understanding they can provide becomes simply a theoretical musing. As he states it as commentator in *Occasional Work of a Female Slave*, Kluge realized early in his filmmaking career that theoretical and ''unused ideas do not keep, they evaporate.''

Closely aligned with the Frankfurt school of aesthetics, Kluge is perhaps the most articulate filmmaker in Germany today in assessing the problems of controlling and effectively using ideas within the production/distribution structure of the contemporary German film industry.[2] In June 1976, he pinpoints the specifics of this structure as such: "our adversaries are these: The Association of American distributors, represented by its union; the producers of the controlling television station, Beta-Film, and the owners of the circuit of 300 cinemas which form the Hauptverband der Filmtheater."[3] Founding his own production in 1963, Kluge has accordingly attempted to counter these monopolies, most importantly by activating a machinery that would allow the filmmaker full control of his or her film since, for Kluge, "the economic and artistic responsibilities must be in the hands of a single person, . . . the directors must be their own producers."[4] This demand for independence, however, has little to do with artistic integrity. Rather, it is a calculated business tactic which recognizes that only in controlling the mechanisms of production as fully as possible can a filmmaker challenge the division of labor through which the relatively monopolistic channels of public information impede and guard what the general public knows.

As a businessman Kluge has few idealistic illusions: for him, film is above all else a capitalistic merchandise which, however artistically unique, remains structured in such a way that production is dependent on consumption and reception. Despite similar political leanings, Kluge is no Godard. And if his first real contact with the film industry bears an uncanny resemblance to *Le mépris*, Kluge resists any tendency to return to zero ground in his films, primarily because he recognizes that the projected reception of a film, its expectation horizon, must provide the conditions for a language with which to communicate. Like Godard in so many other ways, Kluge turns sharply from the isolation of Godard's sometimes radical film language and ultimately from the entire concept of a "politique des auteurs" which supports those individualistic notions of a film language: in Miriam Hansen's words, "while the post-Oberhausen film-makers naturally turned to the French New Wave for a model, German *Autorenkino* was not only less homogeneous than its French counterpart but also developed different notions of authorship. The emphasis was necessarily more on a '*politique* des auteurs,' the political struggle for independent film-making in a country which did not have a film culture comparable to that of France."[5] In 1980 Kluge further specifies his list of adversaries:

> . . . we still have three enemies: the American companies, the bureaucracies—our sacrosanct national bureaucracy—and finally the individualism of the filmmakers. These filmmakers present themselves as auteurs, and their subjectivity becomes the primary point, which in fact this subjectivity is always less than the cinema itself. The cinema is its spectators, the collective imaginary. From now on, it will be necessary to move ahead to a new stage and to make not personal films but collective films. . . . One should make collective films that bear on daily life. Such a cinema could ultimately be the cinema of spectators which is my own goal.[6]

Since this "real film is the one in the spectator's mind,"[7] Kluge naturally fights indefatigably for access to that mind, not by popularizing his perceptions but by attempting to open those traditionally secured spaces of communication, the actual cinemas where information is defined and disseminated. "Our policy is: to produce the greatest number of immediate outlets for public information," he says. "At this moment, we find ourselves before the last barrier, the showcase cinemas. . . . This economic mechanism is assured as long as films make the most money in the center of cities. We must now demand a second kind of programming which doesn't aim all films at showcase cinemas but at marginal zones for their first showings—at the 3,000 other moviehouses and at the fifty or more independent cinemas."[8] Perhaps the key notion in Kluge's aesthetic, *Öffentlichkeit* suggest succinctly his central concern here with expanding the zones of communication and transforming the media apparatuses so that a more diverse public is reached and more pertinent, varied information is made available to many different German spectators.[9] As he implies at many points, the American domination of the distribution networks is again the main obstacle in this regard, the Kluge's task is to locate and use the channels of communication that this established system has excluded from the semantics of its discourse. Both in his socioeconomic dealings and in his films themselves, Kluge sees this problem as one of zones of information in which a kind of spatial security drastically distorts the full complexity of the meanings in a social reality: "Centralization itself is precisely how the American films reduce the film public. For example: with *The Exorcist* the profits are very high but at the same time people who are not interested in this kind of film disappear from the cinemas. . . . Such a development can be reversed only progressively. One can reverse it only if indeed we reclaim those marginal zones of exploitation." For Kluge, these marginal zones are defined in two ways: as geographic areas outside the main cities and as classes and interest groups other than the dominant one. In both cases, Kluge uses that cinematically apposite metaphor of a body in which "blood is not being generated to the veins"; in both cases the essential solution is "the differentiation of responses to needs, and accessibility."[10]

Indeed Kluge has had a modicum of success in expanding these zones of distribution where meaning is produced. But in addition to the opening of these new regions, Kluge demands the development of new powers of receptivity so that cinema not only broaches new topics but activates diverse responses which then become major ingredients in the production of meaning. Along with the increase in social data and diversified audiences, in short, Kluge aims to expand the role and space of cinematic reception, since vitalizing and sharpening the powers of reception initiate nothing less than the full imaginative potential of an art that is also an industry. "Above all else," Kluge argues, "film is not a normal capitalist merchandise since it always requires a form of artistic production; even if it was a mass produced product, it would be produced artistically since it is a merchandise of fantasy and it is the reception that thus constitutes the film."[11] With the communication of fantasy and dreams as a base, Kluge's reception aesthetic accordingly becomes more precisely defined as a materialist aesthetic in which the concrete manifestations of a work of art are ultimately the various responses it elicits. "A materialist aesthetic means," he says,

a way of organizing collective social experience. This collective social experience exists with films or without them. It has existed for about three-hundred-thousand years, and been "actualised" for only about three-hundred of them, because social development grew faster. The invention of film, of the cinema, is only an industrial answer to the film which has its basis in people's minds. The stream of associations which is the basis of thinking and feeling . . . has all the qualities of cinema. And everything you do with your mind and your senses, you can do in the cinema. . . . The real mass media is the people themselves, not the derivatives like cinema or television. And if you have a conception of film which means that it's the spectators who produce their films, and not the authors who produce the screenplay for the spectators, then you have a materialistic theory.[12]

The spectators, for Kluge, can "change the films through the production of their own minds": "the films are enriched by the spectator's experience. And we call this position materialistic because it thinks from the bottom up, *from* the spectator and the cinema in *his* mind, to the cinema on the screen. The cinema on the screen is only a way of organizing experience that already exists before the film is made. . . . And minds are rather flexible, not very fragile."[13] Or, as he puts it in the major work he co-authored on the German film industry: "The concept of production not only includes the manufacturing of the film but also its exhibition and appropriation by the imagination of the spectator who actually produces the film, as the film on the screen sets in motion the film in the mind of the spectator."[14] To encourage this situation, moreover, the traditional controlling force of the director as auteur must give way to a new passivity antipodal to the dominating relationship whereby Hollywood secures the space of the screen as the exclusive place where meaning is active: "If the film is active, the spectator becomes passive. . . . Hollywood films try to persuade the audience to give up their own experience and follow the more organized experience of the film. In my opinion the opposite is right."[15]

With political aims roughly similar to Schlöndorff's and techniques which often resemble Fassbinder's, Kluge practices this program for a materialistic aesthetic as an explicit and graphic conflict with the closed formulas of conventional discourse. Like Schlöndorff, Kluge leans in this effort toward a certain type of realism; yet, more like Fassbinder, he is entirely aware that fictive tropes are the means by which this reality and its significance are produced for the spectator. While Kluge focuses his films on commonly ignored social realities, in short, he does so in a manner meant to activate the audience's sense that these realities are products fundamentally subject to change. "What you notice as realistic," he explains,

given the way our senses have been educated, is not necessarily or certainly real. The potential and historical roots, and the detours of possibilities, also belong to reality. The realistic result, the actual result, is only an abstraction that has murdered all other possibilities for the moment. But these possibilities will recur. . . . The most ideological illusion of all would be to believe that documentary realism is realism. On the other hand—to some extent because it's the reality of our minds . . . I think the testimony of fiction is better than the testimony of non-fiction. Fiction is mimetic, imitative, because it's hiding behind non-fiction; and I think these are two sides of the same thing. Which is why I always try to mix these two things—not simply for the sake of mixing them, but rather to create in any film the maximum possible tensions between fiction and non-fiction.[16]

Kluge's more recent films—*Occasional Work of a Female Slave*, *Strongman Ferdinand*, and *The Patriot*—are surely all good examples of this tension between fiction and nonfiction, between abstraction and a physical reality. But *Strongman Ferdinand* is especially pertinent to Kluge's aesthetic and this study because it not only aims at the reconciliation of these different compositional tensions but attempts more than any of the previous films to reconcile social information with mass appeal.[17] Indeed, while this film may lack the radical montage typical of Kluge's films, it is precisely this anomalous status that makes it such a revealing document: no other Kluge film so explicitly and lucidly attempts to integrate his politics, radical technique, and commercial expectations, and hence perhaps no other Kluge film demonstrates so well the problems and place of Kluge in the displaced dialogue with mainstream cinema. Specifically, *Strongman Ferdinand* raises a political issue as serious and historically relevant as any Schlöndorff film: industry's development of fascistic security forces to counteract the terrorist threat. Yet Kluge handles this subject with a sense of filmic tropes as ironically engaging as the most effective of Fassbinder films. In its intention and in its discourse, *Strongman Ferdinand* demonstrates, perhaps better than any other film, that for Kluge the "cinema has one possibility other arts don't have. Because it's rather trivial and derives from the fairground . . . it hasn't been developed from the viewpoint of a small, educated society; it's made for the plebeian people, for the proletarian component." Yet, beginning with this aim for commercial attraction and mass appeal, *Strongman Ferdinand* then moves to alter the terms of this popular discourse, "to re-invent its possibilities" as a bearer of alternative messages.[18] That this particular film failed to reach those large audiences despite its formal and commercial strategies (including a re-cutting) indicates, moreover, the frustrating paradox at the center of many of Kluge's films, where the dialogue with the audience is also a rigorous training. In Kluge's words, "a dialogue with the real experiences of the audience demands a new filmic language, and this new language initially withdraws from the audience, because they're not used to it and because the largest part of film language is stuck in the habitual grooves. . . . Anybody who has been wrongly trained at anytime . . . knows that they need a bit of practice if they want to become 'natural' again."[19]

Since a basic principle of this dialogic training is repetition, it is not surprising that the precursor of *Strongman Ferdinand* appears earlier in *Occasional Work of a Female Slave* when another security officer addresses the supervisors of an industrial plant:

My name is Ferdinand Schliephake. I'm the chief security officer in a large factory. Gentlemen, what you're asking me for is not a safe factory. I can guarantee you a safe factory by taking measures to evacuate the plant in accordance with my safety regulations. . . . The problem we're discussing here, and it's also my problem, is security *inside* the plant. And security inside the plant means safe and productive manpower, not an empty factory with no production,—and how do we obtain safe people? That's something we should think about—and it's your problem. I can only guarantee you safe buildings and a safe atmosphere in which safe people can produce, but I can't supply safe people, nor precondition them.[20]

Like Ferdinand Rieche of *Strongman Ferdinand*, the Ferdinand of *Occasional Work* sees himself as a "philosopher of safety" whose central maxim is "thinking is making sure." Both Ferdinands are theoreticians—specifically, theoreticians of space. For both, furthermore, their zones of security, like theory itself, are threatened mostly by individuals who, as unmalleably concrete forces, always resist the hermetics of security just as they resist the hermeneutics of theory. Like the central and omnipresent consciousness in *Yesterday Girl* or *Artists under the Big Top*, the strongman Ferdinand becomes the focus of this dialectic between theory and practice, a dialectic which appears in most of Kluge's films and informs their very production. Here, however, unlike most of the other films, theory and ideology are in the hands of conservative powers, and the resulting contradictions generate a logic of development even more ironically disconcerting than that of a woman performing abortions to support her family. Resembling most closely the sequence in *Coup de Grâce* where a slapstick soundtrack accompanies the aristocratic officers shooting birds from their automobile or the long concluding sequence of *The Marriage of Maria Braun* where the impending tragedy looks more and more like vaudeville, *Strongman Ferdinand* transforms a policeman into a terrorist, a celebrated comic personality into a political statement,[21] and a Chaplinesque film about the control of space and mise-en-scène into a horror show about the contradictions and violence of that control.

The chief irony and foundation for most of what follows in *Strongman Ferdinand* is introduced in the first shots of the film when the close-up of Ferdinand is matched with a voice-over commentary: "This is Ferdinand Rieche. Security is his business. He knows everything about it and will never understand that other people don't." Immediately violating the formula of classical films which delays revelation, this beginning succinctly describes Ferdinand's predicament throughout the film whereby his fanatical search for knowledge and meaning remains, from beginning to end, frustrated by the definitions and categories that he imposes on his experiences. Dividing experience into zones of information, in other words, Ferdinand effectively cuts himself off at the very outset from a perspective that would allow him to see how these zones interact politically, socially, and thus semantically. Almost in parody of Schlöndorff's sense of the interaction of experience and its context, the commentator goes on to describe Ferdinand's manically precise ability to detach himself from any interaction whatsoever:

Security zone 1: Rieche himself
Security zone 2: his apartment
Security zone 3: his job, currently a police detective
Security zone 4: police work in totality
Security zone 5: the totality itself

Security is the term Rieche lives by and the concept which becomes, with incredible rapidity, an ideology pursued to the exclusion of all reality. Like Schlöndorff's idea of a historical space, it implies here the protection of an area of social reality from external intrusions, specifically the intrusion of the industrial compound by terrorists. Yet, more importantly in *Strongman Ferdinand*, security suggests the utopian desire for a final stabilization and pinpointing of meaning. Indeed, Kluge may be as interested as Schlöndorff in the dynamics of space and historical perspective (although in films such as *Yesterday Girl* with a stricter sense of dialectics). But in *Strongman Ferdinand* the argument about space and society is most explicitly bound up with the problem of semantics and information, the problem crucial to Kluge's aesthetic.

The second half of the opening sequence merges these two issues of security and semantics from the comic perspective that controls the entire film. As Ferdinand sips his coffee, he listens to a weather report for Europe on the Armed Forces Network, English again surfacing as an early index of that ubiquitous foreign presence in Germany. "Meteorologists are mystified," says the announcer. "A pocket of hot air is drifting toward Wiesbaden." Listening intently, Ferdinand unfolds a map of Europe before him and follows it closely as the radio report describes the movement of the different air masses: obsessively driven here to translate facts into his own geographically manageable patterns, Ferdinand gestures and moves his hands to trace and re-create for himself those vast and mystifying air currents. The result is that, unlike in Fassbinder's hands, spatial demystification becomes a comic simplification and the location of spatial significance appears at best as a parody of itself.

No matter what the circumstances, Ferdinand's ideology of space and security remains consistent. When he quits his police job because the constitutional laws make it impossible for him to act as strictly as he would like, this move from the "public sector" to the "private sector" of industrial security becomes only a change in geography, not in his attitude toward that geography. Through a series of quick cuts, Ferdinand is shown walking through the many different sections of the large plant, while the voice-over remarks: "In 48 hours, Rieche knows every corner of the plant. He divided the corners into map squares: everything's under control." His measures are rigorously intellectual: guards perform elaborate military exercises; electronic detection devices are set up to monitor all areas of the plant; and, most significantly, Ferdinand introduces theory into the security operations, an aspect of his work neglected by his predecessor. Conflicts between ideals and physical facts, theory and practice, arise immediately, however; the results, as throughout the film, are ludicrous. Just as Ferdinand's pudgy, comic appearance jars with his James Bond pretensions, his determined attempts to secure spatial zones stumble and entangle themselves repeatedly. When a guard locks a door with histrionic efficiency, a cleaning woman is trapped inside; whether maneuvering through Ferdinand's imaginary emergencies or attending one of his lectures on security theory, the paramilitary guards slip and slide more like Keystone cops than storm troopers. After an impressive demonstration of an ultraviolet fingerprint detector, a shadowy figure appears at the door to whisper melodramatically: "sexual excesses in storage area no. 10, a cleaning woman and known members of the staff."

While Ferdinand's approach is intensely theoretical, the comic contradictions in his life thus derive mostly from the fact that his work remains thoroughly practical.

As Kluge notes, "the difficult thing about taking sides is that it means a lot of reality; and having the reality sometimes damages your ability to take sides. . . . The more practical a person's activities are, the more faults will emerge."[22] At one explicit point, for instance, Ferdinand gazes out the window at a monument, and while the camera angle moves back and forth, inside and outside the window, the commentator remarks on the problem of security in a country that defends the practical rights of the individual: "Looked at systematically. First imperative: formation and training of an effective force. Rieche's promise: to respect the Constitutional State. No scandals; no bad press. The two imperatives conflict." Likewise, there is Kluge's continual contrasting of the daily practice of physical reality with Ferdinand's efforts mechanically to regulate and control that reality in himself as well as others. Just after the voice-over notes that the studious Ferdinand "would sooner be killed than fail to carry out his mission," which "means learn, learn, learn," the camera cuts to the scholarly Ferdinand glaring at the buxom Gertie Kahlmann crossing the street. Later, when he catches her stealing factory food, he takes her to his apartment, where he seduces her, berating her for "abusing a position of trust" while at the same time taking her hand and fondling her knee. The following bed scene, moreover, becomes a slapstick summary of Ferdinand's continual predicament, the ungainly bodies cramped and turning in a space too small for them and Ferdinand continuing to assert his demand for spatial order and control: crawling over Gertie to the other side of the cot, he growls, "I can only stand women on my right side." Later that same night, Gertie and Ferdinand slump in chairs, as the commentator voices the most evident of Ferdinand's many contradictions: "Rieche ponders the question with hindsight: how do you reconcile a thieving girlfriend with security." Indeed, as reality impinges more and more on Ferdinand's theoretical practice, he enacts with increasing clarity what Kluge calls "the complex and contradictory as the dialectic of things . . . a dialectic we can feel with our fingertips."[23]

As the last sequence illustrates so well, the body in *Strongman Ferdinand* often becomes (as it is in other contemporary German films) the central site for the contradictions and the dialectics in the film. In the sequence just prior to Ferdinand's seduction of Gertie, for example, Ferdinand must submit to a physical examination required by "the multinational parent group in Brussels." Fearing for his job if his body should prove unfit during this examination, he uses his powers and gift for machinations to subvert the machinery he has been hired to protect. In one of the sillier sequences of the film, he summons "a woman suspected of theft" to his office and coerces her into giving him a sample of her urine. During his subsequent examination—consisting of several shots of his laboring through various physical tests—he passes the spurious urine off as his own for testing, which causes the doctor to remark, "if you weren't a man, I'd say you were three months pregnant." Besides indicating once again Ferdinand's ability to exploit his professional stance to serve his physical need and the contradictions that result, this last sequence further delineates the reversals, distortions, and transformations that the body demands (in life as well as in film) in the service of the needs of representation. Here, as in filmic representation, the body must disguise its contradictions in order to achieve a

"How to reconcile a thieving girl friend with security?"
(*Strongman Ferdinand*). The Museum of Modern Art/Film
Stills Archive.

socially acceptable image, an image which would stabilize its meaning to fit society's systems for understanding. Yet it is precisely the contradictions behind these socially demanded postures of the body that Kluge exposes: in *Occasional Work of a Female Slave*, Roswitha performs abortions on other women's bodies in order to protect her position as a mother-figure; in *Strongman Ferdinand*, Ferdinand at one point disguises himself as a terrorist in order to test his own security system.

Disguising himself as a terrorist and finally acting as a terrorist, Ferdinand is, from Kluge's point of view, a radical even as he fights against radicals. Like Kluge's Roswitha and Anita G., Ferdinand is an individual alienated from his society by his unbending adherence to a single form of action and by his ignoring of the contradictions that this position generates. That he has nothing liberal-minded about him changes little, and his sense that "radical security has nothing to do with radicalism" is one of the many seeming contradictions that the irony of the film eventually transforms into a contrary fact. Just as Ferdinand's extreme theory of security absurdly divides him from the concrete circumstances of his life, so too does this security work make him a radical, alienated from both the perspective of the factory workers and the perspective of the industrial entrepreneurs who employ him.

His alienation from the workers is neatly encapsulated in three sequences midway through the film, in which Kluge's camera indicates precisely how Ferdinand is caught between two different spatial perspectives at odds with his own. In the first, the stubby Ferdinand race-walks while the tall Gertie walks alongside him, their appearances and gaits being as usual comically out of line. Gertie suddenly tells Ferdinand that she is being scorned by her fellow workers and that "for some reason you're not popular in the factory." At this, Ferdinand abruptly reverses directions; Gertie walks forward a few feet and then stops; and the camera continues its rapid reverse dolly, so that distance dramatically expands between the two characters, the continuity of action breaks into three different spatial orientations, and the compact medium shot comes unraveled. The next sequence then describes the motivation for this conflict and collapse as Ferdinand sits in his office securing the worker's private lives as if they were decipherable equations that can be abstracted to fit his vision and plan. Later, Ferdinand sits alone in a vast, empty cafeteria, his isolation conspicuously described with a crane shot and bright lighting which dwarf him in the very space he must supposedly secure. The commentary observes: "Rieche is hamstrung by the Constitutional State. Rieche needs an emergency. Without one he's had it." And just then Wilutzki, the company's vice-president, enters and sarcastically remarks, "Nothing to do then?" Whereas with the workers space becomes an abstraction and a division which Ferdinand uses to enforce distinctions, here in the eyes of the bureaucracy space becomes tauntingly too large for Ferdinand's limited perspective.

This conjunction in the last sequence of Ferdinand's double alienation from the perspective of the workers and that of the bureaucracy is indeed emblematic of his distance from both sides of a sociopolitical perspective or, more precisely, of how one creates the other: in *Strongman Ferdinand*, as in its companion piece, Fassbinder's *Third Generation*, the individual's radical adherence to a particular ideology, no matter what its goals, ultimately and ironically can only serve the ruling class insofar as it mystifies sociopolitical relations and isolates individuals in separate fictions of reality (just as Ferdinand is isolated in his medium-shot conception of space). As a consequence, the radical becomes the powerless pawn of the established forces (here capitalistic) that manipulate him or her through various fictions and disoriented spaces, all of which are finally only the tools of economic demands well beyond any single ideology. If individual lives are lived in close-up and Ferdinand's security is confined to a medium-shot perspective, the economic machinery behind these two looks at the world is doubtless a long-shot vision of society that uses the second perspective to control the first. Sounding like Orson Welles in *The Third Man*, one of Kluge's businessmen describes this bureaucratic overview: "I'm interested in the whole thing, not the particulars, not the details. Look at it from my point of view, from a bird's-eye view, from above. When I'm flying my two-seater plane, then I don't see these little things. You've got to see the thing in its entirety."[24]

Whereas Ferdinand fails to perceive the specificity and individuality of his subordinates, he fails conversely to perceive the scope of a bureaucracy in which he in turn loses all specificity. A product of his theoretical tunnel-vision, this mystified perspective is signaled several times in the film, such as when, at different points, Ganter and Wilutzki each tell Ferdinand that he "understands nothing about it." What this mystification mostly succeeds in hiding is specifically the expendability of Ferdinand's philosophy of security: as he perpetrates his ideology of order, stability, and paranoia, Ferdinand supports a bureaucratic reality which separates him from his work, other workers, and physical life, a bureaucratic reality which has no use for ideologies and social fictions except as far as they protect their own interests through mystification and separation.

In this world of capitalistic enterprise, the rapid cycles of production and consumption apply especially to political and social fictions which, as described in one of Kluge's favorite images, are quickly demolished and rebuilt in the attempt to create as much discontinuity in time as they create in social space. And the consequence is that the fully visible relations according to which constructive meaning is made never materialize for Ferdinand. He works at his desk while the office around him is torn down and rebuilt; at the beginning of the film the ouster of his predecessor prefigures the future dismissal of the myopic Ferdinand for in effect living his proper ideology too fully. As an ideology, Ferdinand's security implies the division and closure of areas of reality in order that information and meaning are exactly controlled. Carried too far, however, the fiction necessarily clashes with other realities and perspectives, and the apparatus behind that fiction — which it is the fiction's business to disguise — ironically appears through the cracks; and so the fiction renders itself useless. Put another way: in relation to the close-up reality of the workers and the long-shot vision of the bureaucrats, Ferdinand's medium-shot security methods remain woefully out of focus; his perspective is there only to blur one and to make it impossible to see the other; his eventual insistence on the exclusive reality and definitive borders of his own perspective necessarily clashes with the demands of the other points of view.

This fictive nature of ideology and the relativity of his perspective are ultimately the single truth that consistently evades Ferdinand as he pursues his own ideology as a reality that must be preserved from the pressure of both workers and bosses, the outside and the inside. At one moment, Ferdinand battles a group of leftist demonstrators at the gates, where he pushes and shouts, "this is the boundary, the company boundary. To cross it is trespassing." The next moment, however, the enemy threatens from within: he secretly films a workers' meeting and later kidnaps, injures, and locks in the basement a female scientist whom he suspects of passing information to a competitor. As opposite sides of the same line, these two incidents ultimately cancel out Ferdinand's signifying system itself, since the binary opposition on which it relies immediately collapses when exposed as an arbitrary point of view across what is really undifferentiated space. For Ferdinand, however, these lines, boundaries, and spatial demarcations are important signifying units with precise functions that supposedly lead to precise meanings; as ideological markers, they should be eminently reliable, and, for Ferdinand, their binary structure provides positivistic indices, not artificial symbols. For his employers, of course, these radical and idealistic semantics are especially annoying, since their own semantics are structured in terms of pragmatics and obfuscation. In the context of their language, Ferdinand's signifying practices become merely empty exercises that produce at best false facts and often dangerous demands for linguistic accuracy. After a terrorist bombing of the plant, for example, Ferdinand defends himself by explaining that he "can't worry at the same time about sabotage and the press." However, what for Ferdinand has the logical significance of a binary opposition is for the bureaucracy a dangerously spurious language, which an executive corrects for him: "There is no sabotage here. Only in military installations. Therefore, I don't hear the word 'sabotage.' Do you think we'd have a single customer if there was 'sabotage' in our factory? . . . A simple case of material damage. An accident. There is no more time for jokes. Improve security immediately."

Like any semantic practice that loses touch with the material reality around and informing it, Ferdinand's security system and middle-range perspective finally become a mad exercise in their own processes, a redundant bind like the ones encountered in so many other contemporary German films. His drilling of his security troops soon expands into an extensive drilling of the entire plant (an activity which naturally runs counter to production, the plant's main function). Following this same self-generating logic, the men trained to protect the plant are eventually used instead to raid another factory. For Kluge, this obsessive redundancy of formulas and signifiers is clearly the matrix of a capitalist society, and he relates it appropriately to a kind of linguistic security system that distinctly mirrors Ferdinand's medium-shot sense of property: "The whole culture industry," he says, "is busy persuading people to divide their senses and their consciousness. Even language . . . persuades people not to interest themselves in the elementary basis of their awareness, in their way of observing, in their sensuality. Karl Marx says that the whole of human history made the five senses and educated them; and then the sense of property developed and dominated all the other senses."[25]

Indeed, perhaps the most renowned illustration of these false and crippling divisions is the theoretical distinction of public and private spheres, work and leisure time, a division which, when Gertie and Ferdinand attempt to practice it, degenerates into absurd prattle. The vehicle for this attempted move into leisure time by the couple is fittingly a mobile home impounded by Ferdinand. As they travel down the highway they pass a bulldozer pulling a prefabricated house which the camera angle parallels with their own home on wheels: here, not only does Ferdinand's work travel with them (embodied in the property he secures), but, with the last shot, it becomes quite clear that what is changing sites is the security of property and not the consciousness of individuals. The subsequent long shot of the trailer starkly isolated in the middle of a field is another of Kluge's studied mise-en-scènes illustrating Ferdinand's adherence to limited spatial schemes that jar comically with spatial reality. And the vacation itself consists of Gertie performing a series of quick, routine exercises around the trailer and Ferdinand evaluating it as a training course exactly like the one he institutes at the plant. "Two successes," he notes, "the cold air and the tree. Otherwise the exercise is a flop." As the climax of this dislocation and alienation from experience, Ferdinand then explains to Gertie that this November vacation is in fact merely a practice drill for Christmas, since "Christmas takes training or it never works." The intimate trip into the country thus becomes an insane parody of a security job that divides experience into abstractly segmented perspectives and so drains it of significance. On a November evening, Ferdinand sits in a trailer by a plastic Christmas tree and reads the assignments: "1st, presents: we imagine them.

"The body and the public sphere" (*Strongman Ferdinand*). The Museum of Modern Art/Film Stills Archive.

2nd, candles and tree: we have. 3rd, think of the starving in India. 4th, the search for lodging: sleep in a snowstorm out of which I steer to a warm barn in the nick of time. 5th, records. 6th, miscellaneous.'' Here as elsewhere, Ferdinand remains the radical of security; here as elsewhere, his language, like his spatial perspective, militantly insists on the emplacement of meaning regardless of the resistance of facts, big and small.

If this dislocation is quite obviously a product of the radical theoretical stance that defines Ferdinand's manic demarcations, fictive exercises, and general approach to signs and meaning, its foundation is first and foremost a spatial organization of reality around the notions of property and a medium-shot perspective that sees neither the close-up particulars which it tries to manipulate nor the overview which in turn exploits its position. In this sense, Ferdinand becomes a premier metteur-en-scène and auteur who, like the makers of so many commercial films, works to obscure the concrete interaction of space, as well as the apparatuses that control his framework, by making the viewer the owner of perspective and hence the illusory owner of space. Under Kluge's own critical maneuvers, however, this auteurist perspective in *Strongman Ferdinand* buckles significantly against its own physicality; space subsequently proves to have many more dimensions than those of a malleable mise-en-scène. Moving his office into the production area, for instance, Ferdinand hardly gets any closer to the actuality of the workers, as outside his window large pieces of machinery move past on ceiling tracks to suggest that the window view has clarified not the workers' existence but their position as industrial cogs in Ferdinand's drama and, in turn, Ferdinand's own position as a controlled perspective. Likewise, there is Ferdinand's fishtank. Midway through his trial period, he stares into this fishtank, where different-colored fish swim slowly through a small replica of the factory. He reflects: "The little one, a commie. The black one, an Arab. The spotted one, all the East block spies. Fattie, the revolutionary syndicalist opposition. . . . A wildcat strike committee. . . . Diverse agents of industrial espionage. . . . Amateurs trying for assorted reasons to get inside the factory. . . . Inside agitators. . . . No overall picture. . . . If you got them all in a factory alley and sealed off both ends, you'd have an overall picture." Punctuated with close-ups of the fishtank and shots through it of Ferdinand's distorted face, this sequence describes with an appropriately surreal air the double bind of Ferdinand, a man whose demand to contain reality has left him with a fantastically twisted view of social facts and concomitantly deprived him of any overview outside that of a single-minded mise-en-scène which reduces reality to fit within the borders of its perspective. Like the commercial cinema that Kluge attacks, Ferdinand's point of view is as distorted as his face pressed against the glass; his spatial sense as restricted as the tank; and his visual language as abstracted as the names with which he pinpoints his fish.

Earlier Ferdinand puts into place another scene which again clashes with social reality, this time the overview. In this sequence, Ferdinand prepares a monitoring camera in a laboratory by reconstructing the camera angle with his hands in the position of the frame. As Kluge's camera angle takes over Ferdinand's angle of vision to re-create his panning action, the shot comes to rest on Wilutzki, who stands in the doorway and sharply denounces Ferdinand's safeguarding methods: "what are you doing here? . . . You're paralyzing production. Forget about extending your contract. An insurance policy would work out cheaper." When Ferdinand asks if he disputes its quality, Wilutzki answers, "no, its usefulness." But, Ferdinand exclaims, "you can't look at law and order in terms of usefulness." Meant to trap the enemy, in this sequence Ferdinand's visual equipment in fact discovers the bureaucracy, the irony being characteristic of the entire film: the precision and quality of Ferdinand's perspective, like his ideology of security, perform so effectively and mechanically that the perspective is unable to distinguish data, circumstances, and ends. Whereas the bureaucracy evaluates performance in terms of changing circumstances and long-ranging goals, Ferdinand evaluates performance, like theory, in and of itself. In a very real sense, then, Wilutzki is indeed the adversary of Ferdinand's angle of vision, since he represents a system of evaluation outside Ferdinand's closed, unilateral perspective. Wilutzki and the bureaucratics attribute meaning differently from Ferdinand, from a larger angle of view; in doing so, they threaten to subvert his mise-en-scène by judging it within a wider circumference. Just as Ferdinand directs the image, Wilutzki and his colleagues are truly the producers of the image and hence literally constitute it from their position of power and judgment: as the inadvertent pan demonstrates, Wilutzki *is* the image since he literally decides its status, value, and significance.

This collision of the visual semantics of producer and director begins its final phase when Ganter delivers his mandate "to do more" but "not to do too much." Retreating to his fishtank in despair over this remark, Ferdinand spins another of his pertinent scenarios: "the Chinese premier paints a gloomy picture of the next 50 to 100 years. War is inevitable; only the date of its outbreak is uncertain. . . . Against this background the chairman's ambiguous words." Translating Ganter's ambivalent message into a framework of certain distinctions here, Ferdinand makes an exotic adventure out of his business crisis; later, after a short sleep, he awakes to introduce the climactic sequence into this closed studio of fish, a sequence which completes the logic of his threatened security system: filmed again through the distorting glass of the tank, Ferdinand slowly raises his finger to fire it like a gun and destroy the factory replica that he protects as his job. The factory smokestacks tumble in response to this dreamed power, and, as the camera pans across the room, the commentary remarks: "crisis, catastrophe, general strike, the enemy: from these Rieche's work derives meaning. . . . Most people believe in normal situations; Rieche believes just as strongly in emergency." What Ferdinand desires and demands here is obviously a scenario of general conflict, a fantastic montage of abstractions, which would stabilize the binary opposition on which his semantics of security depends and thus rescue the meaning of his job: as a director of security deprived of an overview, he sees the world through arbitrary signs and medium shots, and the significance of these signs depends very much on a binary structure whose stasis is the very opposite of dialectics. Ferdinand's filmic security, in short, uses a grammar much more like that of Griffith than that of Eisenstein.

The entire tripartite structure of *Strongman Ferdinand*—the close-up of the workers, the overview of the bureaucracy, and the medium-shot perspective of Ferdinand—becomes in a similar manner analogous to the various dimensions of the cinema that Kluge himself works so indefatigably to reshape. Before the titles, a police assignment involving Ferdinand arranges itself with lighting and a set-up much like that of a film production crew. The assignment is, however, bungled because the main actor, the saboteur, has rights that cannot be infringed upon. Exasperated, Ferdinand moves to private industry, where his directorial talents will not be hampered and where he can operate much as if in a studio system: in other words, Ferdinand joins a private production system whose workings closely resemble those of commercial cinema, where lives and realities are organized in the manner of his fantastic fishtank, according to patterns and types which reify and simplify and which distance the viewer from any actual experience. Serving a bureaucracy whose interests are primarily in production and consumption, this commercial cinema, like Ferdinand's perspective, blurs any connection between a spectator's lived reality and the image one watches, each film reinforcing the passivity that its predecessor has initiated, so that the language of film, like Ferdinand's, remains markedly apart from the world and receives its significance precisely from that difference. Exploiting the implications and logic of this way of seeing, just as Ferdinand radicalizes it, Kluge and his film seek, however, to transform this binary system of signification into a dialectic that would function on several levels, a dialectic through which real information can then pass.

As I have indicated, one of Ferdinand's main goals throughout the film is precisely to locate this kind of information and meaning, seeking it, however, only as support or defense for his a priori perceptions and not as a way of changing those perceptions. In the second sequence of the film, Ferdinand gathers leftist literature in a bookshop; when the clerk asks if he "reads the *Red Flag* regularly," he barks back, "I want information not debate." This debate and dialectic is of course exactly what Ferdinand needs, since without it all the information he collects tells him little. His final and most important effort to gather information, tracking Wilutzki to Belgium, accordingly turns up new facts and even confirms Ferdinand's suspicions that Wilutzki is selling the company. Yet the significance of the facts remains completely beyond Ferdinand's comprehension, since he interprets them in terms of his limited, abstract semantics. When he returns to Ganter with the information, Ganter listens unmoved and then tells him he simply doesn't understand the workings of multinational transactions. As always, though, Ferdinand stubbornly insists on deciding for himself "what I don't understand"; he continues the frantic pursuit of his vision (eventually kidnapping and imprisoning Wilutzki) until he is finally dismissed and replaced by Kniebeling, who thus completes the film's circular pattern of demolishing and rebuilding. To the end, Ferdinand insists on the self-contained value of his vision, his scenarios, and his fascistic security methods (ultimately even forcing Wilutzki to admit the *theoretical* validity of his insane actions). Yet, because his information remains almost purely theoretical and myopically located, he misses all practical meaning.

What acts as misinformation within Ferdinand's theoretical mise-en-scène becomes, however, the real information of Kluge's dialectical mise-en-scène in which the audience becomes the accomplice of both the narrative and the image. Within the framework of his image, first of all, Kluge regularly creates an internal montage of elements which works above all else to disjoin the spatial unity that Ferdinand struggles so persistently to maintain as internally consistent. This is clearly not standard Eisenstein montage, since even as an internal scheme it graphically resists all intellectual and abstract tendencies: rather it is what might be called an Althusserian montage of practical ideology:

> *Practical ideologies* are complex formations of montages of notions—representations— images on the one hand, and of montages of behaviours—conducts—attitudes—gestures on the other. The whole functions as the practical norms which govern the attitude and the taking-up of concrete positions by men with respect to the real objects and the real problems of the social and individual existence, and of their history.[26]

Thus, shots such as Ferdinand exercising in an opera box, his cathartic swim in the frozen quarry before his gathered troops, or his comic attempt to search American businessmen at the plant gate—all erupt on a visually concrete level that explicitly exposes the contradiction in Ferdinand's spatial fascism, that is, the contradiction in his effort to mold his practical life and physical environs with less than effective theoretical strategies. In each of these examples, the mise-en-scène establishes unusually rigid and geometrical formations such as the ornately staid box at the opera or the flat, white surface of the ice lined with Ferdinand's paramilitary troops; yet within these static frameworks Ferdinand becomes, in both examples, an absurdly comic eruption of an unwielding physical presence across the surfaces and against the boundaries around him when, in the first example, he begins doing jumping jacks on the far right side of the frame and, in the second, when he strips his flabby body and plunges into the hole in the ice. Indeed, on this point, Schlöndorff's *Coup de Grâce* and Kluge's *Strongman Ferdinand* present opposite faces of the same coin: in the conflict between vision and physical reality, Schlöndorff describes the tragically destructive ability of the former to force itself on the latter, while Kluge shows in nearly every shot the inescapable intrusion of the physical, despite Ferdinand's categorical efforts to suppress it in favor of his idiosyncratic schemes. If, as Godard claims, "tragedy is life in close-up, and comedy, life in long shot,"[27] *Strongman Ferdinand* is a medium-shot film in which the comedy develops out of a double confrontation: first, between Ferdinand's scenario and the physical resistance of close-up particulars and, second, between this internal dialectic and the metaphoric long shot which deflates its tension.

This double confrontation that the mise-en-scène focuses is in turn propelled through a narrative that similarly disjoins more than synthesizes and works to unstructure vision more than to structure it. It is, in fact, an inverted narrative in which the facts that motivate and explain the action are given in the first shots and the narrative moves toward an ever-growing confusion and mystery as to what these facts mean. The separate sequences hence stand out as isolated vignettes which appropriately delineate and highlight the dynamics of the mise-en-scène for attention; if the editing does establish connections, they are usually disjunctions, such as that of the harried dismissal of Ferdinand's predecessor being cut with a medium shot of Ferdinand kicking a can through the street with the commentary "Rieche hasn't an inkling." Additionally, there is the novelistic commentary, which adds very little information that isn't visually present or capable of being said by Rieche: it acts rather to dislocate the immediate illusory experience of the image onto two different yet co-existent sensory levels, just as the music of the soundtrack dislocates the image onto two different emotional levels ("Silent Night" playing as Ferdinand follows Wilutzki to Belgium or circus music when Ferdinand dons his commando mask). While the film visually locates the simultaneous operations of three different points of view, therefore, it similarly shatters the illusion of film's seamless, present-tense reality and redefines it for the spectator as a multidimensional phenomenon whose significance lies in the concrete contradictions it uncovers within the borders of theoretically closed time and space. "Experience is always a question of a specific situation," Kluge explains:

In this concrete situation, there is always future, past, and actual present: it's the same. In the mass medium like the cinema, or in art, it seems as if you have a choice. A great deal of art . . . attempts to counter the dominance of the present, to invent a second reality to serve as viceroy to the forgotten or demolished past. That's one choice. The other choice, which is made by television and by the press, is the actuality principle. It's also a choice made by the film camera, which can only photograph something that's present. And I think it's a false choice, because in a concrete situation, such as we actually live in, you can never make that separation. . . . The three parts which exist in our minds and in our experience are always present. . . . Grammar, for instance, is one of mankind's most interesting illusions. It's a sort of repression of an experience, like logic, or like rationalism. . . . In any concrete situation, these abstractions must be reduced to the concrete situation. And that's the province of film.[28]

The grammar which Kluge creates in his films is thus a deceptively complex one in which the whole production of meaning is juggled with the reality of concrete experience, the burden of the resulting confusion and the information it implies being settled firmly on the spectator. At work throughout the film, this process culminates in the bizarre final sequence in which Ferdinand aims his scoped rifle and shoots a state official. Somewhat obliquely, this action recalls two earlier sequences when Ferdinand fires at moving body-targets in a police shooting gallery and several earlier scenes when he uses a telescopic device to glean and reduce facts for his security system: in the final sequence as in the earlier ones, the body becomes the locus of meaning, the figure to be pinpointed and controlled, the reality to denote. Yet, in this final sequence, the demand for accuracy and a reality secure from confusion reaches its contradictory climax as it transforms a security officer into a terrorist, results in an image of reality with less apparent meaning than at any other point in the film, and thus becomes Kluge's most powerful statement about the black comedy of physical circumstances. Interviewed in the police van after the assassination attempt, Ferdinand explains his grotesquely illogical predicament in a coldly logical manner in which the search for meaning gradually gives way to tragic nonsense: "I'm fed up, us knowing so much about certain groups we see running around scot free, with no right to touch them. We're ready and able. That's what I wanted my shot to draw attention to. . . . I wanted to show that despite their precautions an assassin could get to the minister. If we were running things for the other side we could manage it. That proves there's a need for our services. That shot was my job application." When the reporter points out that Ferdinand's failure to miss the minister (which was his desire) suggests that he and his group are not so competent, Ferdinand grabs the mike and replies: "Tactics, say our enemy—and we're willing to learn from the enemy—is the extension of strategy into practice. If we replace 'strategy' with 'meaning' an uncertainty factor relating to everything we do must have an effect on individual actions. Nowadays, no business can operate without a certain degree of risk. . . . I shot him in the cheek because our lives have no precise meaning. So you can't always shoot with precise meaning." Ironically, only in pushing his semantics of security to its logical extreme here does Ferdinand seem to perceive the large rift between a strategy for meaning and the significance of real events, the way concrete circumstance restructures information.

These last statements by Ferdinand significantly appear, moreover, in the format of a radio interview, so that at the conclusion, as at the beginning of the film, the information network of public media enters Kluge's diegesis as a possibility shown to be clearly inadequate to the demands of a multidimensional reality. As with the newspaper headlines that surround Berthold's firing, this final interview with Ferdinand is capable only of presenting a social reality as if it were a simple actuality, giving that actuality a seeming objectivity independent of the viewer's subjectivity. Thoroughly abstract in its nature, this avenue of information mirrors in many ways Ferdinand's mise-en-scène of security according to which the dominant power relations are simply reproduced and perpetrated as self-evident truths and in which the ideology of the perspective functions primarily to disguise the machinery behind it (as it reduces social facts to fit its schemes). Unlike the dialectical information of Kluge's materialist aesthetic, these conventional modes cannot possibly delineate the complexities through which a security officer can, with radical consistency, become a terrorist assassin. For, in Kluge's words,

> In the system of the monopoly of the press, the mass media and the illusory public sphere, the actual social relations of power are reproduced. Thereby cause and consequence are reversed. Since this power has an effect upon the relations of power which have already been socially produced and internalized in individuals, an illusion arises as to who the perpetrator is, as to who is individually responsible for the crime. Therefore, it is not by chance that demented people and social outsiders appear as perpetrators of violent actions. Their acts are prepared by a social production process which disappears in the act of violence.[29]

The perpetrator of a violent crime, Ferdinand is also the quintessential metteur-en-scène who thus doubly reflects the system Kluge describes here: he is a director whose crime and security practices, like the television camera that describes them, falsify and mask social reality. The crucial dimension of social reality falsified and masked, moreover, is the producer itself, the power structure behind the image and the act, the overview which informs the violence of a limited perspective.

Opposed to these conventional structures of representation, *Strongman Ferdinand* (and particularly its last sequence) aims at a depiction of events which would unstructure the representation itself by exposing the fundamental inadequacies of its abstractions and by unveiling the production machinery behind those abstractions. The film attempts to dislocate the usual spectatorial relation with the screen specifically by introducing the unmalleable presence of physical circumstance into an imagistic framework that has traditionally resisted the theoretical inconsistency of those circumstances. And the result is that, just as the final television interview remains ludicrously incapable of grasping the twisted logic of Ferdinand's actions, physical circumstance and concrete particulars in this film invariably undermine the putative value of an ideologically closed mise-en-scène. Just prior to the opening titles, Ferdinand resigns from his public police work with the challenge "you can't shut me up if it's an official communication." This becomes a marvelously accurate beginning for a film in which an irrepressible security officer's outlandish defense of abstract methods and meanings becomes ironically and inevitably an exposition of the politics of perspective and a call for a dialectically concrete film language that, in every sense, takes account of the many dimensions of the image. In Kluge's words: the mass media, the press, the cinema, and language itself "already mirror false structures" that divide the senses from consciousness, while in fact "the senses are a substance of consciousness, . . . and you can't have consciousness without its substance.''[30] Actuating this notion, the narrative and imagistic disjunctions of *Strongman Ferdinand* become an aesthetic strategy to promote an individual and concrete comprehension based on substantive perceptions of a world made up of multiple fictions amidst a plethora of spatial and temporal circumstances. Kluge's is a semantics of substance whereby meaning is necessarily visceral and circumstantial, and like that of *Occasional Work*, the final message of *Strongman Ferdinand* (much like the final image) becomes a question of meaning itself: ''The film at this point is faced with a problem: that there is no genre for this way of looking at things; the attention of the person watching is not structured'' and consequently ''the film must run the risk of being misunderstood by some of those who see it—otherwise a genre where the people will learn how to orient themselves reliably amidst several antagonistic reality principles will never come about.''[31]

Kluge's attempt to reach this ideal cinema of spectators who actively and concretely participate in the attribution of meaning leads him, not surprisingly, to a more experimental and radically original kind of filmmaking than that of many of his contemporaries. Often his films and his aesthetic resemble those of filmmakers such as Hellmuth Costard or Schroeter who seem well beyond the pale of populist cinema. His desire ''to take a step forward and to make not personal films but collective films'' is very much a desire for a maximum rupture in the individualized, closed structure of the standard cinema: ''Collectiveness isn't a question of founding groups,'' remarks Kluge. ''It's also a question of your single capacities, which are developed in a different historical way.''[32] Always fighting to widen accessibility and to expand the variety of films to meet the needs of an infinite spectrum of viewers, Kluge has recently recognized the dangerous potential for the once radical Filmverlag itself to become a little Hollywood which monopolizes only a small corner of spectators with celebrity names such as Wenders, Herzog, and Fassbinder. And his relentless battle to alter the industry's recurring tendency to circumscribe and limit the cinema and its audiences is indeed a testimony to his utopian conception of film's power to actualize and guard the vitality of individual experience. The power structures of society may, with calculated ease, attempt to repress the concrete and the individual within the mise-en-scène of a particular ideology. But this kind of ''society has nothing to do with living,'' says Kluge, whereas the cinema he envisions ''has a lot to do with living, and with the observation of living experience.''[33]

"At home, at work" (*Redupers*). The Museum of Modern
Art/Film Stills Archive.

SEVEN

___

Sander's *The All Round Reduced Personality—Redupers*

A Depth of Differences

> If the personal is the political, then the traditional
> separation between private and public history must
> be rethought. This feminist rethinking has
> coincided with a general renegotiation of the
> separation of high art from the culture of everyday
> life—popular and mass culture—and the combined
> result has been a reconsideration of both the
> context of historical narrative and the politics of
> representation and self-representation.
> —Linda Hutcheon

> The question that poses itself is which country we
> could emigrate to. Only a rhetorical question of
> course.
> —Helke Sander, ''Men Are Responsible That
> Women Become Their Enemies: Tales of
> Rejection''

Frequently aligned with the aesthetics and politics of Alexander Kluge, the films of Helke Sander represent at the same time a critical revision of those positions. Despite his intentions to locate and activate a new cinematic spectator in the multiple experiences of his audiences, Kluge and his cinema often seem to fashion that dialogue as the construction of another utopian collectivity that recuperates as a more active singularity the very differences on which it is constructed. With their relentless presentation of the varieties of personal experiences, Sander's films, on the other hand, attempt to return that dialogue to the politics of the personal and active differences of the subjective viewer. As perhaps the most internationally acclaimed feminist film of the New German Cinema, *The All Round Reduced Personality* (or *Redupers* as it is usually abbreviated) thus gathers many of the themes that have haunted and motivated the women's movement in Germany through the sixties and seventies and re-presents them through the perspective of a female subject, refigured significantly as a concrete, particular, and mobile reflection of the filmmaker her-self. Contrasting the publicity posters for *Redupers* and Godard's *2 or 3 Things I Know about Her* (from a significantly different "New Wave"), Judith Mayne notes that what distinguishes the poster image of Sander is that the image "against which this image of Sander is projected has depth"—a depth produced in the film through "the disengagement of the female look from simplistic and deterministic definitions of the woman as object of male desire."[1] Within the often flattened space of postwar German film, it is this depth of individual experiences and differences that Sander so trenchantly engages.

Sander has for some time been actively involved in critically refashioning a so-cial and aesthetic space for the audience she would be addressing in her films. Dur-ing the sixties she founded the "Action Committee to Prepare the Liberation of Women" and in 1968 addressed the Socialist German Students (SDS) to loudly pro-test the subsuming of women's specific struggles for liberation under more general arguments about social liberation. As a filmmaker she continued to provoke this split within the resistance: "For me it was additionally hard because not only was I not taken seriously by the TV editors, I didn't have support from my leftist colleagues with whom I worked. Their support ceased in that instant when I became a feminist and started to hear them tell me my films would split the working class."[2] With Claudia Alemann, she organized in 1973 the first international seminar on women and film, and as one of the founding editors and frequent contributors to *Frauen und Film*—since the early seventies, one of the more influential feminist film journals in Germany and the United States—Sander helped initiate numerous debates about the conditions of production and reception in West Germany; the relation of a women's cinema to other interventions in the mainstream circuits; and the relation of personal experience, public politics, and narrative form. Indeed, the crucial difference be-tween her position and project and that of the other directors of the New German Cinema is that this clearing of an alternative space and address lose much of their binary idealism (as, for instance, in the formulation of an alternative cinema di-rected only against an established mainstream cinema). In her 1981 film *The Sub-jective Factor* she recalls and investigates much of this social and personal history appropriately across a fragmented narrative with different voice-overs, cryptic titles, staged performances, and disjointed memories. It aims to represent history as al-ways an incomplete dialogue that tries to contain multiple social discourses and points of view across a single personal and gendered history that is itself far from unified.

Her position within women's cinema in Germany was hardly unprepared.[3] Be-fore 1970 Ula Stöckl, May Spils, Dore O., and Erika Runge were all active film-makers, even if only two (Stöckl and Spils) had made feature films. Produced out of a countercultural atmosphere attending more and more to gender-specific issues such as abortion and women within a social workplace, these early feminist films are often concerned with a kind of political consciousness raising reflected primarily in subject matter that forefronts particular social and identity crises for women. In the 1970s and early 1980s the West German women's film movement attended increasingly, however, to a critique of the patriarchal structure of modernism and the avant-garde and applied those to the representational strategies of narrative feature films, in an attempt to engage mainstream cinema in a more productive fashion. Among the growing number of diverse films made by women during this period, the most acclaimed include Elfi Mikesch's *I Often Think of Hawaii*, Ulrike Ottinger's *Madame X* and *Ticket of No Return*, Margarethe von Trotta's *The Second Awakening of Christa Klages* and *Sisters, or the Balance of Happiness*, Jutta Brückner's *Hunger Years*, and Helma Sanders-Brahms's *Germany Pale Mother*. Through these and a large variety of other films, Anton Kaes has identified two central thematics that chronologically distinguish women's cinema in West Germany: (1) in the late 1970s the central motifs are "the search for female identity, the separation from the mother, the settling of accounts with the father, gender-specific historiography, and the perspective of memory; and (2) in the 1980s these issues would become revised as "a search for identity as a way back to one's own mother, the gesture of memory and the coming to terms with a national past that is reflected and inscribed in personal biography."[4] At the heart of and negotiating this shift in thematic and representational tactics is Sander's *Redupers*.

As Sander's work on and off the screen suggests, the relation of the New German Cinema and the women's movement has been a tense and often contradictory one, many of the contradictions embedded in a dialogue whose address has now had to differentiate itself more than ever more from both the ubiquity of Hollywood images and the largely masculine alternative of the New German Cinema. Clearly benefiting from the inroads in production and distribution (especially through television) that generated much of contemporary German film, *Frauenfilm* can be seen, as Thomas Elsaesser argues, as "in some sense the culmination of developments inherent in the New German Cinema from its beginning":

> It could combine the ideology of self-expression of the *Autorenfilm* with the social responsiveness of the spectator film; it followed the main tendency of the German documentary, in that its aim was to give a voice to those who "had been silent too long," and to lend itself to the demands of social minorities. Finally, its aesthetic strategies had to engage with identification, recognition and false consciousness, since they form such a crucial part of women's social existence.[5]

Within this larger historical and aesthetic context, the critical and distinctive turn becomes "how the women's film tackled the problem of distance and proximity, how it tried to encourage neither a voyeuristic nor a contemplative stance, but an attitude on the part of the spectator at once concerned and self-reflexive."[6] As it evolved through the seventies and eighties, however, this significant reformulation of what I have called a displaced dialogue would, most importantly, take the form of the re-inscription of spectatorial desire within the personal terms of physical and social limitations. In Sander's words: it would mean "being torn back and forth between the women's movement and its demands and its advances on the one hand, and the conditions of artistic work on the other."[7]

In *Redupers*, a tradition of anonymous viewing—often associated with the spectator of classical Hollywood cinema but also with most patriarchal ways of seeing—is immediately signaled and located as a geography. The film opens with a long track through the streets of Berlin, dislocated from any individual point of view as it displays grimly urban sidewalks and buildings from the window of a moving car. Graffiti, Esso trucks, and commercial signs mark the streets as the camera turns corners and continues its unbroken track; the American commentator of "the wires of AP and UPI" counterpoints those images as "a free voice in a free world," where "more and more people are talking about the good sounds of AFN [American Armed Forces Network] Berlin." In the following sequence, the female protagonist Edda Chiemnyjewski receives a letter from a postman in front of her home. On the letter is an English message for the German post office, which Edda translates for the postman: "Berlin has a special status. It's not in East Germany and it's not in West Germany. I hope you'll find it and be able to deliver the letter. Meanwhile I suggest the following: ask President Carter to find out where Berlin belongs." When Edda responds wryly that "Maybe we don't even exist," the postman announces the central theme of the film, a theme that applies equally to Berlin and to Edda's efforts to establish her position in that city: "Maybe we are just being created."

The long surface of that opening track through public streets bound to and contrasted by the fragmented snatches of radio broadcast thus becomes a dense and dramatic prologue announcing the primary motifs of the film: it is a film about a public space divided against itself, like the city of Berlin divided by a wall; it is about a visual perspective constantly in a dialectical relationship with an audio intervention or commentary, an image whose seemingly anonymous and touristic public point of view becomes the fabric into which an alienated and isolated protagonist must struggle actively to insert herself. Across all these layerings, the film might be seen, quite simply and like many contemporary German films, as a search for identity and a home within the postwar crisis of a destitute but defined social space. Yet, as Sander remarks in her 1977 essay "Feminism and Film," for women the shifting contrasts, resistances, and clutter within this place and space make the project of fashioning an identity the far more problematic one of leading "women into the blank regions of unexplored subjectivity."[8]

The story of *Redupers* is a partly autobiographical, partly fictionalized tale in which, significantly, Sander herself plays the lead character Edda. She is a photographer who aims, at once, for self-expression and financial, social survival (a structure and thematics that anticipate *The Subjective Factor* and the 1984 *Love Is the Beginning of All Terrors*, the three being commonly grouped as a trilogy). As a sharp break with the style and thematics of the first two sequences, the third sequence of the film presents Edda and her daughter in a medium close-up in the hallway of their home. While the daughter clings and pleads with her mother not to go, Edda fights to free herself, explaining that "I have to go take pictures. . . . Today I have to work. . . . Don't make it so difficult for me!" Set before a hallway mirror that crowds and flattens the figures, the scene dramatizes the divided person and personality of Edda in all its clumsy, embarrassing starts and stops, in all its undramatic triviality; it suggests a traditionally "natural" bond (between mother and daughter but notably without a father-figure) that now cannot "afford" (in senses from the psychological to the economic) the previously transparent logic of that bond.

The next cut counterpoints that strained domestic moment with a long shot of Edda's Volkswagen driving through the fog and then shows her and three women colleagues in a medium long shot against a grim and cold exterior cityscape. Standing next to their cameras, they peer across the East-West border at a train trestle as Edda's voice-over remarks: "That was the third diesel engine that passed. We're waiting for the last steam engine from Berlin via Hamburg. Assignment one photo: 32DM. . . . A teleshot across the border. . . . Edda Chiemnyjewski, photo journalist, waiting for an event worthy of publication." If the traditional domestic place and bond no longer offer Edda an easy definition, here her public position is equally stranded across the space of personal expectations and their enactment within a meaningful public event.

Through these three dramatically varied opening sequences, *Redupers* presents a central character torn and redefined across the contending geographies she must inhabit in order to characterize herself at all. She becomes, in fact, a multiple, often fragmented, subject whose private and public demands rarely fit with each other and who must work indefatigably to somehow literally figure herself against the flat public, anonymous background that the first track of Berlin depicts. As the narrative develops, she drifts from one small photographic assignment to another ("Curatorium Indivisible Germany, Annual Meeting, 45 DM"; "Senior Citizens Party, 3 Photos"); at one point she decides to risk choosing her own direction and to photograph an antirape demonstration and "hope a newspaper will buy them" since "she thinks that not enough of her socially significant photos are bought." Moving in and out of the darkroom in her home, she alternately prepares photos and blows bubbles or tosses balls with her daughter.

This tension between the spheres of living and working or between expression and a communal forum in which to have an expression motivates Edda throughout the film. Most often these conflicts are depicted in the business setting in which she finds her eye for the "personal situation" conflicting with her professional obligation. At a "Senior Citizen's Party" she has real problems "limiting herself to the saleable shots for the press. Being business-like is difficult. She wastes too much time trying to capture situations." While the male "master of ceremonies" announces from the stage that "we are gathered today to demonstrate that no one has been forgotten, that we are one big happy family," Edda sits on the fringes of that public discourse, talking with some of the old women about the dresses they made for the party. Her home life, moreover, is equally infiltrated with conflicts that are both physical and abstract. Doing her budget, "she has no time for quiet reflection," yet she momentarily allows herself to dream of learning physics. In bed with her very unfatherly boyfriend Werner, she "wonders what it will mean to her daughter if she no longer sees him"; while she is telling him about her photos of Berlin and musing out loud whether "the photos will show us limitations that are more concrete than the wall," he falls asleep. The medium frontal shot of the couple in bed becomes a searingly ironic image of the conceptual limitations that cross from public life into domestic space and communication.

As the drifting focus for her story, Edda becomes increasingly involved with the Women's Photography Collective as the logical avenue through which to try to harmonize her personal vision and the demands of a public life. The project evolves around a Women's Photography Collective's use of funds from the City Council to assemble an exhibition of photographs about West Berlin. The voice-over of Edda explains "the History of the Project":

> 1) the City decides to fund a public relations project and present the citizens with the advantages of their urban environment. 2) The City decides not to hire a commercial firm and launches a photography contest to aid starving artists: "Photographers See Our City." 3) A women's group inside the governing parties decides to support a women's photography project in order to draw the decision maker's attention to their own existence. 4) The respective men give way to the party women's pressure. They thus achieve several aims: a) proof that they favor women's emancipation; b) the crucial point is that other groups had applied for more money than the women.

The logic and terms of this "history" encapsulate many of the political dilemmas that surround Edda as a woman artist. Above all and throughout the film, her artistic endeavors are inextricably bound to financial constraints controlled by larger social, profoundly patriarchal mechanisms. Second, in their precisely enumerated presentation (which echoes the calmly objective enunciation of the voice-over throughout the film), they map and ironize cultural proceedings whose seeming progressions and achievements contain a variety of material contradictions and compromises that inform the work of a woman in a public sphere. Third, this history and its terms are almost indistinguishable from the representation of Edda's home life, where there is also an overdetermined effort to calculate and organize the ironic shifts and compromises at its heart. The photographic project, as well as Edda's involvement in it, becomes then an ironic history of representing the particularities of her personal life as a public history: a venture into what Gertrud Koch calls "the aestheticization of women's everyday existence."[9]

In these movements through her domestic and professional life, there is a clear development—although with an aleatory, often circular movement: (1) from the crisis of an individual trying to survive within the terms of an unsympathetic social environment, (2) to the assertion of her individual perspective against that environment, (3) to the organization of those needs and demands as a shared political project. What becomes most important and distinctive about this development, however, is that it is explicitly *not* a movement outward from the confines and pressures of a personal life to the larger spaces and broader meanings of a professional world, but instead a discovery of, especially for her as a woman, the coincidences and conjunctions between the two. The "event worthy of publication" that Edda seeks in those dreary open city spaces is, as she gradually realizes, her own activity in negotiating her different emotional, intellectual, and physical realms.

Both the images Edda relentlessly seeks and the life she wishes to live thus work to redefine or recreate that distance between her self and the world that they are inseparable from. Driving in her car as images of the city track by, her voice-over reflects that "for years Edda had been impressed by the following: that the aesthetic

imagination was the passion for things alien. . . . Passion for that without meaning.
One should at least be able to choose freely those things alien." While one might
portray the aesthetic imagination of the last two centuries in precisely these terms of
subjectivity driven to transcend itself through some identification with an alien
"Other," Edda's casual proposition suggests a different trajectory: one defined by a
passion for the "everyday," where, with its clear origin in a female perspective and
the rhythms of quotidian work and pleasure, practical invention rather than a transcendent imagination socially represents itself as always part of the complexities
and subtleties of that daily life. Midway through the film, she attends an aikido class
in a gymnasium and follows with the rest of the neatly organized class through the
fluid movements and then becomes part of a still tableau: "All sorts of Asian influ-
ences," the voice-over remarks of the cultural dislocations that permeate Berlin,
"make their way to Berlin via the USA, and help the helpless find themselves."
That night she abandons these exotic movements, and shortly after this sequence she
performs spontaneous exercises in her home. As one of many examples in the film,
here Edda reroutes her desires and how she expresses her body and her self through
a domestic place and movements that are her own inventions. That a bouncy song on
an East Berlin radio program meanwhile urges listeners to "send the Yankees to
their doom, and all Berlin will be happy again" becomes the kind of wry irony that
continually punctuates and recontextualizes moments of true harmony in the film:
unlike the grand narrative of the socialist vision, for Edda moments of integration of
self and environment and of triumph over cultural displacement are invariably short-
lived.

The title becomes consequently a wry parody of a phrase commonly used by
officials in the German Democratic Republic to describe its socialist goals for its
citizens: "the all-round developed personality." Whereas that utopian vision of the
socialist state draws the imagination to an image of a wholly integrated individual,
it is just that totalizing image (usually patriarchal) that reduces the details that give
meaning to the work of the individual subject (usually women and other minorities).
Of the multiple sectors that impinge upon Edda's own efforts, consequently, her socialist or socially conscious colleagues often become part of the problem. When ac-
quaintances approach her about volunteering her time and work for an ecology
project about Berlin, she "finds it difficult to turn them away," yet "can't afford to
work for free." Even within the Women's Photography Collective individual neces-
sities and actions provoke ironic abrasions and obstacles: at one point, one of the
women within the Collective complains about her colleagues, "it's annoying one of
you always bringing your child."

What becomes most compellingly clear is that here, as with Kluge, the distinction between a public and a private life is an illusory one. But, whereas the terms of
Kluge's dialectic usually remain inscribed within a model that glosses over differ-
entiations and particularities, in *Redupers* subjectivity and its intervention in public
life are always complicated by the specific material complications and contradictions that define them—most importantly in this case, the particular history of this
German woman within postwar German history.[10] In this sense, Edda's explora-

tions of Berlin are inseparable from Sander's autobiographical intrusions within the narrative: it is the singularity of Sander's actual lived experiences that disrupts the traditional aesthetic "balance" of the image and the logical flow of the narrative by adding a certain depth to a cityscape that the third-person objectivity of filmic narrative tends to reduce to surface. If Walter Benjamin's model of the wandering flaneur still has suggestive power as a prototype of cinematic perception, in this case that "flaneuse" disavows much of the power of that position, drawing attention to her own personal directions and inclinations to drift off the boulevards onto the back streets.

That Edda and Sander are a photographer and a filmmaker is, needless to say, as critical to the drama as their feminist politics, since representing themselves and their city through their images conjoins in the activity of presenting photographs and films publicly. Both photography and film are traditionally considered popular arts, and establishing them within the hierarchy of public representation, breaking down the borders that marginalize them as cultural representations, becomes a parallel, though not synonymous, activity with the engendering of an image of a woman within a public sphere.

Likewise the space of Berlin becomes both a metaphor for Edda and Sander's drama and the representational terms of its success. As a rich contrast to the driven and (vaguely) directed quest of Wenders's characters (in *Kings of the Road*) along the rural East-West border of a divided Germany, Sander's city of Berlin is crowded with contending images and people and offers multiple directions to a driver through its many streets. Berlin becomes (too obviously perhaps) the counterpart to an arena for the crisis of a female personality and its struggle to insert a subjectivity into a resistant public space: the emphatically public patriarchy of the socialist East is set against the individualism of the capitalist West; across that border (where garbage and radio waves cross regularly), Edda and Sander struggle to make connections, note similarities, and ultimately to visually fracture the wall so that differences might interact. But Berlin is more than this, too: it is the actual daily space and concrete mise-en-scène that must be remade within a photographic and filmic framework whose particular insistence on realism make it the crucial place for contesting whose reality inhabits that space.

In *Redupers* there are three main representational efforts directed at a divided Berlin. The first is Edda's photo montage comparing East Berlin and West Berlin, through which she attempts to show, with images from both sides, how the East and the West are alike and "where the wall has openings." As she shows her photos to the other women in the project, her voice-over ironically envisions the ecstatic merger of differences that these photos can suggest yet demonstrate only as fragmented discrete images: "Edda's secret joy is to watch TV and imagine only five minutes away the all round developed personality watching West TV."

The second—and most celebrated—is a very large blown-up photo of a section of the Berlin wall, its high-angled perspective showing an empty lot on the East side and a single car parked next to the Western side of the wall. "Three of the women mount the photo so it can be carried through the streets," and, in keeping with a size that signals its public significance, they move the photo from location to location,

"Mapping differences: the wall and the image"
(*Redupers*). The Museum of Modern Art/Film Stills
Archive.

measuring its meaning and impact in terms of three different public contexts. Their
different attempts, however, find the photo juxtaposed against advertisements (one
urging "Get Rid of All That Dirt!" and a second for Shell Oil), and these unavoid-
able contexts precipitate the "First Shock," that intervention in the public sphere
always risks reduction to two-dimensional flatness: "Will their photo be noticed
among all the advertisements?" she asks.

At another extraordinary point, however, the women carry the photo into a cinematic frame that replicates the very scene and angle of the photo, setting the image
against the same wall that divides the center of the photographic space. The result is
much more than a postmodern play with mise-en-abyme; it becomes rather a temporary but trenchant measure of imagistic difference as depth. Here the empty ge-
ometry of this street scene—which had developed a certain dynamics across the tension of the wall dividing those spaces—receives a critical turn through its doubling
in the hands of the three women. What is added in the difference between the two
representations of scene is the self-consciousness of the image as always dramatiz-
ing a distance from a "real" scene or another image of it and the presence of a
specific time and point of view (these three women again in this place) as the determination of the "depth" which that particular temporal and spatial position creates in distinguishing itself.

The third project occurs shortly after this sequence and dramatizes the performance of a perspective across the Berlin wall as the Women's Collective constructs a "domestic frame" on an observation platform from which spectators can look across at East Berlin. The scene is introduced by another of the many horizontal tracks in the film, moving from right to left, from fields to city buildings and graffitied walls to the observation platform. A line of people mount the step to the top of the platform, where the women have erected a curtain that is then pulled open to reveal the other Berlin across the wall. "The stage is set for the world," the voice-over exclaims. The next shot, however, is a long shot of a fog-enshrouded sun, the backdrop for an Associated Press radio report: "The AP reports that UN Secretary-General Waldheim in New York and 14 nations formulated a message for intelligent beings that might be encountered by Voyager I on its trip through the solar system: 'I greet you on behalf of people from our planet; we want to teach you and learn if we are fortunate.' " The sequence then cuts back to a medium shot of the women standing on the platform: "Somehow we are all disappointed," Edda's voice-over observes. "The curtain is not impressive enough. Is not the glance into the workers' fatherland enhanced by the curtain? Is this also the motherland for the hopes of women?" The comic contrasting of the search for alien life on other planets and the search for a common life within the particular space of Berlin is, of course, more than just a debunking of a perspective more directed at outer space than at human space. The structures of these two images contrast, more importantly, the blur of an anonymous gaze and a "glance" from a self-consciously domestic frame (associated with "woman's work") that might change the field of vision from ideological abstractions to daily particulars.

That especially these last two interventions into the real space of Berlin are more "invented performances" than they are traditional photographic representations, and that the three progressively move toward defining themselves in terms of the "alternative public" that does (or does not) receive them, indicate both the crucial temporal and the crucial collective dimensions of these images. Invention complements performance in this sense: both are fundamentally arrangements or rearrangements of objects or situations to allow not the appearance of something new but a different (frequently pragmatic) use of the already there. What enriches and complicates each of these projects is their momentary possibilities of success or failure and their changing positions within a variety of social settings or across the multiple points of view of their collective inventors and different viewers. They move through time, changing the position of their point of view according to their emplacement in a specific context or before a specific audience. That movement delineates a variety of perceptual positions within the space they frame as the performance and invention of *depth as a pragmatics of space.*

In a similar sense, what Sander's filmic performance adds to Edda's fragmented and regularly frustrated photographic work is a narrative/temporal voice that, in both a literal and metaphoric way, mobilizes a perspective on and within those images by connecting them to larger narratives and by exploring the social and personal motivations that inhabit them. Rather than the deconstruction and subversion of narrative found in *The Bitter Tears of Petra von Kant* or *The Left-Handed Woman,* the history that *Redupers* documents is best characterized as paratactic and aleatory, absolutely committed to narrative potential, but only as it can be reinvented to reclaim a space for the woman subject. As the primary organization of the narrative structure of the film itself, the conversational address of the voice-over is at once personal and collective, constructed from quotations, well-known political and literary sources, and off-hand personal reflections. It becomes a shifting combination of both Edda's and Sander's voices, dispersed like the fragments of the radio broadcasts and fluctuating between an identification/enunciation as "I," "we," and "they."

Expanding on Christa Wolf's description of the tension in women's representations between "diary writing" and imagistic "miniatures" as forms of perception,[11] Judith Mayne rightly characterizes this narration of Edda's story as the effort to interject a first-person perspective into the third-person address that has characterized especially classical Hollywood cinema: "Voice-over narration is quite common in the cinema, and is in particular associated with the documentary film. But the female voice in *Redupers* is no authoritative commentator. . . . Rather, the voice emphasizes the plurality of truths, the proliferation of perspectives that are possible. The female voice in *Redupers* exists as an ungrounded presence, emanating from a number of sources, none of them privileged as the center of the film."[12] This transparent remaking of Edda's story through the experiences and reflections of Sander's life then refigures the traditional opposition between narrative fiction and documentary forms as a blend of autobiographical story-telling or a diary of the everyday. The documented space of Berlin quickly fragments and reassembles around the imagistic interventions and personal inventions of Edda/Sander as the presence that narrates and so temporalizes that space.

The inevitable action to move this narration to more secure and stable frameworks within which personal expression and exploration can more easily survive becomes part of the ironic conclusion of *Redupers*. Beginning this series of false endings to the film, Edda dries her hair while talking with a friend on the phone and explaining that their billboard photographs are not so "political" as other projects but rather are attempts to "document Berlin." In the next shot she arranges to leave her daughter with someone while she attends a gallery opening where she and her colleagues plan to "make contacts" that will assist their work. The "politics" of these efforts is casually underlined as Edda takes care of the details of her makeup and jewelry, and these details of personalized social tactics then smoothly dovetail with their networking across the conversations of the opening's cocktail party where various individuals counsel them "to first exhibit in a smaller gallery" or to "use more cunning in your tactics." When Edda corners an established male artist, his advice becomes almost a parody of the formula that led to the success of the more renowned members of the New German Cinema as a way of securing personal vision in a commercial market: "the tactic vis-a-vis the government is always the same: we find support from abroad . . . ," he explains; he then quickly begins to patronize her through his position ("I'm in touch with a photo gallery in New York City"); and that in turn becomes the prelude for a sexual advance. On the street she rebuffs his advances and vomits in the gutter. (Inventing herself within this artistic network begins with an exercise in repulsion—an all-too-graphic emptying of self in the streets.) The subsequent aerial shot of a map of Berlin then transforms a splotch of the city into a flattened and networked grid of that city, a visual analogue perhaps for the potential reductive power of the traditional public sphere itself. While an air raid siren signals the climactic crisis that pervades this drama of place and subjectivity, the geometrical flattening, fragmenting, and division of the city space recalls that catastrophic event in modern Germany and the inseparable link between the struggles to narrate the histories of personal lives and the divided public boundaries inherited from that war.

In the final sequence, Edda's daughter approaches to meet her from the depth of a street that recedes into the back of the image. The two join and then separate, with Edda walking into the distance, from the front to the back of the image, emphatically marking a new depth within this street scene. The voice-over's final quotation is from Wolf's "The Diary: an Aid to Work and Memory":

> I don't want to go any further. Anyone who asks about a person's diary must accept the fact more is concealed than said. It was not possible to speak about plans, clearly set forth in the diary, that have arisen, been changed, dropped again, come to nothing, or were carried out, unexpectedly suddenly there, complete. And it wasn't possible to bring into focus through strenuous thought the stuff of life that was very near in time. Or the mistakes made in trying to do this. And, of course, no mention of the names that appear once or more often in the diary.

Just as the depth of this image describes the distance from the flat tracking shots that begin *Redupers*, so too the single voice of Edda's narration contrasts the fragmented public voices of the radio that open the film. If this deepening of space and personalizing of narration is the product of an always detailed, sometimes reluctant, and often annoying mapping of gender differences and differences within the female gender across a quotidian space, it becomes, as importantly, the difficult and strenuous *invention* of that space as a different kind of communal bond (represented here in terms of the mother and daughter). This is a forecast of the Berlin that needed inventing for the American postal system. Earlier Edda reflects on the painful stress of daily life: "Before falling asleep, I think that life is made of days like this." The immediate solution has nothing epiphanic about it but instead evolves from the daily work of arranging space according to one's own history in which (from Wolf again) "only constant effort gives meaning to the units of time in which we live."

Within this concluding space, after all, this mother and this daughter meet not in the painful moment of separation within the tight, angular interior that describes the second sequence in the film but as figures who can momentarily meet and release each other on the street, within the gendered depth of their generational variety. This indeed locates a particular and different public within the larger context of Berlin, and it is why *Redupers*, as a central political document in women's filmmaking in contemporary German cinema, is a feminist intervention that is so much more than a feminist inflection of the New German Cinema.

Elsaesser has noted that the distinctive and critical role of Sander doubling as the protagonist-photographer Edda mobilizes an "approach focusing on spectator-positionings and narrational strategies" that "encompass both sets of determining instances, author-oriented as well as audience oriented."[13] In the case of *Redupers*, an ironic, if not parodic, perspective circles the character of Edda and her desires, which, at the very least, complicates this path of identification from auteur/protagonist to the identifying subject/spectator and which recasts, unlike Kluge's, the primary voice of that dialogue as located within the particular activity of a female viewer to see herself through and against the film. Across these ironies of identification, an audience member is asked not so much to imagine herself—against the background of the film, as a single Other position—but to invent herself, like Sander's invention of herself in the figure of Edda, as a variety of particular narrative positions in which subjectivity develops itself in the space of intersubjectivity. This is a space (like a cinema) where interior lives actually come out.

Of the many examples of these tactics, the most stunning and summary in *Redupers* is, near the conclusion, the image-collage made from three different films by women overlayed on a newspaper that fills the frame. Just after Edda assembles photographic negatives for her project on Berlin, there is a full-frame close-up of a newspaper page. Overlayered on that background are sequences from the three films that, like Edda's work, concern the intersection of a woman's public and private life: a close-up of a woman from Ursula Reuter-Christiansen's *The Executioner*, a beach scene of a family from Yvonne Rainer's *Film about a Woman Who . . .* , and surreal shots of a woman cutting up fish and opening a refrigerator to find a baby from Valie Export's *Invisible Adversaries*. Edda's voice-over introduces the image: "Obsessed by daily life as other women see it," and then reads a letter from "Aunt Kate":

Dear Edda, Please don't stop showing women and the problems they have with their tyrant men. Tyrants are even worse in old age! They drive everyone mad. Your father sent Hatschi a good book written by a doctor from Berlin. We are both reading it. And Karlemann sent us one of his poems. He wrote it during the war in Russia. He was thinking of your mother Erika. The sun is shining into my room, but it rains alot. Makes me sad somehow. You can always call us, at night also. Please write soon—or phone. Yours, Aunt Katherine.

In addition to the Sander/Edda introductory voice, three different discourses intersect here as three different spatial arrangements that individually suggest other positions and spaces within them and outside them: the writing of the public newspaper suggests both a public forum and the subjective inflection of Wolf's "writing"; the miniature images are third-person discourses and interventions into "daily life"; and the personal letter from Aunt Katherine mixes complaints about the history of patriarchal abuse and private anecdotes.

To "read" these voices, newspapers, images, and letters as an act of positioning oneself is to necessarily reflect on them as different ratios of gendered and nongendered space but also as materially different discourses that offer and define subjectivity in the substantially altered terms of an intersubjectivity. In Kaja Silverman's words (about *The Subjective Factor*), a response requires a "productive synthesis" that "refuses to adopt a classically oppositional relation to other discourses, knowing full well the complicity and homage such a relation implies. Instead, it raids the existing discursive field, carrying away what it can use and abandoning the rest."[14] Here spectatorial identification must become a somewhat difficult mobility not only through the spatial and material particulars of each of these contending spaces but through a refiguring of itself in the material terms of the particular discourse that is mobilizing it. What prevents these interventions of personal perspectives from becoming a free-floating narcissism or terrorism across public space is, moreover, that the materiality of the discourses demands that one respond to them, that one's sense of them be made across (not necessarily "in") their terms: Aunt Katherine needs to be called or written back, and the missing quadrangle of films overlaying the paper invites a fourth film.

I would characterize the kind of identification that this particular sequence and *Redupers* as a whole elicits as "off-balanced invention," much like the frequent, and frequently humorous or awkward, attempts by Edda to fit her work and her body into the myriad of predicaments and situations that do not exactly fit or that fit with some discomfort (office spaces, cocktail parties). Sander has claimed, tongue-in-cheek perhaps, that the film is "a rather comic contribution to the question of why women so seldom make much of their lives,"[15] and this "comic" tone strikes me as central to the address of the film. In a very important way, the triumphant peculiarity of this film is that, like the doubled voice/body of Sander/Edda, its different identifications emphasize the physical nature of that process as inevitably clumsy, temporary, and comic in the most liberating sense: measuring and testing space against one's own "interiors" and body, the identifying figures at once invent shared geographies and a knowledge of the material limitations of that action; the comedy of those different positions available as gendered subjects generate different positions in that public space.

In terms of the actual reception of this film, what is thus produced is a synthesized image of self not as an object-image but as a self-producing activity where tangential and everyday materials (which *Redupers* is constantly forefronting) refer to a space and where one's disrupted temporal movement through that space becomes the terms of productive *identification as intervention and invention*. To watch this film is to arrange one's self, with some irony and humor I think, as a constant daily movement outward (from the cinema), where the personal life will inevitably align with the expanding common ground and the public spaces of other moving (here firstly female) arrangements. In this sense, Sander's cinema is again a doubled address, a clearing of a space where "We are not only building a house, but simultaneously gathering and assembling the materials for it ourselves."[16] "The work space and the space of creation," says Trinh Minh-Ha, "is where she confronts and leaves off at the same time a world of named nooks and corners, of street signs and traffic regulations, of beaten paths and multiple masks, of constant intermeshing with other bodies'—that are also her own—needs, assumptions, prejudices, and limits."[17] For Sander and her audience, in short, an active intervention in public images must be the continual invention of public spaces with different personal depths.

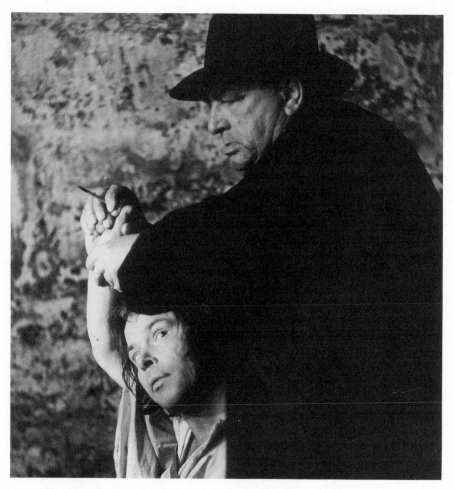

"To write a beginning: Kaspar born in the shadow of
death" (*Kaspar Hauser*).

The Original Tradition

Hypnotic Space in Herzog's
The Mystery of Kaspar Hauser

> Actually the grotesque . . . discloses the
> potentiality of an entirely different world, of
> another order, another way of life. It leads men
> out of the confines of the apparent (false) unity of
> the indisputable and stable. . . . The romantic
> grotesque does this too, but in its own subjective
> form. The existing world suddenly becomes alien
> . . . precisely because there is the potentiality of a
> friendly world, and of the golden age, of carnival
> truth. Man returns unto himself.
> *Bakhtin*, Rabelais and His World

> And lovely apparitions,—dim at first,
> Then radiant, as the mind, arising bright
> From the embrace of beauty (whence the forms
> Of which these are the phantoms) casts on them
> The gathered rays which are reality—
> Shall visit us, the progeny immortal
> Of Painting, Sculpture, and rapt Poesy,
> And arts, though unimagined, yet to be.
> *Shelley*, Prometheus Unbound

At a 1979 panel discussion, Werner Herzog proclaimed with characteristic enthusiasm and exaggeration that "there is one filmmaker here in the United States who is
very important for me—who is like the Shakespeare of filmmaking—and that is
Griffith. So, if you ask me to say who is the *most* important filmmaker here in this
country, I would say, 'It's Griffith . . . and Griffith . . . and Griffith again!' "'[1] Despite Herzog's status as one of the more radical contemporary German filmmakers,
this excess adulation of cinema's grand patriarch is not as incongruous as it might
appear to some. For, while Herzog is certainly a revolutionary experimenter with the
forms of commercial cinema, it is no less true that his films work from a very
strong, if peculiar, sense of history and tradition. Indeed, what most distinguishes
his association with this tradition is that the causality on which it generally relies is
the very idea Herzog resists most. For Herzog, the danger in a history or tradition is

precisely that it binds one to the inevitability of its logic, and his first feature-length film, *Signs of Life*, accordingly becomes a kind of historical symbol for the original state that his later films continually aspire to: "I always have the very strong feeling that this particular film," he says, "is my *only* really innocent film. It was made somehow as if there was no film history."[2] The tradition and context out of which Herzog works, in other words, is one of pristine originality, where the source or wellspring of the tradition is the only acceptable influence on creation. Whether the filmmaker is Griffith or Murnau, these images arrived first, bearing the mark of an unblemished eye; this mark is doubtless what Herzog seeks to retrieve through his own pseudo-mystical transformations of narrative form.

First and foremost, of course, Herzog's films attack and counter the rigid tradition that has intervened between a visionary like Griffith and himself. This tradition, according to Herzog, is responsible for the facilely realistic syntax and images which have abraded and blinded spectators for years. Earlier at the same film conference, he rails against the stale preconceptions that have resulted from this historical training and that have consequently made it impossible for audiences to share Herzog's vision of things: "they are always coming toward my work," he contends, "with plans for certain sorts of 'prefabricated houses' already in their minds, and for some reason they expect that my work should follow exactly the pattern of those prefabricated mobile homes which they happen to have sticking somewhere in their brains."[3]

The reference here is obviously to Herzog's study of American culture in *Stroszek*, where mobile homes function as a metaphor for that artificial and mechanical rapport with the environment often associated with American society. On one level, in fact, *Stroszek* becomes a parable for the American culture's brutalization of the fresh and ridiculously innocent vision which Bruno S. and his comrades bring with them from Germany. These contemporary voyagers expect to find the pure frontiers of an ancient America. But they discover a reality impoverished by industrialized farmers who defend their borders with tractors and shotguns, mobile homes which are given and repossessed with the speed of a salesman's pitch and an auctioneer's sell (the ultimate poetry of late capitalism according to Herzog), and landscapes that are experienced mostly through the disenfranchised distance of a television screen. *Stroszek* is not, however, simply a blanket indictment of American culture; it becomes an indictment, rather, of the dull and destructive commercialization of the culture's original energy.

For Herzog, Bruno's encounter with America in *Stroszek* becomes an analogue for his own encounter with the Hollywood film industry. "In Western Europe," he explains, "there is such a strong domination of American culture and American films. And all of us who are working in filmmaking have to deal with this sort of domination. For me, it was particularly important to define my position about this country and its culture, and that's one of the major reasons I made *Stroszek*."[4] The distinctive energy of D. W. Griffith and other filmic explorers resembles, for Herzog, that of the American Indian who at the conclusion of *Stroszek* has been reduced to a carnival display amidst a sideshow of animals transformed into mechanical entertainment. In both the film industry and this cheap sideshow, the energy of the objects and the beauty of the landscapes have been subjected to that circular and senseless figure of mechanical rotation which Wenders and others see as so debilitating and so much a part of contemporary filmmaking, and the end of *Stroszek* indexes the monotony of this murderous cinematic formula, as a burning truck spins in circles and Bruno, just prior to his apparent suicide, mounts a mechanical chair lift that rotates up and down a majestic mountain.

In contrast to this pointlessly redundant relation with the world that Hollywood often epitomizes, Herzog offers an experiential immediacy through his films, a visionary encounter with the real rather than a regurgitation of flattened tropes. Writing about *Aguirre, The Wrath of God*, Herzog differentiates this kind of spectacle from Hollywood's and, with typical self-heroics, describes it as a financial as well as aesthetic victory over the giant American studios. The film's attraction and "the advantage it has over Hollywood," he argues, "is that it is real. The spectacle is real. It is the real life of the jungle, not the botanic gardens of the studio. . . . It is easy enough to make a film in your own living room; but imagine trying to make one with 500 people in the Amazon tributaries. We had a budget of a little over $300,000; but to look at *Aguirre* is a 3 million dollar film."[5] Needless to say, the realism that Herzog extols here has little to do with documentary realism or more contemporary movements such as *cinema verité*. On the one hand, it refers to Herzog's somewhat legendary need to confront and embrace the dangers and destructive energies that define the natural world for him, so that the reality of the film and on the film becomes an unswerving look at death on several levels. Isolating a film crew in the jungles of South America, attempting to film the eruption of the volcano La Soufrière, supposedly walking from Germany to Paris to show Lotte Eisner a film, working regularly with the mythically hostile Klaus Kinski, or insisting on actually dragging a ship over a mountain in *Fitzcarraldo* become for Herzog extra-filmic means of establishing the authenticity of his filmic reality. On the other hand, this Herzogian realism demands that the texture and matter of the film products themselves bear the same signs of life, namely, the signs of an eruption or violence that should visually tear the placid surface that classical cinema usually represents as life itself.

This is where the naturalism that Herzog praises begins to take on the colors of a supernaturalism. For what Herzog does through his films is imaginatively search out energies and irrationalities that at once challenge and dwarf humanity's social conception of itself as a universal center. Indeed, his insistence that these irrationalities are in fact hard, material realities is attested by his frequent return to seemingly documentary subjects that stand alongside and support the radical perception of his fictional narratives. *The Flying Doctors of East Africa*, *Fata Morgana*, *Land of Silence and Darkness*, *The Great Ecstasy of the Sculptor Steiner*, and *La Soufrière* are some of these films whose documentary proposition is consciously undercut and redefined by a perspective that transforms the visual facts into a grotesque carnival.[6] In each of these films, like the mountains in *La Soufrière*, the presence of the irrational and extreme continually threatens to explode the visual surface—and indeed frequently does erupt there—making Herzog's brand of naturalism, even in its most realistic form, seem as mocking of the travelogue realism of commercial representation as Herzog's vibrant desertscapes in *Fata Morgana* are of the concluding entertainment parody in that film, in which a pianist and a drummer flatly go through their motions before a stationary camera.

Herzog's film art is hence clearly at odds with the packaged notions of entertainment that Hollywood purveys, his films reactions to the debilitating formulas of commercial cinema. This is not to say, however, that Herzog is unwilling to use certain commercial avenues and modes of expression. His self-promoting of his own films across America, for example, may be typically heroic and idiosyncratic, yet it is nonetheless a version of Hollywood's own distribution tactics. Likewise, on his own initiative, he cut and dubbed *Nosferatu* for American suburbs, and for the same film, he and his cameraman, Schmidt-Reitwein, worked carefully to create their special effects while staying within the confines of the genre. "For *Nosferatu*," he says "we did these scenes so precisely because we knew we were working in a very special field—namely the field of a particular kind of 'genre' film which had its own specific rituals and narrative laws and mythic figures that have all been well-known to audiences for at least half a century now."[7] In a similar way, the special history of Herzog's *Kaspar Hauser* becomes indicative of his give-and-take dialogue with commercial audiences of Germany (as well as that of the other filmmakers in this study): after little success when it first appeared in West Germany in 1974, the film did extremely well in the United States and at the European festivals; the film then returned to Germany in 1975, the crucial year for the New German Cinema, and with its novelty more or less legitimized by these more confident taste-setters, German audiences welcomed Herzog's unusual vision back into the cinemas.

Yet, this ability to work within conventions and to attract regular audiences should never detract from Herzog's role as an experimenter in new sights. For Herzog, the smug and mostly academic distinction between art and entertainment, between experimental and commercial cinema, is a dangerously false one. For him, this opposition has itself created certain audience expectations, and has little to do with the way audiences *can* potentially see when and if the opposition dissolves. As experiments within commercial cinema, Herzog's films seek to erase that culturally inculcated distinction which has wrongly conditioned viewers to see a certain way, to avoid the new and radical, and to remain satisfied with the commercially commonplace. He seeks, that is, to make commercial audiences radical seers; the relative success of films like *Nosferatu* and *Fitzcarraldo* in the showcase cinemas of Germany and America indeed seems to further this goal of integrating within mass entertainment a radical evolution of cinematic vision that is, paradoxically, a return to historical origins.

In this evolution, *The Mystery of Kaspar Hauser* appears at nearly the midpoint mark in Herzog's career up to *Nosferatu*. As he admits himself, the film serves as a kind of watershed, summing up what went before it and opening the way for the outstanding films that follow. (According to Herzog, the film refers in one way or another to every film he made prior to it.)[8] In addition, the original German title of the film, *Jeder für sich und Gott gegen alle (Everyman for Himself and God against All)*, contains that fundamental irony of brashly announcing the revolutionary and iconoclastic stance that informs all of Herzog's films and, at the same time, having its source in Roger Corman's *The Trip*, a solidly Hollywood production which nonetheless offers a truly Herzogian sequence featuring a dwarf on a merry-go-round repeating Herzog's title again and again. The realist demand of Herzog's aesthetic is likewise dramatically evident in this fantastic tale: not only is the story taken from the well-known (and often adapted)[9] historical account of the mysterious young man found in 1828 on the streets of Nuremberg, but Herzog's attention to certain factual details is astonishingly painstaking in many cases. There are of course some considerable alterations in the facts of Kaspar's life, the plot, and the dialogue; yet concomitantly Herzog strives for historical accuracy to the extent of re-creating Kaspar's clothes and reconstructing characters, such as Lord Stanhope, to look uncannily like the originals.[10] As in his other films, the force of Herzog's imagination demands a commensurate force from physical reality.

Yet, more important to its status as a central document in Herzog's work, *Kaspar Hauser* is the story of an unsocialized man, the parable of a vision that comes into the world relatively untouched by the strictures of society. This theme is obviously a favorite one in film history, and Truffaut's *Wild Child* and Hal Ashby's *Being There* are recent examples whose differences indicate Herzog's special handling of the theme. In Truffaut's film, the interaction of the uncivilized boy and the forces of society is, despite conflicts and hostility, ultimately positive, both parties learning something from the other and the boy gradually accepting the instruction and friendship society offers him. In *Being There*, the strange, retarded behavior of Chauncey Gardner, educated only by television and plants, is barely noticed by an American society that eventually welcomes him as a messianic wiseman and political leader. Whereas the Truffaut film offers a message of social humanism according to which a primitive man's fundamental sense of justice can be nurtured by the tools of society, *Being There* presents a far more cynical view, the wild child here being a mindless video hoax and the society a degenerate reflection of his moronic ingenuousness. In *Kaspar Hauser*, however, the terms of this theme are significantly changed: there are few benefits specific to civilization, and Kaspar offers a radical awareness of the world which is as uncompromising about the destructive value of society as it is about the remedial effect of this awareness on that society. The humanistic rationalism of the French director and the social cynicism of the American are replaced by Herzog's Romanticism, which aligns the gentle and innocuous Kaspar with the violent visionary Aguirre, the ultimate iconoclast Nosferatu, and the flying skier Steiner. In a world where vision and sensibility have been corrupted by status-quo notions of truth, Herzog's outcasts are entirely inaccessible to the prejudices of society. Depending on his physical means, this outcast is thus both victim and oppressor, both Kaspar and Aguirre, and finally the two at once.

Kaspar's position as victim is naturally much more obvious through the course of the film than are his powers to threaten or tyrannize. The opening shots of him chained in a cavern and attended to by a black-cloaked figure that beats him foreshadow the more subtle oppressions he will suffer later when introduced to society. Of all Herzog's heroes and anti-heroes Kaspar is perhaps the one most purely misfit for this society: in these opening shots he is taught to write, to speak, and even to walk for the first time; for the remainder of the film he carries the signs of this late entry into society and his subsequently always marginal position there. From his first appearance in the town square, he is a curiosity for the townspeople, an object to be examined and guarded against: he is exiled to a horse stall, to the local jail, to a traveling carnival from which he tries to escape, and finally to a philanthropist's home, where the civilizing comforts he receives are never entirely comforting. When Daumer, the philanthropist, sadly observes that "it just can't be true when you say that your bed is the only place you're happy," Kaspar replies, "It seems to me that my coming into this world was a terrible fall." Later, when brought to an aristocratic party which is meant to be the pinnacle of his social achievement, he shocks the group when a lady asks what it was like "in that dark cellar of yours," and he answers, "Better than outside." For Kaspar, the amenities of civilization are more torments than aids, and, like Herzog and his forefathers of the twenties, the peace Kaspar seeks is offered not through social advancement but, as Jan-Christopher Horak has observed, through a return or regression to an original state of chiaroscuro.[11]

What Kaspar yearns for and what society attempts to frustrate in him is not, however, simply an original prenatal unconsciousness but an original vision which is extraordinarily attuned to the vibrancy of nature and in which the separation of an individual from the world is merely a question of space. Herzog is without doubt the nature poet of the German cinema, and Kaspar's rebuff of aristocratic curiosity suggests a desire not so much for the cavern of his youth but for the pristine world that suddenly moved before his eyes when released, a vision that originates not actually in a place but in a first unchanneled encounter with a world in which human sight is not its center but a participant dissolved in its energies. Herzog's camera appropriately presents this encounter with lengthy static shots such as the one of the fields of grass during the credit sequence of, later in the film, the equally long take of swans on a pond. In both cases, the shot is consciously devoid of any narrative value and of human subjects. And, as with the similar kind of shots that appear early in *Heart of Glass*, they introduce a world whose meaning lies not in any significance attained from the human order but in their own self-conspicuous vitality. The integrity of this presence outside human consciousness is the primitive wisdom of Kaspar's perspective, provoking his blunt reply to Lord Stanhope's request to "tell us whatever comes into your natural head." Making the self-evident enigmatic to the socialite Stanhope, Kaspar answers that "nothing lives in me but my life."

This life which Kaspar is particularly sensitive to is not, moreover, merely a pastoral beauty, for it is primarily the product of an energy that can easily become anarchy or chaos (as it does so quickly in *Even Dwarfs Started Small*, *Heart of Glass*, and *Nosferatu*) and its peace is ultimately a kind of death. Over the shot of the fields of grass that introduces the film, a quotation (from Büchner's *Lenz*) announces this other face of that image: "Don't you hear that terrible screaming all around us—that screaming that men call silence." And this same anarchist energy, hidden from the eyes of social beings, mildly erupts at one point when Kaspar and the other carnival freaks dash madly through the fields toward freedom. When caught near a hut swarming with bees, Kaspar remarks, "I would like to fly like a rider—midst the

"The sacrificial icon of self" (*Kaspar Hauser*). The
Museum of Modern Art/Film Stills Archive.

bloody tussle of war," thus recalling that archetypal symbol of loosed energy, the
horse with which Kaspar is identified early in the film when he plays with a toy one
in his cavern and later when he sleeps with one on first arriving at the village.

Tightly linked to these eruptions of energy are the shadows of death which obtrusively appear throughout the film as prognostic signs of the inevitable destruction
that befalls all forms of nature and, most noticeably, the constructs that the human
mind imposes on the world. Immediately after Kaspar is dragged from his cellar-
prison, for instance, Herzog ruptures the narrative with several expressive, nonnarrative shots that literally stop the plot flow in order to foreground those energies of
nature. In this instance, the extreme background contains one of Herzog's brilliantly
lit landscapes of a mountain valley; perpendicular to the camera axis in the foreground Kaspar lies senseless on the ground; just behind Kaspar and vertically perpendicular to his body sits the mysterious black-cloaked stranger, his back to the
camera. As usual, the camera does not budge, and the cross-like figure that Kaspar
and the dark guardian form contrasts sharply with the brilliant landscape of the
background and so creates a stunning icon of tragedy and death. This Christian reference occurs again in the film when the jailer and his family try to teach Kaspar to
eat properly, Kaspar's unnatural movements and obvious strain being punctuated by
shots of a bird in a cage and a small crucifix with Christ. These metaphoric identifications of Kaspar and Christ are not, however, orthodox ones, since Herzog, I believe, sees Christ mostly as the emblem of a human tragedy enmeshed in the forces

of nature (somewhat as Yeats does). A similar point is made in a more profane manner when later in the film Kaspar mourns the loss of the small garden in which he had sown his name with seeds. While the camera cuts to a heron killing and eating a frog (nature most naturally brutal) Kaspar's voice-over relates how he "took some cress seeds and sowed my name with them. And it came up right pretty. And it made me so happy that I can hardly say. And yesterday when I came back from boating, somebody had come into the garden and stepped on my name. I cried for a long time." The most salient mark of his individuality, Kaspar's name, is destroyed here just as he himself is destroyed in the end by that mysterious harbinger of death, his former guardian, who in introducing Kaspar to the world introduces him to destruction and death. The significance of the coupling is unmistakable: an acute perception of life's energies such as Kaspar's derives from the proximity of death and an intimacy with the annihilation of self.

His end prefigured in his beginning, Kaspar's life thus becomes a sort of anti-*Bildungsroman* and a story that continually tends toward a nonnarrative form. Most notably, the education that is the foundation for a character's development in this novelistic genre is depicted here as an interference and hindrance which Kaspar's original vision must regularly overcome. As I have indicated, this vision originates in a sensual imagination that grasps those energies at a much more authentic level than the rational categorizing of social beings. The close-up of Kaspar playing with the bird in the prison window thus diametrically contrasts the local peasants' geometrical game with the chicken meant to terrify Kaspar in the same prison. More specifically, there are the several direct attempts to educate Kaspar that he consistently befuddles with an illogic that rings truer than the logic his instructors force on him. The theologians, for example, struggle to have him accept ideas which are not at all sensually apparent to him. When one says, "What we really want to know is didn't a Higher Being occupy your thoughts in prison," Kaspar replies, "In my prison I didn't think of anything—I can't imagine that God created everything out of nothing like you say." Angry and frustrated, the theologians insist, "You must have faith!" And immediately following a cut to the garden where one of the ministers and Daumer pick apples, Kaspar demonstrates his version of faith, so simplistically unlike the abstract sensibility of the ministers. "Let the applies lie; they're tired and want to sleep," Kaspar says. Daumer, however, tries to explain human supremacy ("Apples don't have lives of their own; they follow our will") by rolling an apple which the minister is supposed to stop. But the apple hops over the minister's foot, and Kaspar observes, "Smart apple—it jumped over his foot and ran away."

A second formulaic attempt to educate Kaspar is also stymied by a perception which again dramatically subverts logical pedagogy. A professor of logic presents Kaspar with the riddle about a man at a crossroads leading to a village of liars and a village of truthtellers. Kaspar must ask one question to discover his hypothetical way. The pompous professor eventually gives the solution and explains that "by means of a double negative a liar is forced to tell the truth. . . . That's what I call logic via argument to truth." Kaspar, though, offers another solution: "I should ask the man whether he was a tree-frog. The man from the liar's village would say yes; the man from the truthteller's village would say no." The professor then sums up the convoluted philosophy of a society whose aim is to reorient Kaspar away from his radical vitalism. Kaspar's explanation, he says, is "not logic"; "logic is deduction not description. What you've done is describe something, not deduce it, . . . Understanding is secondary: the reasoning's the thing."

Most prominent in this drama of rational deduction set against illogical description is society's language and writing opposed to Kaspar's relative muteness, "that screaming that men call silence." Even before Kaspar sees the light of the world, his guardian initiates his tragic separation from it by putting a pen in Kaspar's hand and paper before him. Over Kaspar's grunts and groans, the caped figure commands, "writing . . . writ—ing. Remember that: writing." These first words of dialogue in the film then form a unit with the next phrase, delivered again later when the guardian abandons Kaspar: "Repeat after me: I want to be a gallant rider like my father was before me." Together these two sentences indicate the double structure of a language and a patriarchal society that will challenge Kaspar's perception throughout his life yet which he must adapt, in one way or another, if he is ever to communicate that perception. In those first shots, that is, a moribund father-surrogate with pen stands over Kaspar and his toy horse; shortly thereafter, another father figure, the Rittmeister, and his scribe stand before Kaspar and a live horse, making the terms of Kaspar's growth quite plain: language and the father or, more precisely, the language of the father becomes for Kaspar—as it is for Herzog himself in his engagement with the tradition of cinematic language—the obstacle and often the enemy that must be reconciled or overcome with a vision of the world that seems forever just outside the borders of communication. (That Herzog's Romantic conception of the individual here tends to imagine a self that precedes language suggests, however, his major differences with what would no doubt appear to him as the overly mechanistic vision of modern psychoanalysis. For modern psychoanalysis, of course, Herzog's communicative self, Kaspar with language, is ultimately the only self.)

The diminutive scribe who accompanies the Rittmeister when Kaspar is first discovered is doubtless an extreme version of all that is comically absurd about society's demand for records and verbal logic. In that first encounter, the camera pans back and forth from the policeman to the Rittmeister to the scribe, who, as a caustic parody of human distance from actual experience, records every self-evident detail that is muttered by the Rittmeister. This clerk pursues Kaspar everywhere in an effort to gather in writing all that can be discovered about him and thus to translate this human mystery into a comprehensible critique. When Kaspar and his sideshow companions rebel and run for their freedom, the clerk chases them across the field while shouting, "Stop in the name of the law," entirely unaware that it is precisely this law that threatens them. After they are caught, there is a long shot of the small scribe walking across a resplendent field which visually inundates him, while he notes to himself, "what a fine, what a beautiful report this will make. I shall write a report the likes of which has never been seen." As manifested in the clerk, writing thus becomes an absurdly repetitive exercise generated by its own self-serving momentum and remaining unbreachably distant from the more arcane centers of life. At its worst, this writing dissects in a search for simple explanations where there are none;

at the conclusion of the film, as a final illustration of this irony, surgeons cut up Kaspar's body, and the clerk gleefully remarks, "what a wonderful, precise report this will make. Deformities discovered in Kaspar Hauser's brain and liver. Finally we have got an explanation for this strange man—as we can not find a better one."

Perverse and terribly deleterious in the hands of the clerk, writing cannot, however, be simply dismissed in favor of brute silence or animal solipsism. For, writing, along with the other instruments of culture (like opera in *Fitzcarraldo*), is finally the means of communication that Kaspar desperately seeks and needs in order to pass on his vision and understanding. Transformed into a kind of poetry to match his perception, language can act as a liaison between Kaspar and the natural world and hence a means of reestablishing the connection that language originally deprived him of. After his arrival in the village, the jailer's son Julius gives Kaspar his first language lesson, during which Julius holds up a mirror so that Kaspar sees the separate parts of the body he is naming: language thus becomes commensurate with the segmentation of the body, the breakdown of imaginative unity signaled by a mirror stage during which the body first recognizes itself as other than the world. Emphasizing this breakdown, the next sequence shows Kaspar being washed by the jailer and his wife, nature literally being stripped from him while he cries, "Mother, my skin is coming off." Yet, the possible redemption of this lost unity is also present when, in the following sequence, the jailer's daughter Agnes attempts to teach Kaspar a children's poem. The rhyme is too difficult for Kaspar; but the language that divides Kaspar has in this new form the potential for imaginative transformation and the ability to regain the harmony with nature that the final shot of this sequence captures: Kaspar plays with a bird on the ledge of the prison window that separates him from the outside world.

Indeed, at several points in the film, this positive power of language appears as a corrective for the fall that invariably comes with its acquisition. Kaspar's autobiography and his admiration of Daumer's knowledge both testify to the benefits of culture and its languages, just as Kaspar's mimicking of the ministers' gestures illustrates his ability to turn their own tools against them when they press him too far. Similarly, music represents an unusually immediate communication for Kaspar. "Why can't I play the piano like I breathe," he exclaims; for without these imaginative reconciliations with the world "everything is so hard" and "the people are like wolves." Yet perhaps the most revealing metaphor for this reconciliation is planting his name in the earth, where the signature flowers as both verbal and visual sign of the individual's bond with the energies of the world—a bond that is, however, always ephemeral when subjected to those energies.

This visual translation of the verbal in the last example is important for two reasons: first, as a figurative recollection of an undiscriminating unity of vision that psychoanalysis locates before the mirror stage and the formation of a social self;[12] second, as a summary of Herzog's own communicative goals. The blooming of Kaspar's name, in short, becomes the verbal sign and symbol of the imaginative penetration into the world that Herzog aspires to himself with the language of his cinema, as it works to see the world with infant eyes. Like Kaspar's name, this vision and its language are singularly unconventional, holistic, and resistant to narrative patterning, and more than the language of any other commercial German director, it remains a struggle toward an effacement of a homocentric perspective. Like the medieval artist with whom he identifies, Herzog aims to lose his signature in the imaginative unity he seeks to re-create. And perhaps the central paradox in his work is precisely this aesthetic movement toward a kind of medieval loss of self which couples with the extravagant display of self whereby he sells his films.

The nature and terms of this cinematic language evolve in *Kaspar Hauser* specifically around the divisive structures of vision: namely, a logic of space, spectacle, linear development. Space and its visual apprehension are certainly central elements in all of Herzog's films, and in *Kaspar Hauser* they are the key terms in Kaspar's confrontation with society. From the perspective of society (and classical cinema for that matter), space is a function of perceptual proportions which define and limit a field according to geometrical and thus illusively objective dimensions. Incisively parodied in *Stroszek* when armed farmers guard a border strip between plots of land, this rigid demarcation of space haunts and stifles Kaspar until his death, his vision never quite adjusting to the boundaries of a social perspective. After his release from the cellar, the film describes Kaspar's transition to the village and indexes the contraction of this space (and time) with a series of shots that move from open landscapes and meadows to rooftops, houses, the face of a clock, and finally to the closed village square where Kaspar is left by the guardian. After being crowded in a horse's stall, he is moved to the prison, a transition Herzog makes with an extreme low-angle close-up of that tower which distorts both its size and proportions. Continuing these semi-subjective shots of Kaspar's spatial disorientation, Herzog cuts to the inside of the tower, where a medium close-up shows Kaspar in profile clutching the large wall and staring wide-eyed; the camera then executes a marvelously emphatic 90-degree track so that it repositions itself just behind Kaspar's head and refocuses on the small window that mesmerizes Kaspar, a refugee from the comparative largeness of the room. Ending the sequence, the camera cuts back to the original profile shot of Kaspar hugging the wall and now closing his eyes tightly. Without a word of commentary, Herzog thus describes the confusion of realms that overwhelms Kaspar as he is chaotically shifted from a borderless outside to an inside where he must confront proportions seen as dislocations entirely foreign to a socially inured eye. The re-creation of this point of view, in shots such as the track around Kaspar's head, offers an interpretation of space that is anything but stable, and expresses nicely the fear and anxiety that result when an undifferentiating vision must limit itself to the procrustean proportions of mostly arbitrary boundaries. In this case the spaces of the world become a funhouse afloat.

Later, after his tutelage with Daumer, Kaspar overcomes most of this anxiety, but he retains amongst his new social accoutrements his sense that the boundaries imposed on perspective distort the significance of space as well as the original powers of perspective itself. The geometrical and dimensional relations through which societal men or women normally decipher space according to patterns of difference and similarity simply never make much sense to Kaspar. Walking by the prison tower with Daumer, he remarks that "a very big man must have built it." And when

Daumer tries to correct him and explain how he once "lived in that tower where the little window is," Kaspar replies, "that cannot be—because the room is a few steps big. Wherever I look in the room—to the right, to the left, frontwards, backwards, there is only room. But when I look on the tower . . . and turn around, the tower is gone. So the room is bigger than the tower." For Kaspar, the powers of space over perspective are in short mind-forged, the size of space being relative to the force of its perceptual limitations. He, like Herzog, possesses a physical knowledge of space rather than a geometrical one: in Herzog's words, it is "a *physical* knowledge . . . of a certain order that existed in that space, and it is that kind of knowledge which has decided many an important battle."[13]

A tension is established, therefore, between Kaspar's fluid participation in space and the strict definitions of it that society insists upon. Somewhat as in *Coup de Grâce*, this tension is dramatized most frequently as a dialectic between closed, inside structures and the energy of nature outside (although the significance of these two structures is obviously quite different in Herzog's film). In *Kaspar Hauser*, space inside houses always appears cramped and consciously unbalanced in a manner that suggests the precariousness of its forms: the theologians' interrogation takes place in a crowded medium shot which is coupled with a low-angle, medium-long shot which draws together three walls and what appears to be a very low ceiling; during Lord Stanhope's reception, the seemingly perfect arrangement of tightly packed groups of aristocrats is momentarily broken at one point when Kaspar wheels distortedly across the camera angle nearly flush with the lens; after the first attack on Kaspar, the camera follows Daumer and Kathe on a frantic track through the house while doors, corners, walls, stairs, and windows seem to obtrude and clutter their search. Kaspar consequently is continually on the brink of claustrophobic fits that drive him again and again to open space: he flees the carnival; he excuses himself from Stanhope's party in order to recover by an open window; and, as he awaits death, he stares out a window to the place where he retreats to enjoy an Edenic moment prefiguring his death. Here societal space is like its language, an instrument of dissection, a montage of scenic unity, an atomization of what is otherwise vital, and a closed system of signification. Outside, nature releases space, silence, and meaning.

This division of experience and space, through language and a limited perspective, occurs at its most fundamental level when Kaspar learns words by using a mirror to divide the parts of his body and see himself for the first time as self-spectacle. Developed throughout *Kaspar Hauser*, space as an arena for spectacle thus becomes one of the tenets that Herzog shares with Fassbinder and Schlöndorff, although for Herzog it is specifically the human intrusion into and demand to control space which denigrates it so tragically: under the domination of a human perspective, nature becomes a cheapened sideshow, and its mysteries freakish oddities to be displayed at a distance. *Kaspar Hauser* can in fact be described as a series of exhibitions in which the internal placing of the scene exposes, under its own strain, the debilitating and destructive practice of dividing the viewer and the space viewed, of enforcing dramatic space. There is in this regard the previously mentioned sequence in which Stanhope directs and displays Kaspar at his reception. But as early as his first appearance in the town square, Kaspar stands stiff and mute in the center of the square, while the camera cuts from window to window where the imperturbable townspeople watch the curiosity below. Similarly, when Kaspar is transferred to his jail cell, long lines of men and women mount the steps leading up to his cell; at the top they peer through the small window in the iron door, the barrier maintaining the separation of space that provokes voyeuristic curiosity. As in a cinema or at certain kinds of theater, the screening or curtaining of space here allows the spectator a privileged position from which to manipulate the exotic and to demand from it a special symbolic significance where there in fact is none. Two town officials remark at this point: "he's beginning to be a burden to the community coffers. Perhaps he should begin contributing to his own upkeep. . . . One could turn the public interest in him to good use." Thus, the theatrical demarcation of space and the voyeuristic curiosity it inspires receive official sanction as a valuable economic and social structure—as a commercial cinema.

Kaspar is subsequently leased to a traveling carnival that turns the social ideology of spectacle into an economic venture. As the villagers arrive to view the show, the master of ceremonies, a slightly awry version of Dr. Caligari, warns, "minors, please keep your distance," leaving no doubt about the importance of spatial divisions. He then introduces his "Four Riddles of the Spheres": the midget King of Punts; the Young Mozart; Hombrecito, the South American Indian; and "the final and greatest mystery of them all, Kaspar Hauser." Except for Kaspar, each of these oddities is something of a sham, their powers and mysteries being exaggerated for the purpose of the spectacle. Yet it is here that Herzog's rarely acknowledged irony transforms the significance of these spectacles within the frame by positing a second point of view outside the societal spaces that define internal actions. This kind of visual irony is present in most of Herzog's films, such as in *Nosferatu*, where the conventional interpretation of the vampire is ingeniously overturned, remaking him as an heroic iconoclast, or in *Aguirre*, where the apparent madness of Aguirre is powerfully reversed when the jungle around him erupts with spears, monkeys, and treed ships that seem to objectify his apocalyptic vision. In each of these cases, it is a new order of spatial reality that relocates the geometrical order within the frame, and in doing so generates its ironic significance.

Less striking in some ways than the last two examples, the carnival sequence in *Kaspar Hauser* illustrates the same process whereby the person or object, drained of its vibrancy by a societal perspective, has that original significance reinvested through what is literally a reframing action—ironic in that it recontextualizes.[14] Emphasizing the imposture of the carnival freaks, in other words, Herzog makes it clear that these postures are the product of a cultural look which positions these individuals outside the norm in order that they serve as objects of pleasure: exhibitionism always follows from the demands of a spectator's desires. But, as Herzog says of Kaspar, "he's *not* an outsider: he is the very center, and all the rest are outsiders."[15] And by recasting those spectators as exhibitions themselves, Herzog returns Kaspar to the center from which meaning emanates, reversing the angles of significance and translating those voyeuristic fantasies into an imaginative reality. Put another way, the risible and the grotesque become truth itself when the angle of vision changes.

The midget king's tale can thus be read as an allegory describing Kaspar's original Titanic rapport with the earth, which, as civilization gradually encroached on his space, shrank to a state of paralytic exile: in the master of ceremonies' words, "last link in an ancient line of giants, each king of this line was tinier than the last. Another few centuries and the King of Punts will be made invisible. . . . The very last king will be no bigger than a flea . . . cowering like an outcast in the corner of his throne. . . . And as kings have grown tinier, so have their kingdoms. His kingdom is no larger than the spot he sits on—for neither can he leave his kingdom without outside help nor can he enter it." The noble savage, Hombrecito, likewise resembles Kaspar in his other-worldly speech and rather mystical contact with music: "he plays his wooden flute night and day, because he believes if he stops all the people of the town will die." Lastly, there is the child Mozart who, like Kaspar and Hombrecito, remains entranced and in touch only with music and imaginative space. Like Kaspar's own performances of Mozart's music, the child's relationship with the civilized world is riddled with gaps and irrational lacunae: "one day," the master of ceremonies recounts, "he fell into a deep trance and asked for nothing more than the music of Mozart. Now still in a trance he looks for dark holes in the earth because they tried to teach him to read and write in school. . . . Day in, day out, he peers into dark holes in the earth looking for entrances to caves and underground watercourses. His mind is completely engrossed in zones of twilight."

Roped off for exhibition, Kaspar hence inhabits an increasingly diminishing area of the world, while his vision embraces new vistas that society has no conception of. The strain of this conflict is what ultimately drives Kaspar, along with many of Herzog's other characters, into a visionary seclusion where the force of his difference from society marks his insights as both psychotic and iconoclastic. As Kaspar says to Daumer, the result of his education and social acclimation is that he is happiest alone in bed. And, when attacked the first time, the wounded Kaspar mysteriously makes his way to the small, dark cellar of the house, a last refuge from society and a return to the original space of his first cavern, the place of an infantile imaginary.

This visionary retreat into a contracted space is in turn reflected as a blank hypnotic stare that describes Kaspar throughout his life: as vital space grows smaller for him, his look turns further and further inward for the geography of its life. Certainly most fully developed in *Heart of Glass*, this glare is, as Herzog explains, best described as a look back through the encrustations of civilization to a primal scene and is explicitly connected with the mnemonic powers of hypnosis.[16] Best exemplified by the several shots of Kaspar staring blankly out of windows, this hypnotic look remains radically insulated and unresponsive to human aggressions. When the town officials test Kaspar by having a sword thrust at him from several directions, he stares straight ahead without any reaction to the rapid movements, and one of the more disconcerting details in *Kaspar Hauser* is Kaspar's constant subversion of eye-line matches through the wandering focus of his eyes. Just as he resists language and the demarcations of space, his gaze resists the optical dialogue which, in classical cinema, becomes an erotics of exchange, an aggressive duel of spectacles described in terms of eye-line matching.[17] Signaling and culminating this resistance is a shot just before Kaspar's death in which he stares at his own reflection in a tub of water, a shot which re-creates Herzog's Romantic version of the mirror stage that marked Kaspar's entrance into a world of self-spectacle. With a brush of his hand, however, the image dissipates, and Kaspar's fascinated gaze merges, through the subjective camera angle, with an image of self that literally dissolves in a space of featureless fluidity.

This fascinated stare obviously fortifies Herzog's connection with those filmic origins which in America may mean Griffith but in Germany mean above all else Fritz Lang and Murnau, the masters of fascination. For, despite considerable differences, Herzog clearly follows these early German directors in their continual concerns with the dynamics of vision and spectacle and, more importantly, in finding an approximation of the ideal cinematic experience in the hypnotic look. "If you look at a film under hypnosis," Herzog argues, "you *may* be able to have visionary experience of a type that you have never had before."[18] As part of this project and tradition, therefore, Herzog's films regularly seek to re-create something of Kaspar Hauser's hypnotic vision, and *Kaspar Hauser* itself works specifically to generate that imagistic fascination which would engage the spectator's eye not in the titillating fashion of Hollywood cinema where voyeuristic distance maintains the spectacle but as an exploration and hypnotic participation in the energies of space.

In this regard, Kaspar's dream-visions become the keys to Herzog's own cinematic vision and the alternative space he wishes to present, a space, like Kaspar's, where the outer side is also its center and where the distance between the viewed and the viewer collapses.[19] To be sure, the changes in filmstock which differentiate these dreams from Kaspar's more socialized visions immediately indicate the alternative status of these visions, the rough filmstock correlating to Kaspar's primal imagination. Yet, equally important are the realistic roots of these dreams, again establishing Herzog's notion of the fantastic documentary: the dreams (of deserts, camels, etc.) all originate in actual stories or daily events, and Kaspar's early inability to distinguish his dreams from reality suggests that the distinction is a moot question for the true seer.

The first dream which Kaspar recounts for Daumer is of Caucasus, the region where, aptly, the Titan Prometheus was supposedly chained to a mountain for stealing fire from the gods. The dream is short and slow, a meditative shot in which the beauty of the image is fascinating rather than exotic: here, as in the meditative shots of nature which permeate *Kaspar Hauser*, the image becomes a strange landscape of shared energy, familiar like the new vistas of a dream. Like the other stationary shots in the film, moreover, the filmic image appears as a kind of painting without action or movement except for the slow panning and flickering of its surface. Disregarding action, it immobilizes the look within its own hypnotic space, a vast and luxurious oasis of unbounded directions.

Kaspar's second dream adds the darkness of mortality to the vibrant spaces that the first dream sketches. Occurring after the first stabbing, this vision describes a procession through blue fog toward Death. In Kaspar's words: "I saw the ocean and I saw a mountain. It was like a procession. There was a lot of fog and at the top was Death." Certainly a premonition of his own imminent death, this dream is more importantly an image of the end of humanity in the grip of nature: here, linear pro-gression becomes an illusion culminating in death, and the crowd of faceless and blurred figures that wander up and down this stationary, low-angle shot character-izes neatly the actual status of human individuality enmeshed in the darkened mass of nature's process.

If these first two visions encapsulate that anonymous energy with which the im-age leads the look through foreign landscapes, the third dream acts as a summary statement of the film's imagistic and narrative direction. Kaspar relates this dream-vision just before he dies, but hesitates at first because it is actually only the begin-ning of a story and he has been warned that he must learn to tell a story according to its conventions, that is, with a beginning and an end. Like the Caucasus dream, the images of this desert story appear old and glowing. Kaspar narrates:

> I see a long caravan coming through the desert, across the sands. And this caravan is led by an old Berber, an old blind man. . . . Now the caravan stops because some believe they are lost and because they see mountains ahead of them. . . . They look at their com-passes. But it's no use. . . . Then their blind leader picks up a handful of sand, and tastes it as though it were food. . . . My sons, the blind man says, you are wrong: those are not mountains that you see; it is only your imagination. We must continue northward. . . . And they follow the old man's advice and finally reach the city in the north. . . . And that's where the story begins. But how the story goes after they reach the city, I don't know.

Like the sands of *Fata Morgana*, this is a place where arbitrary human divisions of space are useless: neither compasses nor distances assessed by the eye are pertinent; only the blind seer can look beyond his band's false homocentric assumptions about space and direction, assumptions that are of course the underpinning of the society that surrounds Kaspar's death bed. Like Kaspar's, the seer's is a sensual imagina-tion: he relies on the feel and taste of the earth's energies to guide his sight. Like Herzog's, his is a physical knowledge of space.

More significantly perhaps, the very images and structure of the dream of the Berber become a condensation of Herzog's own story of Kaspar. In both cases, the luminous presence of nature makes the appearance of humans almost incidental. In both, the fluidity of space engulfs the demarcations of time so that linear develop-ment and closure, the foundations of narrative form, dissolve, just as the closing song of *Kaspar Hauser* merges with and returns to the identical opening song to form Herzog's figure of a spinning circle, that mark of chaos preparatory to icono-clastic vision. Like the endings of *Heart of Glass* and *Nosferatu*, the conclusion of the Berber's tale becomes not an ending but more precisely a beginning, a narrative opening or return rather than a closing; as such, it mirrors the whole of *Kaspar Hauser* as an attempted subversion of narrative structure itself: iconoclastic in terms of traditional imagistic linkages and closure and in terms of anthropocentric images themselves. In one sense, *Kaspar Hauser* does not even have a proper beginning, the introductory images being a series of loosely connected and unmotivated shots: an oar lightly touching water, a man in a boat, a woman's face, a shore line, an extreme low-angle shot of the tower that later imprisons Kaspar, and a woman washing clothes. Preparing the foundation of the film, each of these shots evokes a discrete reality in and of itself, each unrelated to the logic of the other and each as boldly assertive as the close-up of the woman who looks directly into the camera.

But, above all else, the narrative structure of *Kaspar Hauser* is the promise of a solution to a natural mystery whose solution never arrives. On one level the film provokes spectatorial desire, as do all narratives, to search for a conclusion and resolution of some sort. Yet here the black-caped guardian, that figure of birth and death who begins and ends the film, focuses the frustration of motivation that replaces the standard resolution of this desire. His final note, left in Kaspar's hands, offers a solution but one as opaque and cryptic as the silence that precedes the note: "he can tell you exactly what I look like and where I come from. To save him the trouble, I'll tell you myself who I am and where I come from. . . . MLO." Like this false missive in which language offers no solution but only more mystery, moreover, the clinical dissection of Kaspar's body and the clerk's ludicrous contentment that the puzzle has been solved become simply other ironical stagings whose purported conclusions are undercut by the vivid mental image of Kaspar that remains. Like the river on which the opening shots of the film surface, the narrative flows open at both ends, the scintillating singularity of the images fully resisting the weight of a closed interpretive structure.[20]

Paralleling the tale of the Berber that ends with the possible beginning of a new city, *Kaspar Hauser* thus concludes on the edge of new and radically altered narrative structure, on the edge of an alternative narrative form with which to communicate new images. In large part a stripping away and debunking of society's imaginings, *Kaspar Hauser* is a sort of last mediating gesture before the almost impenetrable images and elusive narrative of *Heart of Glass*. Yet in its turn *Heart of Glass* ends with a beginning, and Herzog's own quest seems at this point less a question of a final vision than a problem of articulation and communication.[21] "I am *still* searching," he says. "But I can assure you I *do* see something at the horizon. . . . I am still trying to articulate those images that I see at the horizon. I may never be able to succeed completely . . . but I *do* know that I won't give up."[22] For Herzog, like Kaspar, that fascinated vision must find an adequate language and an audience, or its power dissipates as solipsism: "My films are born out of a very strong fascination, and I know that I have seen there things that others have not yet seen and that others do not know. This is what I wish to make visible to other people. It is a need to communicate, very strong and very alive."[23]

Indeed, the mode and matter of Herzog's communication is as far from the political cinema of Fassbinder and Kluge as his visionary eye is from their reflective eyes. Besides the obvious differences, the politics of Herzog's communication involve a dangerously self-defeating dimension, according to which the articulation of vision in a communicable form is ultimately a death sentence: Kaspar tells his tale only on the brink of death and Herzog makes his film only when the reality of destruction sufficiently threatens. Yet, despite this Romantic moribundity, Herzog's films remain communicative efforts, specifically directed, he insists, at a social amelioration and a new imagining of cultural reality. Herzog's films are not simply images of iconoclastic despair but rather images meant to renovate a society that desperately needs new spaces: "we live in a society that has *no* adequate images anymore," he claims, "and, if we do not find adequate images and an adequate language for our civilization with which to express them, we will die out like the dinosaurs. . . . We have already recognized that problems like the energy shortage or the overpopulation of the world are great dangers for our society and for our kind of civilization, but I think that it has not been understood widely enough that we absolutely *need* new images."[24] Utterly asocial in one sense, Herzog's films thus locate themselves, somewhat paradoxically, just as earnestly within a social system of communication and the need to reach and engage audiences. Defined by this dialogue, Herzog's apocalyptic vision of defeat consequently becomes only the message or figure which is more fully defined by the positive communicative framework that is its medium or ground. Ultimately and at their best, the two should become a phoenix image, which would infuse the viewer with a visionary energy to be then actualized in the world and which would entrance its audience into the original perspective needed to transform the boundaries and open the borders of societal space.

"Recalling Hitler from the grave of Romantic art" (*Hitler*).

NINE

The Exorcism of the Image

Syberberg's Hitler, A Film from Germany

> The screen is a dim page spread before us, white
> and silent. The film has broken, or a projector
> bulb has burned out. It was difficult even for us,
> old fans who've always been at the movies
> (haven't we?) to tell which before the darkness
> swept in. The last image was too immediate for
> any eye to register. It may have been a human
> figure, dreaming of an early evening in each great
> capital luminous enough to tell him he will never
> die, coming outside to wish on the first star. But it
> was *not* a star, it was falling, a bright angel of
> death. And in the darkening and awful expanse of
> the screen something has kept on, a film we have
> not learned to see. . . .
>
>   Thomas Pynchon, *Gravity's Rainbow*

Hans-Jürgen Syberberg's position and practice within contemporary German cinema has been as ironic as it has been extreme. In many ways the most classically German of the recent generation of German filmmakers, he nonetheless frequently refuses contact with the German public and is in turn blasted by German critics and directors alike. One West German writer has labeled him "a manic egocentric beset with a persecution complex, sniffing out conspiracies all over the place,"[1] while his more sympathetic colleague Fassbinder describes him as a "merchant in plagiarism" who simply imitated Werner Schroeter's techniques and "competently marketed what he took from Schroeter."[2] Syberberg's rapport with the American film industry has been no less ambivalent. He has regularly denounced Hollywood as "the great whore of show-business," derided other German filmmakers for their successful manipulation of Hollywood formulas,[3] and consistently made films antithetical in every sense to the traditional cinematic models. Yet, despite these belligerent stances, Syberberg's *Hitler*, has been received by American audiences with an enthusiasm rarely equaled by other contemporary German films, an enthusiasm concretized and encouraged by Susan Sontag's glowing essay on the film.[4] The message is clear: whether expressly or unintentionally, Syberberg's films have become demiurgic projections whose radical difference has generated much of their spectatorial fascination and whose extreme nationalism has been their most effective commercial ploy on the international market.

While the films themselves are naturally the matrix for these extreme and often contradictory responses, the dynamics of Syberberg's career clearly establish the patterns from which the films and the responses to them spring. Particularly in his relations with the film industry and its audiences, Syberberg shares in this regard many of Herzog's independent attitudes about filmmaking, just as Schlöndorff and Kluge share, in their own very different way, mutual concerns and strategies for revamping Germany's film business. Whereas the latter two are committed to remaking the industry from the inside, Syberberg, like Herzog, remains the iconoclastic outsider whose projects for working with the available means of filmic communication are as imaginatively innovative as they are frequently unacceptable to conventional producers and audiences. His virulent and sometimes whining attacks on German critics and the audiences they represent are well known, culminating in the rather vitriolic and self-indulgent *Syberbergs Filmbuch*, where he at one point contrasts German reactions to his films with the acclaim they have received outside Germany, most particularly in France.[5] For Syberberg, his self-proclaimed victimization and these narrow-minded responses to his films by German viewers reflect the general degeneracy of an industry whose original potential has been supplanted by vulgarized versions of democratic entertainment. He therefore returns for models, like Herzog, to historical precedents—Méliès, Griffith, and so forth—that seem to have avoided the shallow mass-media formulas and propagandistic tyranny that reached its peak in the film industry during the war and later when Hollywood invaded postwar Germany. Most significantly, for Syberberg, under the pervasive control of this entertainment industry, Germany and America have come simply to reflect each other's closed production methods and a mechanical critical reception of films that naturally excludes the exceptional. "It is astonishing," he says (in a statement that clearly distorts some facts),

> when one discovers the coincidences, to see at what point . . . Germany and America truly have to be seen one closely involved with the other. It has been ten years since German films first sparked an interest the U.S.A. through the projection of about thirty films at the Museum of Modern Art. The people responsible for this program were at this time terrorized by the mighty and all-powerful critics who . . . despite the most insistent urging by Herzog refused even to glance at *Ludwig*. Richard Roud, director of the New York Film Festival, has refused to show no matter which film of Syberberg. . . . But without the New York Film Festival, it is useless to think of distribution in America. . . . The radical nature of this control and how it happens is indeed comparable to that of the film business in Germany. The two stories that appeared one in *Newsweek* and the other in *Time* about the New German Cinema were the work of a team of journalists who were informed and in the service of some specialized German journalists, an exchange that functions exactly like the feedback process of the media, with its perfectly democratic character.[6]

What democratic feedback implies here is a closed system which levels inspiration and reduces imagination to commonplace and prosaic comprehension.[7] Just as the

German and American spectator/critic practices monotonously exchangeable perceptions under the banner of democratic art, films, in the same way, adapt themselves to a similar kind of response under the banner of commercial viability. The result is that the filmic experience becomes a simplistic masturbatory rite in which accessibility becomes synonymous with harmless and bromidic stimulation. This is the "cinema as brothel," Syberberg notes, "with much to laugh about, if it wasn't so serious."[8] Despite his self-avowed Brechtian connection, Syberberg thus quickly and decisively disassociates himself from any notion of proletarian aesthetics (such as Kluge seems to tend toward): film, he argues, "is an extension of life by other means and not its mirror"; it is not "the democratic form of theater in the age of mechanical reproduction as multiplier in favor of the masses."[9] For Syberberg, those proletariat aesthetics have become the Hollywood art of the most banal pleasure for the greatest number, and this art is precisely the foe that Syberberg and his films aim to undo. Insisting on a radically new audience rapport, his films are "a declaration of war against the present forms of cinema dialogue and of boulevard-type cinema in the tradition of Hollywood and its satellites. . . . A declaration of war against psychological chitchat, against the action film, against a particular philosophy endlessly linking shots and reverse shots, against the metaphysics of the automobile and the gun, against the excitement of opened and closed doors, against the melodrama of crime and sex."[10]

For Syberberg, these boulevard cinemas and their entertainment codes become the mainstream industrial projections whose immense power serves mainly to trivialize and subjugate the real potential of the individual imagination and its ability to project vital myths alive to reality. First and foremost, the cinema is "light and things projected";[11] these commercial projections have become the myths of our time, as they mold the spectatorial imagination, through the anonymity of the mechanism itself, into a community or national consciousness.[12] Unlike some of his more rationalistic contemporaries, Syberberg does not question the inherent direction of this mechanism as a medium for the mythic and the irrational, but instead directs his argument against using it to enforce a spectatorial passivity and to cheapen the visionary resources of humanity. Against the established projections of Hollywood, Syberberg sets out to establish counter-projections which would at once scrutinize the mythic products of an age of mechanical reproduction and introduce new potentials for that projection mechanism, which would originate not in the mass industry behind the spectator but in an audience interaction with the screen.

This remaking of the industry of mythic projection is, however, at its base a financial and material matter; and notwithstanding his grand aesthetic schemes, Syberberg, to his credit, has rarely lost sight of this fact that all cinematic projections begin with money and equipment. Unlike Herzog's mostly textual practices, Syberberg takes quite literally the task of refashioning the cinematic machinery that makes perception, and, as for other contemporary German filmmakers, this task leads inevitably to economic and social tensions that ultimately inform the image on the screen. However extreme and unusual, Syberberg's cinematic practice shares with his peers the understanding that film art is an aesthetic of economics, manufacture, and marketing;[13] even more so than his peers, Syberberg's principal accomplishment may well be his ability to manipulate the very machinery of the film industry so as to create literal counter-projections within this socioeconomic framework that serves the boulevard myths.

Almost as an act of defiance against the dominant financial structure, for instance, Syberberg continually makes films whose subject matter and scale are inversely proportionate to the small budgets he receives. Particularly as evidenced in the trilogy of films—*Ludwig*, *Karl May*, and *Hitler*—the financial repression that situates his films apparently becomes the necessary test, obstacle, and final proof for his authorial imagination. This does not mean, naturally, that Syberberg necessarily takes a masochistic delight in setting the force of his singular creative talents against a Goliathan industry that stands in his way: if part of the miracle of *Ludwig* and *Hitler* is that the first was shot in ten days with 300,000 DM and the second in twenty days with 1,000,000, Syberberg insists that because of these limitations, each is merely "a sketch of the potential project that will now never be realized."[14] Nonetheless these budgetary hindrances that so bother Syberberg's filmic art do finally serve him in a manner he could only welcome: first, as testimonies to the heroic force that successfully overcame these obstacles, and, second, much like Herzog's strategies, as a familiar marketing tactic whereby the shooting of the film becomes one of the outstanding attractions of its showing.[15] As Serge Daney has suggested, Syberberg discovers, much like Herzog, a large part of the moral force of his films in that "he risks something . . . with the maximum of his powers,"[16] so that, even as a sketch, a film like *Hitler* remains an aesthetic testimony to its making and maker: "I cannot, as Hitler could do," he says, "command all that I need to make a film; my energy and force must find their source elsewhere than in such power."[17] Just as significantly, moreover, Syberberg, like many of his colleagues, has had to turn to financial sources outside Germany for a film like *Hitler*, and thus, at its economic base, he begins the international dialogue which has been the key to the success of so many films from Germany.[18] As he does on nearly every level of his work, Syberberg manages here to transform difficulties with financial sources into resources of his counter-aesthetic, to turn the economic machinery that so confines him into a vehicle that valorizes real creations.

In much the same manner, Syberberg confronts the actual machinery of film in order to make a counter-reality of the material conditions that position him outside the avenues of traditional commercial cinema. Financially disadvantaged, Syberberg is likewise deprived of the usual tools of the trade with which the film industry works so successfully to create its reality effect. Yet, rather than struggle against these conditions, Syberberg seems to embrace this second disadvantage as imaginative potential from which his special spectacle can arise. In this regard there are two notable innovations which, particularly in *Hitler*, are the marks of Syberberg's cinema: the continual use of frontal projection and the ubiquitous presence of marionettes. (This frontal projection uses a complicated camera set-up in which the camera shoots the scene through a glass positioned at a 45-degree angle before it; a projector angled below the mirror side of this same glass projects a scene in the same direction behind the actor or action onto a special glass.) As I have suggested, the use of both this frontal projection system and the marionettes derives in large part from financial and temporal constraints.[19] Yet, however maternal necessity might be here, the singular importance and value of Syberberg's films follows from the aesthetic significance to which he puts these tools. Thus, the marionettes become far more than a cheap substitute for a cast of thousands: "Behind the marionette, there is someone who holds it. And, this, for me, is the spiritual background of this technique because my idea is that Hitler was manipulated by others. And in this specific case, by us. . . . All these techniques used with the marionettes elucidate the fact that it is we who have given life and movement to Hitler."[20] Likewise, although the frontal projection system that Syberberg uses could be simply an inexpensive way of creating a reality illusion, for Syberberg it becomes the mechanism of a uniquely imaginary space which directly confronts the cinematic *vraisemblable*: "Sometimes in *Hitler* there is a normal approach to reality," Syberberg points out. Yet, by means of the frontal projection, the film fluctuates "between the normal and the surreal in the double sense of the term: in my conception and in the concrete fashion in which the technical equipment was used. This play with the apparatuses, foreseen in advance, was much more important to the spirit of my film than the attempt to recreate a normal and plausible reality."[21]

As both a complaining exile from the established industry and an ingenious innovator who develops a new aesthetic out of the bonds of that position, Syberberg is consequently even more the artistic exception than Herzog. Yet, like Herzog, this pariah independence is partly a ruse and a strategy, since Syberberg's aim is ultimately to gain access to the centers of commercial cinema in order that his mythic counter-projections become part of a true dialogue. This displaced dialogue with commercial cinema is particularly evident in his rapport with America, where— interestingly and somewhat ironically—his iconoclastic frontal projection was developed and abandoned fifty years earlier in Hollywood, only to be rediscovered by Francis Coppola through Syberberg's films. Coppola, in fact, has become a kind of American godfather for Syberberg's films as he has initiated and come to represent an attempted recuperation of the German director by an American film industry and audience. Indeed, like Coppola himself, this particular industry and audience are marginally located in relation to the massive centers of Hollywood; but, like Coppola's films, they are nonetheless very much products and forces of this commercial scene in the United States. However negligible in terms of numbers, Coppola, Sontag, *Rolling Stone*, and others represent the importance of American reception to Syberberg's films and the ability of these films to locate themselves within a certain American tradition (even one simplistically characterized as that of von Stroheim, Lang, and von Sternberg).

Snubbed and annoyed by German critics and spectators, Syberberg has petulantly turned toward more receptive audiences in America and elsewhere who either *while* or *because* they are displaced from the incisive focus of his extraordinarily German topics seem better able to appreciate them.[22] The double irony here—which in its various manifestations underlies this entire study—is that while American audiences have enthusiastically welcomed Syberberg's Teutonically imbued investigation of German history (the Hitler trilogy), German audiences have rejected it in favor of more standard Hollywood treatments of the issue in such films as *Holo-*

caust.[23] In its relation to both German and American audiences, therefore, the dialogue initiated by Syberberg's films has become as displaced in terms of the audiences of these films as they are unsettling in terms of their techniques and topics. Theirs has become a dialogue whose dialectical projections have created an aesthetic dislocation as extreme in results as uncompromisingly imaginative in methods.

As an equally extreme version of his peers' concerns, Syberberg's films direct this dialogue almost exclusively at history, its figures, and its cultural myths. "That our history is in everything of necessity our most important heritage, both for good and evil, is the fate laid upon us at birth," Syberberg writes, "and something that we can only work our way through with an active effort."[24] Actively examining the myths of history, Syberberg's films invariably focus on the generative dynamics of mass appeal and ultimately on the culmination of those dynamics in the technology of cinema, his interrogations thus becoming types of critical reflections in which a product of mass appeal is examined by its most powerful instrument, the camera. He calls his film *Fritz Kortner* "a document witnessing an epoch";[25] and he has gone so far as to propose a library/archive of video-memoirs which would collect an expanding number of these films and video records as testimonies to the collective myths of the age.[26] Clearly, neither these future videos nor Syberberg's past films could be classified as documentaries in the traditional sense. For what Syberberg's representations of history realize is both an interrogation and a participation in the myths of history, a double perspective which becomes that celebrated aesthetic scandal that conjoins Brecht and Wagner.[27] With the counter-aesthetic that results, Syberberg looks at history by turning the myths that organize it back on the very figures at its base; like the special screen used in the frontal projection mechanism, this kind of representation becomes at once a transparency and a mirror through which a counter-projection, from the direction of the audience, is both screened and recorded. Through a bilateral perspective (*on* the history *of* the audience), Syberberg exposes the fascination at the center of historical myths as a way of understanding the present, an exposition that situates itself *inside* the mythic apparatus itself. As he says of *Ludwig* and *Karl May*, these are "positive mythologies of history, filtered through the medium of film, by means of the spiritual checks of irony and pathos."[28]

As the beginning of his inquiry into the crisis of the present, Syberberg therefore returns, as he does for his cinematic tradition, to a historical source: "I chose the way back into the past of our last hundred years," he says, "to see if I could seek out the origins of many contemporary developments."[29] Present in most of his films since his first study of Brecht and later description of contemporary youth culture in *San Domingo*, this search for historical motivation and generations has, however, far less to do with a chain of events than with the development of the imaginative structures, irrational desires, and psychological projections that form a cultural identity, tragically climaxing in *Hitler*.

Although the first two parts of the Hitler trilogy, *Ludwig—Requiem for a Virgin King* and *Karl May*, were not originally conceived as a trilogy, it is completely in keeping with Syberberg's historical perspective, consequently, that the three films

"Figures of mourning: Syberberg and daughter" (*Hitler*).

have an explicit and organic relationship that goes well beyond the exchange of citations and formal similarities. Separately, each describes an epoch in terms of the personality that drew together the sympathies and imagination of the masses; together they map the rise and fall of twentieth-century Germany, as the irrationalities at the heart of its identity go through the various permutations that lead to its horrific collapse in Hitler. Syberberg's Ludwig is in every sense the dream king on the verge of an industrial age: as a child-ruler eccentrically resisting the pressures of the new age, he becomes the true forefather of the petit bourgeois tyrant who uses the mechanics of that new age to control and exploit the same mass sympathy and individual desires. Between the two is Karl May, who becomes the odd but accurate link that unites two so ostensibly different rulers in a mythic consciousness: as the epitome of popular art, he and his literature are the essence of the imagination trivialized in the age of mechanical representation. Despite the pervasive music of Mahler, *Karl May* carries the spirit of Wagner from Ludwig, Wagner's benefactor, to Hitler, his bad conscience;[30] as a writer about exotic lands unseen and Romantic quests in a visionary's America, May strangely represents the aesthetic projections of an overly precious Ludwig in the process of becoming the aesthetic nightmare of Hitler's war. "Anyone who knows the significance of Karl May for the German people," Syberberg says in the introduction to his Hitler book, "how every schoolboy grows up with his works, also knows how close we are here to a history of German sentiment, to its adventures of the soul and its myths of the Good Man, the German who fights and conquers for all that is noble."[31]

As the end piece, *Hitler* is thus the climactic episode in the projection of a cultural imagination manifested through the age of masses and mass technology: in the words of Harry Baer, one of the narrators of the film, "the twentieth century made *Hitler, A Film from Germany*."[32] A massive recuperation of this century as myth and identity, *Hitler* is in nearly every sense an encyclopedic document which literally overwhelms the spectator with the range and density of its textual surface. Jean-Pierre Faye has called it an "immense dia-monologue" made into Germany's "Third Faust"; Elsaesser remarks that the film describes "the end of a (film-) historical development"; and Sontag's appropriately multifaceted and resonant essay concludes on the Wagnerian note that the film "is on another scale than anything one has seen on film. It is a work that demands a special kind of attention and partisanship; and invites being reflected upon, reseen. The more one recognizes its stylistic references and lores, the more the film vibrates."[33] The vehemence of its many detractors seems, moreover, to support its very goal as a piece of war machinery militantly at odds with the placidly superficial ways Western cultures have recuperated their past and their historical unconscious, a recuperation accomplished through the mechanisms of conventional films as well as through the internal mechanisms of each individual. As a historical counter-projection and dialogue, *Hitler* elicits and listens, just as its narrator Koberwitz (played by two actors in turn representing a film producer, a strolling player, a society host, and others) always looks askance and speaks directly to no one, so that visually and verbally the film insists that the audience find its own place in a text which indeed belongs to this audience yet which is concomitantly too much for it. Not surprisingly, there is a stubborn resistance, especially in Germany, and using terms remarkably like Metz's Syberberg describes the confrontation which the film initiates as an engagement with a filmic *vraisemblable* that so effectively censures and limits the image itself. "It is not that" the spectators and critics have rejected the film; "it is that this rejection is unconscious. . . . It's interesting to note that in our society, there is no real need for external censorship. . . . The censor is elsewhere. And this is much more difficult to overcome. The film is indeed blocked but blocked inside people. There is an economic censor and also a media censor."[34]

What has been interiorly censored is specifically that unspeakable historical absence that Wenders delineates in the frame of *Kings of the Road*. Yet here it is less the consequences of that absence than the source that must be confronted: like *Kings of the Road*, the object and instrument of investigation in *Hitler* is the projection mechanism itself, yet here the question is less what are the alternatives than what are the deeply embedded lies that must be faced, accepted, and thus exorcised. The difficulty of *Hitler* is that it painstakingly *reprojects* a representation which a democratic century has condensed (as satanic) and displaced (as past), and so forces the spectator to admit it directly.

Like *Kings of the Road*, *Hitler* is thus a quest in its own right, a map of a people's motivating desires, the search for the beginnings of a paradise lost, and a journey through the mechanism that fulfilled those desires. It is a trial in the double sense of the word: as a Wagnerian encounter, it is a test of endurance in which the questor (the spectator and Syberberg's camera) faces repeated horrors and psychological obstacles which must be overcome; as a different Nuremberg, it is a cross-examination of the representation of Hitler itself ("a trial," says Andre Heller as the narrator in the opening sequence, which "has never in effect taken place"). Certainly more than a musical background, Wagner's *Ring* becomes the closest approximation for this four-part quest, which begins with an image of Ludwig's lost paradise below the title "The Grail" (successively in German, French, and English). In this first section, a beginning, metaphorically embodied in the puppet of Ludwig carried by a young girl, is introduced as a question linked to the burned body of Goebbels that lies on the table at the end of the sequence, a question that is both historical and psychoanalytic, a question in which the past and the present interrogate each other, and a question in which Hollywood has a significant role:

> Where does it all begin? Money, business, invitations to parties, ideology, careers, opportunism. . . . Where does it begin? And who can be said to be free of the plague: the culpability in respect to art? When McCarthy bribed witnesses and extorted confessions, how many Jews in Hollywood decided to collaborate? And it was no longer a question of Hitler before whom they fled to save their lives. The stakes were no longer lives but jobs in Hollywood. This same Hollywood that made so many anti-fascist films. Was it then for the money, this hatred of Hitler in books, films, and journals? . . . More capital extorted and more work in hell. . . . And at the end of our days and our path, what does one say? How to make oneself understood by a Ludwig, how to explain to him our distress and what it has engendered, to him who crossed the Wagnerian fire for art and power?

Part 2, "A German Dream," next introduces Karl May and the Germany of the twenties into the context of these opening inquiries. Amidst the sights and sounds of the Nazi rise, the popular vision of May and the paradise lost of Ludwig become transformed into a mass dream of a cheapened paradise regained, populated with ice-age giants. Before the Wahnfried House in Bayreuth and the prelude to *Lohengrin*, the Führer arises to bring, in the cosmologist's words, "the golden age, paradise saved from the flood by the force of man and his concentration on the essential: punishments and ceremonies, the German dream of death opening on a new life." In "The End of a Winter's Tale," part 3, the extermination of the Jews then becomes the logical extension of the quest, which, like the frontier of May's American Indians, must accept "the curse of greatness that its path is strewn with corpses." In a parody of the interrogation of the accused, Himmler's masseur assuages the conscience of this Grand Inquisitor; and, as before, the quest into and questioning of the past returns on the present, the Hitler-in-Us: "Germany of the Third Reich," claims the Hitler marionette, "was only the prologue" to a world which would succeed it with an endless list of dictators and atrocities from Idi Amin and Vietnam to the PLO terrorists and the Russian mental institutions. Last, "We Children of Hell" follows this German dream as nightmare into the postwar present where Hitler remains alive in the trivialization of the spirit, "the reign of true popular taste." Hitler as questor becomes the film hero as politician, "Siegfried, grand amateur of Westerns"; the dark twists of a world's bad conscience universally acquit Hitler through new democratic fantasies and touristic desires in which "free commerce is the liberty of democracy'' and politics is supposedly replaced by ''leisure time, distractions, show business and the cinema of tourism.''

Thematically, *Hitler* thus comes full circle: the quest toward a historical source found in the Disneyland castles of Ludwig reappears in the Disneyland imagination of a Hollywood culture; the trial of a demagogue dramatically reverses the direction of the accusing eye, so that the juror/audience is likewise indicted in the questioning. As Baer requests at the opening, Hitler is given a chance, since this is a maieutic inquiry in which what really stands trial is the projection of Hitler and the mechanism behind that projection, the democratic audience that regards him. An essentially deflected interrogation, the questions which the film asks its historical subject (Hitler) double back repeatedly and sharply on the spectator as the actual and more pertinent filmic subject: Hitler-Us, that impossible exchange of looks which is the film's circuit, mediated by a narrator who rarely matches eye-lines with either party.[35]

In brief, *Hitler* becomes an investigation of the constitution of the twentieth-century subject as a projection of its worst desires, a trial of cinematic representation itself in its role as technological mindscreen for the modern age and vehicle for its Romantic quest.[36] In Syberberg's words, ''the fundamental question is the debate over democracy: how a Hitler can be democratically elected to power and how democratically one can stop a Hitler.''[37] The answer however is less easy, since the medium for the debate and debaters themselves is fundamentally democratic, and hence this medium is the very object being tried. As used by Hitler, cinematic representation has become at best impoverished and usually criminal, and having the accused testify against itself without using the tactics of the accused demands strategies for communication as iconoclastic as they are tentative. ''How does one seize him, present him in our time with old images?'' begins Heller in the opening monologue of a film about ''the medium who hypnotized the masses.'' For, what is at stake is nothing less than the possibility of a filmic communication and the future of cinematic discourse, a discourse whose value and authenticity have been brutally exploited by its past and a discourse which can only be resurrected by confronting the continuing presence of that past with the forms and material that empower it. A documentation of history like no other, *Hitler* becomes a psycho-social quest located in the perception of history's audience, a counter-projection onto the screen of history, where the trial gradually takes the form of an exorcism.

Unequivocally, therefore, the quest and the trial of *Hitler* concern the cinema and the spectatorial subject of that cinema. As Syberberg points out, ''film is the most important art form that the democratic twentieth century has produced. It is the darling of the age of masses, an age which has been both reviled and heralded as progressive.'' And, as the antenna of a race and its era, film ''should register a few things about the condition of the general will of a country and its current situation.''[38] For Syberberg, what this art form has registered is clearly the perversion of irrational desires in the climactic form of a single figure; what the inquiry of his film sets out to accomplish is the retrieval and banishment of that figure *as cinematic representation*. As Yann Lardeau puts it, the film ''conducts its attack exclusively at the *representation* of Hitler such as it has put itself in place and such as this scenography has historically mobilized the masses—and not his physical presence. . . . Through a new projection, only cinematographic and concerning only images," Syberberg proposes "to unmake the *image* of Hitler, to disclose the fundamental *void* of the Nazi projection of the masses: the *absent* body of Hitler."[39]

"My thesis," says Syberberg, "is in effect that Hitler made an art, and at its base he organized the entire war like a consequence of the fact that he had already begun the spectacle, let's say, with Leni Riefenstahl, with *Olympia*, and after that it was necessary to make a war in order to be able to watch it each evening as newsreels."[40] Continually bordering on a precarious aestheticization of politics here and in the film itself, Syberberg would argue that this conjunction is finally the only way to understand an individual and a social phenomenon which are inseparable from the industrialization of an artistic impulse: the physical reality of Hitler was that of a petty bourgeois and failed architect; only the representational projection of him can account for the power and scale of his political presence. As a tension throughout *Hitler*, these two dimensions confront each other most specifically and clearly through the person of Ellerkamp, Hitler's projectionist and sometimes servant, who describes the cinephile passion of this common man, for whom the projector becomes the instrument and reflection of his status as an imaginary force:[41]

> I am the man who knew Hitler's most secret wishes, his dreams, what he wanted beyond the real world. Everyday two or three films: *Broadway Melody* with Fred Astaire, *Snow White* . . . Fritz Lang's *Nibelungen*. . . . Yes, whoever controls films, controls the future, controls the world and there is only one future, the future of film and he knew it. . . . I know that he really was the greatest, the greatest filmmaker of all time. . . . Again and again, six to eight times in a row he would watch films in order to burn into his memory every frame and every angle. And then I saw him bring the whole thing to a halt at the beginning of the war, no longer looking at feature films but only at newsreels alone with himself, . . . a war made on film exclusively for him.

Yet, while Hitler may be the director of this film, the democratic audience of this demonic screen has been the force which originally put the film of Hitler in place as a viable commodity and which has kept it there ever since as a repressed image of its complicity.[42] As a product of a spectatorial exchange, Hitler's image, film, and war are, that is, equally the product of the audience that regards them, and, in this crucial sense, each of them becomes a function of the psycho-cultural repression that motivates that vision: on the one hand, this repression can be described in terms of the many historical referents that lead through the Weimar Republic;[43] yet, more pertinent to Syberberg's notion of Hitler as a cinematic repression, this repression becomes specifically identified with the figure of the castrated phallus that a psychoanalytic semiology locates as the veiled motivation of the spectator's voyeuristic relation to the cinematic image. "If any historic explosion *proves* the fact of the sexual unconscious," Philippe Sollers has remarked, "it is Fascism. It does so at every level of reality, in its very way of producing, or reproducing, of destroying, of identifying, of representing itself."[44]

Behind Hitler as fascistic representation, in other words, stands the psychoana-

"The displaced dialogue with history" (*Hitler*).

lytic image of the castrated phallus seen before in Wenders's *Kings of the Road*, an image repressed and maintained through this century as a continual displacement of the lack it represents and the anxiety it generates. Underlying the entire argument of Syberberg's film, this image is indexed most notably in the film with the frontal-nude shot of a mother figure partially draped with judge's robes and holding a scale in which two castrated penises balance with three blonde heads of dolls: a dense condensation of how a terrible artificial beauty is born from the archetypal denial that is the operation of the Law, a law of repression here exposed as the process by which the severed heads of beauty (female and filmic) become a function of the severed phallus. Just as Hitler as representation has been put in place by this psycho-political repression, moreover, the demonic representation has been maintained in its turn through history by this same model of repression held in place by Syberberg's hypothetical audience: in modern Germany, particularly, the denial of Hitler's representational presence has been the main support of its strained self-image (cinematic and cultural) and the source of the absence which Wenders, among others, unveils.

To banish the presence of this image as denial means first retrieving it at its origin, its historical mirror stage. The repressed presence permeating the vast majority of commercial films since 1945, Hitler is additionally the product of film history before that time, and the trial which is *Hitler* accordingly becomes a recalling or summoning of the past behind the projection of Hitler's image. In this regard, the stage setting of Syberberg's film is an aesthetic necessity (and not merely an economic one) since this setting becomes the investigatory scene on which the history of the cinematic medium can be properly examined through a dramatic limiting of its tendency to disguise itself and its powers as a signifying practice. The pull of the imaginary, which is film's special province, remains solidly balanced here by the obtrusive symbolic operation that takes place on a stage where the imaginary is markedly reframed and the perceptual experience dislocated.[45] In this way, *Hitler* examines the historical formation of cinema's dark identity as an explicitly symbolic movement.

Here one of the most important and ubiquitous objects on Syberberg's stage is Edison's Black Maria, the symbolic origin of cinema's projections. Like most of the objects and figures that appear in the film, this original studio takes a variety of shapes and sizes: (1) as a large replica in the corner of the stage from which the actors appear and into which they disappear; (2) as a toy model; (3) as an even smaller version inside a snowy glass ball; and (4) as a large photograph of that glass ball. These various reproductions of the studio emphasize most obviously the usually disguised materiality and relative scale of a representational medium whose birth was this very studio; in a similar manner the large replica in the corner of the stage becomes the metaphorically visible source for both the actors and their scenarios (presented so unmistakably as written texts). Yet perhaps the most penetrating use made of this primitive studio and laboratory is its inclusion within the snowy globe which explicitly recalls *Citizen Kane*, the story of a tyrant who attempts to build an empire and a self-image on the fantasies of a plebiscite. In *Citizen Kane*, this globe represents the lost world of a child's imaginary, a loss which drives the adult through an endless series of grandiose replacement images; placed literally within this context, Edison's Black Maria thus becomes in its turn the symbol of a culture's lost imaginary, an origin that this culture sought to recover and fulfill through a history of images that culminate in Hitler.

As a trial that recalls and summons, *Hitler* moves (with intentional disregard for chronology) from this beginning in the Black Maria (into which Baer carries the Ludwig marionette at the start of the film) through the various manifestations and displacements that cinematic history produced in its trek toward its Hitler film: the "archetypal pictures" of August Sanders's photographic democracy, a blown-up cut-out of Eric von Stroheim in Hollywood, an enlargement of Méliès's fantastic moon, a re-creation of Peter Lorre's accusatory plea at the end of *M*, and of course *Caligari*. These and many others appear as blatantly abstracted representations whose form as figures of representation is precisely what makes them crucial testimonies in the inquiry. For, as part of a maieutic trial, the audience/jurors must view and relocate a dislocated past not as some sort of factual evidence but as the movement of a dark imagination through which they as spectators are in complicity with the forms of cinematic representation they now regard: their position as viewers makes them participants in the representations they must now judge as part of a film history they have refused to mourn.

Following this logic, the dialectic of this film/trial is not a montage of opposition through which the encasing representation takes control of the debate but an extraordinarily calm dialectic between the cinematic representation displayed and a measurement or assessment of it. Both Baer and Keller's quietly questioning voices establish the tone for this dialectic; as the multiple layers and figures of the film appear, this narrator acts, in both senses, as a simple *reflection* on the *material* presence of the various representations. Surrounded by mannequins, photographs, and replicas of all shapes and sizes, these actors patiently and imperturbably describe the representational significance of the figures as a way of assessing them. For the spectator, moreover, the disjunction that results between the representation and the assessment becomes the heart of the film as it seizes the exposed materiality of representations in the context of their historical and imaginative significance. Most generally, this disjunctive dialectic appears in the inordinately long monologues which are ironically placed amidst a sea of artifacts and images that mutely resist the queries put to them. In Baer's several tête-à-tête confrontations with the Hitler marionette, for instances, he indeed *seizes* the diminutive figure as the material of fascination, yet the spate of tentative words never seems to designate the force (and hence the significance) that the figure represents. At the end of part 3, Baer sits at a table and speaks with the Hitler marionette, changing its costume repeatedly through the conversation; ''Götterdämmerung'' plays in the background and a replica of Goethe's tree stands on the table before them. After Baer (speaking through the marionette) recites a litany of fascist atrocities past and present, he (resuming his voice as Koberwitz) reflects, ''thus spoke the devil. Cynic or moralist? Or, on the contrary, very human? The Grand Inquisitor living in the world today. . . . His heritage received for a long time, under the most diverse forms.'' But the marionette responds, ''forms so banal that they are born neither of god nor the devil. Long live mediocrity. . . . Thus spoke the cynic, and he is always right.'' As the light grows blindingly bright, the camera moves in on the tightly closed eyes of Baer and so acts almost as a correlative for the impossible rift in this scene between the visual representation of Hitler and the words that signify him, between the forms so materially banal and an assessment of the historical consequences.

These disjunctions and dissimilarities pervade the film, of course, and, outside the narrator's voice, there are two other important ways this dialectic functions. First, there are the staged representations and images themselves, which, as mentioned, continually disturb the stability of their own meaning as they are constantly reformulated in different sizes and material. Second, the film itself uses the materiality of *its* medium to manipulate disjointedly a pastiche of representational realities as a montage of signifiers (visual and aural) which create a dense yet ruptured pattern across the textual surface of the film. In each of these cases, Syberberg's frontal projection plays a crucial role since it dislocates cinematic space as at least two representationally disconnected realities in which the material presence of the one never subdues the other (as would happen with rear projection).[46] As these various disjunctions become part of the linear movement of the text, moreover, the material montage within the sequences establishes a pattern of development which always remains on the extreme fringes of narrative. In the film's first real sequence, for instance, Amelia Syberberg, the child-mourner who walks through the film as a kind of leitmotif, plays amidst a pile of dolls, including a stuffed dog with Hitler's face. She next appears on a platform holding the dog while a Hitler marionette swings from a gallows beside her, various other symbolic figures clutter the background, and the equipment of the film-stage (lighting, beams, etc.) remains conspicuously visible on the edges of the frame. Before a detail from Blake's "Europe, A Prophecy" projected on the back screen, she then carries the dog to another set of gallows, where a dark mannequin hangs. Finally she arrives amongst disproportionate figures from various Expressionist films and places the Hitler dog in a crib. During this sequence, the narrator's voice-over description naturally reinforces the poetic unity of these strange and disparate settings through which the child-mourner wanders. Yet that material and symbolic disparity of the scenes is meant explicitly to counterpoint and rupture that unity as a *representational* disjunction on levels from the engraved visions of Blake's cosmology to the cinematic chiaroscuro of Dr. Mabuse and ultimately to Syberberg's staged wake itself. As the girl stands before the crib awaiting the birth of Hitler amongst those figures of the dead, a final material representation enters the scene in the form of a documentary recording of a 1932 Hitler speech ("I have a project in mind"). A voice-off then shouts "silence"; the title of the film begins to appear for the first time; Heller's own voice whispers how the world ends "by consuming itself"; and Heinz Schubert lights up in center stage as a ringmaster prepared to begin this film as trial, as circus, and ultimately as wake. An exact overture to *Hitler*, this last sequence orchestrates diverse and disjunctive materials precisely in the manner of a circus of representations in which there is no more attempt to synthesize their material realities than there is to unify the simultaneous dance of clowns, fierce animals, and fantastic costumes in a circus.[47]

In this disjunction between diverse images and materials, the figure of the child-mourner who reappears in various guises or contexts acts as a kind of interpretive center for the myriad of forms around her. Like the narrator Koberwitz, she opens a space between the excessive materiality of the representations and their possible meaning; like the various actors, she appears purposely nonconfrontational and ultimately serves only to locate a disjointed place for the spectator in which he or she can both reflect and be reflected, participate in the trial as both judge and accused. This figure acts as the center for "a montage within the cinematographic means of irrationalism" whereby "everything is presented" and "the decision is up to the spectator."[48] And in the overture specifically, what becomes clear through this figure is that this space is the place of mourning, a trial in which the summoning of the representations of Hitler, those repressed images of history, necessarily becomes a wake for the death of cinema and its traditional representations.

A quest, a trial, a wake: *Hitler* is a summoning of cinema's dead, a new Nuremberg whose model is the Nuremberg of Dürer, where melancholy marks the felix culpa of the fall from grace. Yet, the film, as Syberberg puts it, is "more than the work of mourning . . . it is the art of mourning."[49] Like Dürer's print, *Hitler* aims specifically at a liberation from the binds of melancholy through an artistic exorcism of the repressed figures that shackle the consciousness in melancholy, an exorcism that would release the spectator toward a new cinema.

The child-mourner of the film's overture is of course only one of several references to the Dürer engraving, which, as Lardeau remarks, produces "a curious torsion whereby the categories of God, Man, and the Devil involve one in the other and absorb each other reciprocally."[50] As I have suggested, the film creates this same sort of twisting action whereby the spectator becomes absorbed into the diabolical outcome of Hitler's desire to become a filmic god: as the viewer of the spectacle, the audience becomes part of Hitler's deistic and cinematic holocaust, bound together through an imaginary signifier and sharing the body of Hitler as repressed representation of the past. Melancholy indicates the persistence of that body buried in the imaginary, and only through an exorcistic mourning which calls up its representational projection along the imaginary circuit of its presence can the viewer escape its haunting: "Even if the historical person is dead, he becomes a metaphor within historical reality. . . . I have transformed Hitler into a legend, into a mythological figure in order to be able to seize, to have power over him and also the power to destroy him. This is a historically negative figure transformed into a negative myth, into a legend, and this is what permits me to destroy him."[51]

The strategy for this exorcism is descriptively easy: to evacuate the body of Hitler of its representational forms and thus to expose the void of its presence. No doubt the film's most celebrated example of this argument is the shot of Schubert as Hitler wrapped in a toga and rising from the grave of Richard Wagner: connecting Hitler's democratic and Romantic roots, the shot literally calls back from the dead that most glorified iconographic pose by which Hitler is known. That Schubert, the famous comic actor from *Strongman Ferdinand*, is at the center of this imagistic séance entirely dislocates, however, the usual value of these iconographic gestures and dramatically divides the representation from the equally evident body of the actor. The recollected representation of the dead Hitler becomes simply that, a collection of icons and imagistic indices kept alive by history's audience and not as a historical substance.

This cinematic exorcism of Hitler's projected body is clearly the main motif of the film. The constant alteration of his form, shape, and size—as a marionette, giant image, actor, stuffed dog, mannequin—all work ironically and humorously to define his presence precisely as a representational figure *without an actual body* and hence dismissable. Just as the actors play several and mutual roles to call attention to this disjunction between a physical reality and the fiction they must present and be controlled by, Hitler and the nightmarish film he created out of history are continually recalled from their grave in a historical unconscious in order that they present themselves as representations and projections whose power derives only from their position as repressions in the imaginary. As Baer interrogates the marionette, Hitler's most telling response is thus not his bombastic words but that his costume is repeatedly changed. It is surely significant that the only Nazi body to be physically represented in the film is Himmler's (Schubert's): his fat and sweating physique rolls grotesquely in the hands of his masseur while he explains his buddhistic notions of spirituality and the necessary extermination of so many bodies that interfere with racial purity. During this sequence, Himmler's strained face and ungainly form are repeatedly counterpointed by giant documentary photos of naked Jewish victims projected on the back screen before a physically dwarfed Peter Kern in an SS uniform. These and other sequences make it clear that Nazi representation as an imaginary signifier has been maintained specifically through the denial and repression of the physical body (even to the extent of exterminating it). What Syberberg's film accomplishes, moreover, is a recalling of the signifiers of the imaginary body that has resulted from this repression in order to reveal the vacuity of its presence and the at once ludicrous and horrific impossibility of subjugating the corporeal to an imaginary representation.

The most remarkable sequence in this effort is the testimony of Krause, Hitler's other valet, which takes place midway through the second part. Like the first valet, Ellerkamp, Krause (Hellmut Lange) has special access to the machinery behind Hitler's image, and, like Ellerkamp, he dwells partially on Hitler's fascination with and use of the cinematic apparatus. Krause's chief concern, however, is with the actual physical details and quotidian formulas by which the man lived and represented himself: the clothes he wore, his dining habits, and his physical idiosyncrasies. Not surprisingly, Krause's long monologue is insufferably banal and painstaking: ''In the twenty-two or twenty-three minutes which would pass since his waking, Hitler took his bath, shaved, and dressed. He rang for breakfast only as he put on his jacket. At whatever hour he awoke, he spent invariably twenty-two minutes getting ready. Yes, Hitler always shaved himself. To do this he used two razors: one for the first shave, and another for the second. The blade of each razor was changed daily, so that in total Hitler used two blades per day.'' While delivering this very long monologue, Krause *figuratively* walks through the vast halls and rooms projected on the back of the stage, and, as the image changes, the proportions of the rooms and their objects (books, chairs, etc.) repeatedly establish different and strange disproportions in relation to the body of Krause/Lange as he recounts the daily events within these rooms. Somewhat like Koberwitz's dialectical conversations with the marionette, the valet attempts to locate the actual body of Hitler through a minute and pedestrian description of that body's functions, to reduce Hitler's imaginary body to its physical actuality. What appears within this framework, however, is only the body as a representational void that eludes physical detail, a dramatic absence like the frontal projection which overwhelms the valet with its spaces of giant emptiness. Between the dictator who dressed his body clumsily and without taste and the Goliathan image that subdued history, in other words, there is a corporeal void.

The cardboard figures like Wiene's Cesare and Murnau's Nosferatu that punctuate the film are consequently more than simply references to a psychological sociology: like Hitler, they are figuratively and literally the living dead and phantom bodies who continue to survive as cinematic representations and imaginary signifiers without substance or body. To summon these phantoms for testimony and exorcism is then to summon the imaginary body of the cinema itself so that it becomes a material absence that can be seen, grasped, and confronted; to recall Hitler for exorcism is fundamentally to make his cinematic presence as an imaginary signifier a physical and material signifier which empties the original sign of its power as a repressed presence: the place of this operation is naturally a stage whose conspicuous and empty spaces are spread with material relics and bordered by the tools of representation.

In this cinematic exorcism, Syberberg's precedents are Chaplin and Lubitsch, and the references to *The Great Dictator* and *To Be or Not to Be* are certainly intended as homages to these early attacks on the fascist body as representation. Yet, as Syberberg notes, for him these earlier films are too much a part of Hollywood's commercial discourse and its tradition: in *Hitler* he would ''integrate them into a system that would function otherwise, . . . would create a distance in relation to heros such as Hitler and Himmler'' by going ''beyond the conventions'' of the boulevard cinemas.[52] Syberberg would exorcise, that is, not just the fascistic body as a representational structure but the complete structure of the cinematic image used in all classical-fiction films, since it is this image whose spectatorial relation, no matter what the content, has traditionally disguised the material absence behind the dictatorial projection of the apparatus. The excess of the film's running time (seven hours) and the excess of signifiers from such an incredible variety of sources are an attempt to defuse and sometimes deride the very history of this cinematic signification by exposing the full scope of the fascistic projection: exorcism must be a calling out of *all* names in order that the phantom presence finds refuge in none.[53] As the body of the filmic image works through a democracy of vision to generate the figure of Hitler, so too does the body of that image maintain that figure's presence as the repressed structure of scopic desire, the Hitler-in-Us. For Syberberg, consequently, the entire body of the image must be recalled and dismissed *from the inside* of filmic perception itself, at the center of spectatorial fascination where the filmic dialogue itself has been replaced by an absence.

How an exorcism of fascination in fact works is best indicated by Syberberg's term *aufklärerische Trance*, an ''enlightening trance'' which unites Brecht and Wagner in that conjunction so central to Syberberg's aesthetic, a term which suggests the twofold movement of *Hitler*. On the one hand, Syberberg's efforts are directed quite specifically at the materialization of the absent body, a Brechtian exorcism that literally enlightens the void behind the image; on the other hand, the film consciously provokes a fascination or cinematic trance (in part like Herzog) by means of which it draws the spectator into what becomes an in-quest into imagistic fascination itself.

In this double movement, operatic discourse becomes the key underpinning, since it offers a model that both elicits that irrational fascination and challenges the conventional structures on which it is based. As Catherine Clement has remarked in an exceptional essay titled ''Le rire de Déméter,'' operatic discourse provokes a fascination primarily by exposing, through the person of the woman and her song, the unseeable, repressed expression or object. ''In opera,'' Clement says, ''the voice gives itself up to a measured excess'' which ''produces the myth of the singer's death.'' This apocalyptic combination of word and music, she says, moves from a cultural *Heimlich* to Schelling's *Unheimlich*, and, in doing so, involves the viewer/voyeur in an irrational violation of Law, spatial order, and conventional discourse:

"the euclidean space" which situates the listener (viewer) "is thus perturbed, displaced at its center," and just as one is whirled around space when dizzy through the emotion of the song, certain landmarks disappear, "creating the effect of nonsense."[54]

A miming of Wagner,[55] *Hitler* approximates this same action, I suggest, on one important level: it unveils that repressed and unsayable figure of history (specifically related to the exposed and castrating woman); in doing this, it creates mammoth dislocations in space, scale, and euclidean representation itself as a fantastic and mesmerizing dream meant to entrance the spectator. As in both hypnotism and exorcism, repetition combines here with excess to elicit this fascination, as the multiplicity of material signifiers—on the stage, the soundtrack, and the frontal projection screen—generates a mounting dizziness which truly engulfs the spectator in its amazing in-quest. "The entire film," Syberberg remarks, "is a child's world of puppets and dolls, full of stars and music, the material of a child's huge nightmare, such as has never been dreamt, tormenting and bright. A montage with the cinematic devices of the irrational."[56]

Schubert's first appearance as ringmaster is exemplary in this regard: he stands as a glowing object in the center of the frame, a hypnotic master of fascination surrounded by images of death and objects of entertainment; the large megaphone which he turns on the universe and the audience becomes a metaphorical hole in space into which the projection of the film draws the audience's vision as if toward a dark vanishing point. In this film, he announces, it "is a question of the projection of the divine into the human, . . . a question of adventures in the head and their bloody passage into reality. Mephisto before a full house which burns." More specifically, what this film projects is the representational reality of a repressed darkness, a demonic angel, that is in every sense the exhibition of an excess and the source of the film's fiery and hypnotic attraction. "I wonder," Syberberg writes, "how it is possible, for example in San Francisco, that a room of 1,000 spectators is able to follow, for seven hours, a film which has no story in the classical sense of the term, and which creates no tension, no suspense, which provokes no joy. There are other laws which keep these people in the room."[57] These are the dark laws of opera, into which one stares as into a fire.

The projection of excess as an exorcism of the repressed dead thus becomes the operatic space of fascination in which *Hitler* works. Yet this trance is likewise an enlightenment, since, within that space, the film works concomitantly to expel the spectator from the circuit of its dream: while the exorcistic rite itself and the repressed cinematic figure of Hitler are what attract and hold the audience, *Hitler* aims, somewhat paradoxically, to exorcise precisely that mesmerizing structure of cinematic representation, so that the unilateral power of the image on the screen would give way to a counter-projection from the audience. If the figure of Hitler is indeed the Hitler-in-Us, the film attempts to exorcise, *from the inside*, the circuit of that exchange, to call out the Hitler "in Us," and to relegate him to the status of Hitler as material representation on the screen. Ideally, there are then two overlapping circuits of projection, one which originates in the traditional cinematic apparatus and one which originates with the spectator; it is this second from which Hitler must be exorcised by locating him solidly within the first *strictly as the material* of fascination.

Syberberg's enlightening trance is subsequently not a trance which enlightens something or someone but an enlightening of the trance itself through an interrogation of or in-quest into its circulation. Whereas this trance works primarily through repetition and the exhibition of excess, the enlightenment is obviously a product of the reduction of the representation to a materiality and kind of banality: this is the horror of the banal, the physicality of the body apparent throughout the film but especially in the postwar tourist sequence. Transformed and translated into a blend of kitsch, soap opera, and touristic relics throughout the film, the representation of Hitler consequently becomes an exchange based in a kind of laughter which, in effect, negates the imaginary body of Hitler by calling it out of the spectatorial consciousness as a material or symbolic body—distanced, silly, and trivialized. Since two symbolic bodies cannot share the same space, laughter removes Hitler's to the material screen and allows the viewer the vacant relief of his departure, the laughter fully exorcising the body of Hitler from the perceptual body of the spectator. While the fascination of the operatic song relates specifically to the scream rendered tolerable, laughter therefore engages the same psychoanalytic circuit and renders it insignificant.[58] While the excess of signifiers hypnotically recalls the repressed presence of Hitler, the trivialization of these signifiers as material signs expels with finality his diabolical status (as ruler in hell) from its place in the viewer's unconscious.

At the conclusion of *Hitler*, therefore, melancholy returns transformed. The child-mourner reappears draped in celluloid and dressed in the black cape of the film's beginning. She throws off the cape, however, to reveal a white dress, discards the celluloid, and retrieves the Hitler dog with which she opened the wake. Before her stands an enlarged model of Ledoux's *Coup d'oeil du théâtre de Besançon*, in the pupil of which is Kane's snowy globe containing the Black Maria. Moments earlier, moreover, Heller likewise recalls his opening monologue delivered before the life-sized replica of Edison's studio: opening the film, he muses on "the extension of myself into the universe of montage, fragments of an interior projection, memories of an ancient world in the black studio of our imagination." Now he retrieves those words before an interiorized studio: "this black mother of our imagination and of the last stories of the stars of cinema, the Black Maria. . . . Such as we are, and all our projections, memories, and dreams, from the epoch of Light." The inquest into the demonic image and its projection onto modern history thus returns to a large extent on itself, and the circuit of filmic signification binds itself like the loop film in *Kings of the Road*, back into its own circulation. The blocked letters of "The Grail" resurface in the very last frames of the film, and the quest is completed as a circular inscription closed in on its own materiality. The cinematic circle that Wenders so convincingly opened is thus closed again but here as a material body to which the exorcised image of Hitler has been exiled: his presence as an imaginary signifier becomes inscribed and locked into the material of fascination, and this material can only call attention to his actual absence. For Syberberg, the cinema of Hitler and the boulevards is dead, killed not by an external dismantlement (as is Wenders's way) but by an internal exorcism of projection and fascination that frees the spectator from the circuit of traditional projection as it is inscribed in the circle of its own material, on its separate screen. The trial of *Hitler* is finally an admission, its wake, a wake for itself.

The return is then a ritualized return only. For through this return, *Hitler* in fact measures the displacement of the filmic subject/spectator to a new distance and the exorcism of a repressed memory which has been called up and out from its phantom existence in the perceptual and cinematic unconscious of the spectator. The child-mourner's rejection of her celluloid crown of thorns and black cape signals the spectator's release from a half-century of nightmarish memory kept alive through the structural complicity of the cinematic image. Like the fallen angel of Dürer, the girl's glance looks down and away at the underworld from which she now returns. Tossing the Hitler dog aside, she then retrieves it to carry it like a corpse into Ledoux's theater of the eye, where new projections and myths can begin at a new source. While the camera moves closer, the glass ball of Kane and Edison gradually becomes a dropping tear amidst the landscapes of Ludwig; in that tear the child appears at first praying, then directing a look directly at the audience, and finally closing her eyes and covering her ears. Strains from *Tristan and Isolde* again mark the liberation from a memory ("Give me forgetfulness that I may live"); and, like the girl's last gestures in the mind's eye, Syberberg's own words end the film within the black spectatorial void left by the exorcism of the old cinematic body: this is indeed a call to the viewer for "a projection into the black hole of the future."

As the film absorbs itself, what remains for the spectator is a cinematic void, a black hole into which must go counter-projections that will create the history of the future and its new myths. Unfortunately for Syberberg, the price of this exorcism, of revealing the denied, has been, especially in regard to the German audiences of Hollywood cinema, an excommunication from conventional circuits that matches the extremity of his communication of these circuits. Countering the projection of Hitler, Syberberg has indeed dislocated his spectator as no other German director has done, creating a film most spectators have truly not learned to see and leaving only his flamboyant signature to mark the subsequent void. With *Hitler* nostalgia dies, and with it the ease and comfort of having images and memories, projected from outside the mind, control the individual imagination. In the disturbingly dark and empty space that remains, the past film of the democratic masses must become the counter-projections of imaginative individuals: the passivity of a cinematic memory must give way to the difficult task of a varied and active cinematic future.

"Other selves in a drama of images" (*Willow Springs*).

TEN

Schroeter's *Willow Springs* and the Excesses of History

Ought we not to remind ourselves—we who
believe ourselves bound to finitude which belongs
only to us, and which opens up the truth of the
world to us by means of our cognition—ought we
not to remind ourselves that we are bound to the
back of a tiger?
>   —Michel Foucault

With the sort of irony common to the world of
production and distribution, the same factor that
has made this cycle of Schroeter films [*Salome*,
The Death of Maria Malibran, *Willow Springs*]
available here at this time has also rendered them
historical.
>   —B. Ruby Rich (1980)

Inspiring father and prodigal son, Werner Schroeter has been the unresolved paradox at the heart of the New German Cinema. While one of the defining marks of this celebrated new wave from Germany has been the coherency with which its family of filmmakers has addressed movie markets at home and abroad, Schroeter has drifted (passionately, perversely, and insouciantly) in and out of that community of *Wünderkinder* as they developed in the last twenty years into adult entrepreneurs. Indeed, what has united these new German filmmakers through the years has been, as I have been arguing, an engagement with the cultural and cinematic history that contextualizes them. Anchored in the specter of a Nazi past and a postwar colonization by America and Hollywood, these films—from Wenders's nostalgic broodings about the United States to Schlöndorff's political parables about fascism through the ages—have consistently aimed at reexamining the meaning of history for themselves, their characters, and their audiences. Yet to describe Schroeter's films as part of the same family history would seem, especially to viewers acquainted with the earlier films, the most procrustean of academic exercises. Unlike many of his contemporaries, Schroeter and his films have usually appeared to eschew the reality of those historical events that have anchored Fassbinder's Maria Braun, Schlöndorff's Oskar, Wenders's Tom Ripley, or Kluge's Roswitha. Instead, Schroeter's operatic

"Death-mask of expression" (*Maria Malibran*).

characters have inhabited a kind of allegorical twilight where the excessively theatrical settings and elliptical narratives have made his work look more like experimental dreams of mythical times than like pictures of a known world. His recurrent themes of passionate love, erotic death, and *Leidenschaft* (commitment beyond restraints) have focused his films on exaggerated sufferings and stylized beauties ("the beauty of pain" says one of his characters) whose very definition seems to contradict most logics of history or the coherency of a social viewpoint through which an audience might be figured and addressed.

Unlike the work of experimental filmmakers, whose films his early cinema misleadingly resembles, Schroeter's films are, however, located clearly in a narrative tradition: the life of a renowned opera singer who battles for expression within a patriarchal order (*The Death of Maria Malibran*) or the tale of three women isolated in a California desert where they attempt to create an emotionally intense commune free of male interference (*Willow Springs*). Yet the presentations of these narrative histories then disjoin and overlap such a variety of perspectives and materials that most viewers find themselves either confused or fascinated by the presiding unreality of the events. Operatic sound tracks merge with pop tunes; characters strike long and outlandish campy poses in excessively theatrical costumes and makeup; extended silences and poetic overstatements ("life is very precious, even right now") describe the dialogue; the stories themselves often seem random pastiches that shift chaotically not only in time but in subject. If *Maria Malibran* focuses on a historical topic and personality, the historical contours of that topic become largely subverted in the more abstract question of a female creative will, described again and again through close-ups of various combinations of three women set against black back-drops. If *Willow Springs* clearly foreshadows Altman's *Three Women*, the remarkable resemblance of story lines is mostly superficial, since Schroeter's comparatively fragmented film moves the drama, for the most part, out of the desert reality and into the closed, mirrored, and artificial spaces of the house in which this psychic drama is bared and stripped of any distracting realism.

Schroeter's career can, in fact, be divided into two narrative phases. Until the 1978 production of *The Kingdom of Naples*, his films seemed exiled to the underground tradition of low-budget cinema, funded by television (specifically the artsy ZDF network); after 1978, Schroeter made a conscious effort to translate those original themes onto a more commercial and accessible level, into what he has called the more ''humane'' form of traditional narrative patterning. He insists, however, that the move from the more private and more difficult experiments to the more realistic and more public narratives has been mostly one of style, not vision, aimed at finding a larger audience, and that the ''hyperrealism'' of the recent films simply locates the psychodramas of the first films in the historical forms through which they are best communicated.[1] As a paradox and a problem, Schroeter and his film have consequently remained, at base, consistent: if he shares a modernist's critical concern with history and film narrative (as in the work of Godard or Oshima, for instance), his films have detoured that concern through opera, Romantic mysticism, and a gay sensibility through which camp and kitsch become the critical vehicles for self-conscious emotion.

The irony of this practice and Schroeter's place within contemporary German cinema is that he is one of its singularly most influential filmmakers. Moving among theater, opera, and film, he has been a major presence within the general aesthetic climate of Western Europe throughout the sixties and seventies. He has acted in Fassbinder's *Beware of a Holy Whore*; relentlessly pursued a now legendary obsession with Maria Callas; and in Syberberg's *Ludwig*, a narrator describes him as one of the truly revolutionary artists of our age. Seemingly always at the center of controversy, he and Rosa von Praunheim opened a loud, public, and important quarrel about a homosexual perspective in the cinema,[2] but despite his growing international status he has been conspicuously ignored by the New York Film Festival (and hence by most American distributors). His personal behavior has, moreover, preceded and confirmed the flamboyant and eccentric flavor of his films. Whether at Berkeley or the Cinémathèque Française (where Henri Langlois hailed him in 1970), Schroeter and the leathered entourage that follows him have descended in the theatrically outrageous fashion of his films. And his unusually intimate rapport with his actors, matching personalities with roles, has become as celebrated as the passionate relationships of his characters: the locations for his films (such as Naples or Sicily) are, apparently, a kind of home where he closely involves the community and his troupe in decisions about shooting and dialogue; his actors, most notably the striking Magdalena Montezuma and later Antonio Orlando, have followed Schroeter from film to film as the centers for his radically private families on and off the set.

With the 1978 release of *The Kingdom of Naples*, however, Fassbinder went public with this eccentric paradox and proclaimed, in a crucial article, that the best-kept secret of the New German Cinema was Werner Schroeter: "Germany has not only three or five or ten directors to offer," he says; "Germany has one who has certainly been absent." According to Fassbinder, there are few filmmakers who "had chances to make films who didn't borrow from Schroeter," including Daniel Schmid and Ulrike Ottinger, and many recent student films "are fundamentally experiments on Schroeter." While Fassbinder readily admits his own debt (best illustrated perhaps in closet dramas like *The Bitter Tears of Petra von Kant* or *Querelle*, which Schroeter at one time was supposed to direct), the most famous example of Schroeter's influence is Syberberg, whom Fassbinder calls a "merchant in plagiarism," "an extremely capable Schroeter imitator, who while Schroeter awaited recognition competently marketed what he took from Schroeter." Likewise, Herzog has frequently acknowledged the importance of Schroeter's films to his work, and a summary instance of the Schroeter paradox is doubtless the fact that most viewers might know his name and style only through the opera sequence that opens Herzog's blandly commercial *Fitzcarraldo*. Indeed, the separate fates that awaited Herzog and Schroeter after they both shocked audiences at the 1970 Cannes Festival (with *Even Dwarfs Started Small* and *Eika Katappa*) indicate, in Fassbinder's words, how, with singular injustice, Schroeter's films "acquired that very convenient underground label, which in a twinkling has made them into admittedly beautiful but exotic plants, flowering so far away that one basically couldn't deal with them."[3]

Even after *Palermo or Wolfsburg* won the prestigious Golden Bear at the 1980 Berlin Film Festival, Schroeter and his films have remained barely on the visible fringes of the cinematic family and historical movement that he, in many ways, helped to deliver. Or, to put this in broader terms: if a defining characteristic of many contemporary German directors has been their sensitivity and adjustment to their historical situation as filmmakers addressing an audience weaned on Hollywood cinema, Schroeter would seem to have chosen a detoured course in time; and what has made this course so distinctive and central to the project of the New German Cinema is that its starting point and constant focus has been precisely the individual's ability to live radically on history's edges, where both filmmaker and audience are forced to continually re-imagine themselves. For Schroeter and his films, history has become not so much a surrounding and determining predicament where the world and events are privileged so that they structure an individual's sense of self. Rather, for him history becomes a recurring moment, where time and place are an almost arbitrary stage on which the individual releases emotion, where one chooses to enter history from outside in order to perform oneself as a spectacle of time.

This radical notion of the subject's relation to history is best recognized perhaps in Schroeter's *Kingdom of Naples* (1978), fittingly one of the recent films that began to offer Schroeter public and historical recognition. Through its use of fairly traditional narrative formulas and its explicit dramatization of history as a succession of large purple dates on the screen, *Kingdom of Naples* pinpoints an overt argument about history through a biographical and surprisingly naturalistic account of the Pagano family living in Naples between 1943 and 1972, an account that the film furthermore places quite visibly in the larger context of Italian history (the resistance, the economic boom, etc.). A mimicking of family chronicles like Bertolucci's *1900*, the historical realism in this film is, however, repeatedly undercut by the inflated melodrama of exaggerated emotional response and the constructed settings of the stagy courtyard surrounded by apartments. Similarly, the direction and movement of this family or internal history becomes markedly different from what one would expect from a more neorealist film, since in *Kingdom of Naples* the relation of private history to public history develops as a kind of dance of death in which the private life moves primarily to escape entirely the public history, to stop it and abolish it as its source. The characters struggle relentlessly to escape their historical condition of poverty, and for each that escape can mean only death. Apartments open onto nothing but the sea; and, like the swelled red curtain in the film that reveals only a wall, only in their deaths are the characters able to affirm their lives and to color the moments of their personal histories, those moments of passionate excess that public history cannot accommodate or adequately express.

Significantly, in this drama of histories, Schroeter's female characters are the figures who resist history most effectively, quite literally freezing the passage of time into a statically wearied and timelessly wrinkled expression of mortality. Equally significant, moreover, this film of two histories takes place in Naples and begins about 1945: the country and time of cinema's most famous historical realism and the city that, in nineteenth-century opera and literature, became a celebrated location where history was ironically debunked and overturned, the place where historical "codes, genres, figures were converted into masks, unsettled, uncovered."[4] With a cinematic form that at least approaches historical realism and through the formal and narrative play between two kinds of history, in brief, *Kingdom of Naples* enacts a subtle and complex critique of historical reality as such or, more precisely, a critique of the classical representation of historical reality as it has traditionally been constructed for its film audiences. In this critique, *Kingdom of Naples* describes and focuses most crucially on a historical "instant," a temporal period extended across three decades as a rite of passage, when subjective history and public history cross not as an Althusserian articulation but as a seam between the relatively boundless capacity of individual need and the restrictions of historical possibility, the point where a carnivalesque indeterminacy borders the representation of official history. As a sort of summary episode, this potential moment on the edge of history crystallizes in the film when Rosaria is about to give birth to her first child: to the men waiting below, she passes before the window hailing this extended moment of pure potential as a victory over the public history and world that awaits her child: "It isn't born yet!" she triumphantly exclaims.

The heart of Schroeter's narratives is then this radical conception of a performative relation to that historical world that history has consecrated as stable. It is here that one can pinpoint two ideas that focus both the difficulty and importance of Schroeter's films: namely, the notion of an excess lost in a filmic performance and that of the cinematic subject made by this performance. The second of these has of course received a great deal of critical scrutiny lately, mainly because the Lacanian model of the subject, appropriated by Metz for the cinema, has proved at once to

"An aesthetic of excess" (*Maria Malibran*).

offer little understanding of sexual difference as performed by the cinema and to idealize the different positionings of the spectator/subject through the course of history. The first, however, is both more problematic and more central: for, whereas the critique of the cinematic subject has had the advantage of a relatively large vocabulary and literature, the idea and representation of excess (psychoanalytic, cinematic, historical, or otherwise) stumbles precisely on the rock of formulation or articulation.[5] In a sense crucial to Schroeter's aesthetic, a filmic excess—the violent murders that erupt across the narrative, the inexpressible emotions, the inordinately long takes, the multiple reflections within the frame that dizzy the perspective—becomes itself the fulcrum for that critique of the cinematic subject, becomes itself what dramatically and intentionally does not fit that desiring machine of filmic representation; and, as such, its meaning and force are precisely the associative or differential definitions on which it relies: lack, more than, overdetermination, outside, or, in a metaphor from Schroeter's *General Rehearsal*, that homeless place of the passionate soul.

Despite the problem of terminology and despite its Romantic connotations, excess as a filmic strategy in Schroeter's cinema is therefore more than a mystification and is instead a critical attempt to locate a textual subject/spectator or textual place for the viewer that would be quite different from that subject/spectator as it has been discussed in recent years (in terms of the specific way that dominant or classical cinema positions its audience). Rather than an inscription of the subject as a symbolic and historical production, Schroeter's cinema works to make a place for the spectator that would remain a place (unlike the displacement of strictly experimental film), but a place outside the confines of history and the strictures of the historical subject, a place where history is redefined finally by the excesses and possibilities that escape it, that place of undefined potential within which contemporary German cinema has constructed its acute and various dialogues with history.

A filmmaker whose demanding perspective has mapped an aesthetic territory (for two generations of German directors) that he has willfully moved in and out of, a young man crossing the geographical, temporal, and social bar between Palermo, Italy, and Wolfsburg, Germany, three women creating themselves out of a desert that stands in stark contrast to their personal passions: these are all then figures describing Schroeter's history as the stage awaiting the individual's emotional entry from its wings. Within this theatricalized process of history, it thus seems entirely fitting that a film as early as the 1973 *Willow Springs* depicts a narrative trajectory that could describe many of the films of the New German Cinema through the following decade and that, at the beginning of Schroeter's career, the self-conscious performance of that narrative history, somewhere near Hollywood, prefigures its own end as it enters history.

The story of *Willow Springs* neatly coincides with the story of its making. With television funds from ZDF, Schroeter set out for Los Angeles to make a film about Marilyn Monroe. There, however, "everything was too obvious," and instead he made *Willow Springs*, a film in which the specter of Marilyn Monroe (appearing in the film on a ratty calendar) might be considered part of a polemic involving that image as the epitome of a cinematic type. The film opens with a traveling shot of a road in the Mojave desert; a motorcyclist arrives at an isolated house and in English asks the woman at the door, "Do you live here alone?" The subsequent long shot of the exterior of the stucco hacienda records screaming from inside—presumably a violent rape but conceivably a sadomasochistic fantasy—and the following close-ups show a woman on the ground and then, after the man leaves, her weeping. Although the film later indicates that she becomes pregnant from the attack but loses the child, the narrative jumps ahead five years at this point to when three women live in the same house, apparently murdering men who pass along the way.

While *Willow Springs* may ostensibly be the story of three women secluded in the Mojave Desert, realistic distinctions quickly give way to a psycho-aesthetic drama in which it becomes increasingly difficult to tell whether the drama concerns three versions of one woman or three different women, each perhaps representing different dimensions of human creativity and subjectivity: Magdalena, the dominatrix; Ila, the dominated will; and Christine, beauty itself. The three are united in a precarious harmony that the stylized shots pervading the film construct themselves literally as a tense embrace with the exile, suffering, and beauty that the pose demands. "Life is like a wave" says one, "on which you float, taking care not to drown, but you die anyway. The only hope is within myself." After the opening attack, the evasive narrative describes three general movements: the women form a kind of cult of almost mystical passion, psychologically enclosed in and around each other, seducing and killing men; a thirteen-year-old boy Michael, who "has heard about this place," arrives, falls in love with Ila, and disturbs the intense singularity of the group; finally, responding to this threat, Magdalena shoots and kills Christine, Ila, and the boy and walks down the road, arms spread triumphantly. If the vague and elliptical story that follows can be characterized as the effort of a female will to recreate itself out of that original violence and domination (which just precedes the titles), the film image enacts the painful and perhaps doomed struggle to express images of beauty within and against the law and history of a repressive system of representation—a system in many ways like the one that generated and violated the figure of Marilyn Monroe. In the words of one of the women, Christine, "the beauty of Magdalena's face is the beauty of pain."

Around these operatic actions and excruciating emotions, both the exterior desert and the interior rooms glow with a surreal light and color that overwhelm the naturalistic setting and redefine this place as a strangely theatrical space. Inside, a darkened mirror bordered by a string of lights doubles all the characters and reflects faces and heads as if disembodied images. Characters drift and speak like ghosts trapped in an isolated haunted house, and the violence that frames the narrative becomes the poles in a slow movement from seclusion in a vampiristic dream outward to where desires are actualized in a public space. Gary Indiana has described a common theme in Schroeter's films this way: "the male is identified with society, law, power; the female represents the creative will. Sacrifice of the latter by the former is often a metaphor in Schroeter's seemingly frivolous imagery."[6] In *Willow Springs*, however, that pattern becomes the prelude to Magdalena's rebirth within the theatrics of her new perspective: in one important sense, she performs herself, in an act of excess and violence, out of a denaturalized interior and its tripartite sadomasochistic bonds, onto the theatrical potentials of the world beyond.

In this film, what is often a bit difficult to make out but is regularly indexed in the pastiche of cultural codes and historical references—such as the military photo of Michael's father, the use of German and English for the same piece of dialogue, the calendar with Marilyn Monroe's picture, the constant repeating of the Andrew Sisters' record of "Rum and Coca Cola"—is again that curious insistence on history (in its restrictive violence, of the father, as a stage) as a way of materially fixing and reducing the individual within time itself. Magdalena's passage into history marks specifically the formation of a symbolic or social self, but this new self is achieved in *Willow Springs* (and other Schroeter films) only with the conditional death of the more vital imaginary self of Ila. This figurative instant when one's personal story adapts the contours of Public Space and History is where the self is formed as memory, where the self is born into a determining memory; yet, for Schroeter, this birth of memory necessarily signifies the death of a kind of presence. Entering History is always a nostalgic farewell, such as the tattered poster of Cupid that hangs on the wall over the lovers in *Willow Springs*; entering History is always an exchange whose economics barter death as Rose is bartered to an American soldier in *Kingdom of Naples* (the prelude to her actual death). In Serge Daney's words, in Schroeter's films "There is the time of History and the time of biography, and between the two sometimes nothing."[7]

History in *Willow Springs* manifests itself primarily as a material and fabricated spectacle in which the individual must adopt a singular and limiting role, as a spatialization of time that is ultimately a spectacle of death. In the climactic section of *Willow Springs*, after Magdalena witnesses Ila and Michael making furious love, there is a close-up of Magdalena's face and then, in what is presumably a dream or a vision, a cut to her shooting the boy as he and Ila try to leave the house; she chases Ila to the car and kills her also. The next shot returns to the couple making love as the scratchy record ends; a shot of Magdalena and Christine doubly reflected in the darkened bar mirror precedes a long take of the tattered red Cupid poster. With no external logic to the cut, the next shots are of Magdalena fondling a gun, Ila cringing in recognition of what is about to happen, and, after the arrival of two sheriffs in police cars to ask "What do you girls do here," Magdalena reenacts, presumably this time in an actuality mediated by "the law," the same murder, filmed this time from a different angle. In these sequences Ila as a historical figure becomes a version of what Stephen Heath has described as a memory-spectacle whose very nature is to create, "in advance," the subject as a contextualized figure of the past, reified and reduced, like the poster of love on the wall, the action now shifted from the realm of imaginative desire to that of symbolic realism. The final cut is from the triangle of the three dead bodies in front of the house to the same scene emptied, as Magdalena leaves the house and walks down the road, arms spread. In effect, Magdalena thus destroys the triangular structure of her self-image put in place by male violence at the start of the film, a sadomasochistic and narcissistic image of desire and beauty whose destruction is also her release into the world.

History therefore again finds its course and expression as a performance, and specifically a performance based in desire: for Magdalena, this is not only a performance of her self but one in which the voyeuristic demands of desire direct the illusory and holistic emplacement of that memory-spectacle for her and the spectator. In *Willow Springs*, history for Schroeter's characters is not an independently propelled series of chronological events but rather a memory through which desire articulates itself mortally on the world, where history is always between quotation marks (like a scene repeated), indicating its remove and its nature as a productive instance. Put in terms of a recurrent metaphor in Schroeter's films, this meeting between the individual and time can be described spatially this way: as a window onto historical reality that invariably reflects back on the perceiving subject just as a mirror describes the plastic space where the subject fashions a temporal image of him- or herself. In one shot in *Willow Springs*, for instance, Christine sits on the left side of the frame with her back to a window that, because of the shadows and the dirt, appears like a mirror; Magdalena approaches in the reflection, while the camera zooms slowly in on the reflecting window to reveal, at the last moment, that the image of Magdalena does not approach Christine as a reflection but from the world outside and behind Christine. Just as Magdalena in this film represents what Christine calls "the beauty of pain," here her image plays confusedly on a representational edge that merges the reality of the figure and the image of that figure, that concomitantly reveals an intimacy of recognition and a blindness connected with a threatening distance. Like the performance of history itself, this mirror as a window

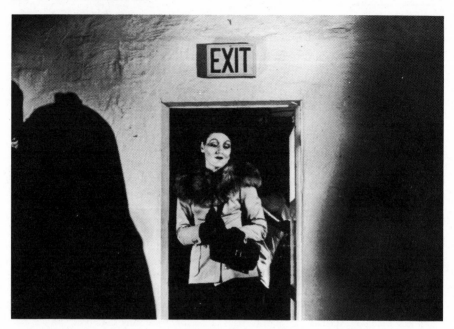

"Entrances as Exits on the stage of history" (*Willow Springs*).

that contains Magdalena dramatizes the two sides of that productive space that inscribes the historical subject in both its beauty and its pain as a single moment, where an external history and a perceiving subject become momentarily and ecstatically lost in each other.

Another metaphor with which to focus this historical moment in *Willow Springs* as a specifically temporal action is that of the urban pastoral,[8] a notion that recalls both that camp tradition of which Schroeter is obviously a part and the troublesome Romantic tradition of Rousseauistic speech, which Schroeter seems, for better or worse, to flirt with. Textually, the pastoral half of this expression is signaled frequently in Schroeter's films by various versions of the bucolic interlude that, for instance, occurs in *Willow Springs* when Christine and Magdalena, in elaborate costumes, glide lyrically together across the desert and unite in a close-up of their two hands slowly rising. Related to other images and narrative stops in the films (such as the androgynous bodies and the composed statuesque faces), these are images and moments of visual or musical excess, unrelated to any narrative logic or at least theatrically reminiscent of something like a lost innocence or purity. As a pastoral, this is a more or less ahistorical or prehistorical moment, which alternates with the tug of history like the boy in *Willow Springs* who, coming to the desert retreat from Los Angeles, sighs, "Back and forth, back and forth, I like the city but I like the country better."

These pastoral signifiers are not isolated, however, and their importance to Schroeter's vision of history lies entirely in the fact that they are ironically bracketed in the quotation marks of their own theatricality or the exaggerated materiality of their production. If this pastoral instant appears as a kind of ahistorical, preconscious state, associated with the extreme passion at the center of the individual's story, its reality is always a nostalgic potential for Schroeter, defined by the urban world of history that surrounds it (as one moves, for instance, from the pastoral Palermo to the urban Wolfsburg or from the desertscape of *Willow Springs* to the claustrophobic and cluttered interiors), defined by the symbolic production into which this imaginary of the pastoral must project itself in order to express itself at all. This urban pastoral describes, in other words, that moment of imaginary excess when the subject dies into history, into representation, like a Wagnerian heroine, like Wilde's Salome, and, if the memory continually and metonymically seeks to reproduce that pastoral purity, for Schroeter this moment is forever retrievable only as an urban pastoral, a material image like the aria on a scratched record that marks the excess of passion as a moment lost. The complement to Rosaria's victorious announcement that her child has not yet been born is accordingly Magdalena's confrontation with Christine in *Willow Springs*: immediately after the boy's wistful description of his vacillation between an urban and pastoral climate, Magdalena tears a plastic doll's head away from Christine and, while staring at it, remarks that "the only person I ever loved was the child that died within me."

That three women or the tripartite representation of a woman figures at the center of this urban pastoral is, however, more than the presentation of a maternal image fostering that lost object on the edge of history. Rather, women play such an important role in Schroeter's films not only because of their status for him as a passionate expression rebelling against a patriarchal history but, equally importantly, because as objects of representation they focus most dramatically the representational repression of the cinema. Engaging history as a memory-spectacle in the process of forming itself, *Willow Springs* necessarily turns, like many other contemporary German films, specifically to the disguised crisis in the cinematic spectacle itself, because it is here that a narrative structure acts out most insidiously the performance of memory, and here that the presence of the female body resists most excessively its material emplacement on the edge of this performance.[9]

The so-called classical narrative cinema is always in this sense fetishized history — *Young Mr. Lincoln* being only the most infamous example. As memories, such films retrieve that lost time, that pastoral instant, as one story or one time that displaces the crisis of the subject entering history from the productive center of the representation to the already produced and continuous reality of narrative fiction. Like the woman in Schroeter's *Bomber Pilot* who notes that "memories interposed themselves between us and our future," the continual present tense of film becomes the illusory suppression of the crisis of history that occurs when the pastoral subject enters that history as a symbolic production.

Exposing this making of history as it is disguised by the filmic text — or, more in the spirit of *Willow Springs*, pinpointing it as a crisis of the subject/spectator — therefore becomes a representational tactic that would counter film's narrative illusion at its perceptual center, where a pastoral body engenders the fetishized time scheme that is its child. For Schroeter, this means not so much (or at least not alone) a deconstruction of the mechanisms of cinema's temporal illusions, as in the cinema of Wenders or Kluge. Instead, in *Willow Springs* Schroeter's strategy for revealing the productive representation of history is primarily and usually to keep intact the fetishizing action of narrative film but to forefront continually its constructive or theatrical nature, so that that pastoral instant of excess, with all its emotional and preconscious force, remains emotionally and explicitly displayed at the very moment it enacts its metonymic and theatrical displacements. Informing the entirety of *Willow Springs*, this Janus-faced aesthetic appears, for instance, in Schroeter's use of operatic scores, from Bizet's *Carmen* to Saint-Saëns's *Samson and Dalila*, which move, as in Syberberg's films, with their traditional emotional force, yet which simultaneously mark their distance as obvious phonographic recordings from another time and place or which are deflated by their juxtaposition to pop or folk music such as the Blue Ridge Rangers' "Jambalaya." Early in the film, Magdalena plays an aria from an Italian opera on a record player and then stares directly into the camera; the next shot shows Ila staring off wistfully while a tear rolls down her cheek, and the sequence closes with a cut to the Cupid poster which recuperates the operatic emotion in its most campy materiality. With painstaking attention, these images exhibit themselves literally as *about* the poignancy of love and pain; yet in so aggressively exhibiting their excess the representations serve ultimately to deflate themselves, so that the portrayal contains that excess only at the cost of admitting the inadequacy of the medium. The tension at the base of the cinematic representation between the transgressing expression of the woman and its trivialization thus parallels that within the image between the Italian aria and the tattered poster of love. In both cases, what is at work is more than a Brechtian examination of the image; rather, what is mockingly interrogated is finally the terms of visual fascination itself — and the violence of its strictures.[10]

Together with the operatic soundtrack, this "representational self-destruction" is no doubt most noticeable in the elaborate and histrionic displays of the female pose of various combinations of the three women, self-consciously constructing different symbolic ratios that seem about to fracture under the weight of the long takes. But, related more specifically to the narrative illusion, this action operates most significantly as a holding in place of film's illusion of continuity or progression while it simultaneously reveals this illusion as a recurring return, as a point of origin whose aura (so unlike Benjamin's) proceeds from its material repetition. Unlike more strictly experimental films, *Willow Springs* does not fully subvert narrative time but instead repeatedly rehearses and recalls — from the meditative dialogue by characters to the doubling of the final murders — its formation as a productive instant: as a material emplacement of the subject into historical time that necessarily entails the loss of an excess reality, a death in a literal sense. Put specifically in terms of the filmic text, *Willow Springs* continually recreates itself as a narrative time and memory spectacle that disintegrate; and, as the subject of that spectacle, the spectator is thus placed repeatedly on that mortal edge of a history, in that pastoral instant that enters excessively into the camp climate of an urban perspective.

Image-repetition is the key tactic here, since it cuts both ways as a temporal

model. In terms of psychoanalytic discourse, repetition serves on one hand to stabilize the subject-ego as it binds that subject to the cohesive narrative of memory's
recollection. In this sense, repetition channels and contains the individual, as in a
classical narrative film where the repetition of shots, figures, and images places the
spectator solidly in a narrative pattern based on recognition. The other side of that
repetition, which is so distinctively Schroeter's focus, is what Lacan calls "the more
radical diversity constituted by repetition itself,"[11] a diversity that marks the dispersal of unity and the disbanding of a historical identity. From this perspective,
repetition functions as "an absence of direction, a failure of coherence: the return to
the same in order to abolish the difficult time of desire, it produces in that very moment the resurgence of inescapable difference. . . . Its edge, its final horizon is thus
death, the ultimate collapse of same and different, pure totality and indifference."[12]
While the first effect of repetition is to inscribe the subject-spectator into a narrative
coherence, this second use of repetition suggests a project clearly at odds with the
first in Schroeter's films; thematically, this second dimension correlates with that
pastoral instant or temporal seclusion into which his characters retreat; figurally it is
the three women that tend to divide and merge at the center of *Willow Springs*, often
reappearing in film after film; and stylistically it is a continual return to the same or
similar image, a return that invariably threatens to undermine narrative suspense
with a kind of boredom, indifference.

This repetition of images becomes in this way a kind of stasis, a nonnarrative
moment that actually stops the fetishized disguise of film's movement in an instant
of death at work. Present throughout *Willow Springs*, this use of image-repetition to
transform historical time into an instant of stasis appears most dramatically in *The
Death of Maria Malibran*, a film that becomes an unsettling documentary of faces
set graphically against dark or entirely black backgrounds. In this film, not only do
these facial poses textually crystallize the expressive look itself as a deathly pale
brilliance, a kind of death mask, born on the edge of darkness, but the repetition of
these poses moreover tends to pull disturbingly against a narrative progression and
to settle the movement of the film's montage in the stasis of these repeated shots.
Within the action of narrative and historical time, in short, the filmic text literally
counters its continuity with the virtual stasis of its recurrent tableaux, tableaux that
significantly strain with the excess of the theatrical postures, tableaux that *General
Rehearsal* metaphorically summarizes when a couple rehearse—again and again
throughout the film—a passionate embrace, a lethargic falling apart, and a return to
the embrace.

What is most distinctively and disturbingly Schroeter here is of course not so
much his subversion of traditional narrative structures, but rather the tense and fragile balance that his films establish on the very edge of these narrative and historical
structures. In this case, for example, image-repetition as the foundation of narrative
works both ways across its temporal model and both ways simultaneously: it at once
secures a narrative history for the subject-spectator and returns that spectator to the
material origin of narrative history by stopping narrative action in the stasis of visual
excess or indeterminacy (suggested in one way by the misdirected eyeline matches
of the frozen faces). Along with the entire narrative of *Willow Springs* and its return

to the performance of an origin, the most descriptive example may be the story of the boy, Michael. Retreating from Los Angeles and a melodramatic history (featuring days at Laguna Beach and the tragic death of his parents in a fire) and arriving at the sanctuary of the three women, this boy repeatedly recites a partial narrative about his desire to flee to a pastoral Hawaii, the repetition of the tale at once calling attention to its own production, defining him as a character, and representing his retardation in the static reality of *Willow Springs*. In terms of this narrative refrain, the present tense in which he lives at Willow Springs becomes a nostalgic desire for a pastoral future, a self-enclosed and circular memory of his future hopes. Yet, when he attempts to leave and to enter an actual narrative history, to complete his past in a real future, this narrative memory dies the death (here the literal death of the boy gunned down by Magdalena) that comes with engaging history. As a distilled instance of the entire narrative of *Willow Springs*, Michael's story thus becomes the narrative version of the plastic replica of the child that died within Magdalena: a material image subsisting on nostalgia, the narrative miscarries at the very moment of its birth.

For Schroeter, therefore, the starting point and consistent focus of his fragile and disjoined narratives are not so much the structures of history (as they are to some extent for more notable followers like Syberberg) but instead the excess that official or symbolic history leaves behind. For Schroeter, facing history becomes largely and ironically a flamboyantly tragic effacement, like that of his Prometheus acting a scene on a burning roof, like the stained-glass phoenix in *General Rehearsal*, whose luminosity overwhelms the figuration. Indeed, this relation to history accounts to a large extent for the marginal place Schroeter has consistently maintained in the recent history of contemporary German cinema: a place emblematic of the original potential of this cinema, lost by other directors through their metaphoric deaths at the hands of history (as in Wenders's *State of Things*) or through more tragically real deaths like Fassbinder's. With some dark irony, moreover, Schroeter had not only been figuratively exiled from this history but for a time quite literally exiled when a scandal erupted over his 1979 efforts to produce *Salome* for the stage. Driven to Paris by a newspaper campaign that depicted Schroeter in the anti-Semitic caricatures of the Nazis (e.g., as a rat), Schroeter made there *General Rehearsal*, perhaps his most autobiographically direct work and one that refers explicitly to this personal incident of historical and cultural violence. In an almost playfully contrary response to this historical pressure, however, Schroeter asks himself within *General Rehearsal* what the theme of the film is. As the question hangs fire, the film cuts to a series of close-ups of individuals whose isolated expressions stand by themselves as the passionate focus of Schroeter's cinema, outside and in excess of both a contextual history and the narrative logic of the question itself.

If, therefore, Schroeter's relation to the history of contemporary German cinema has been contradictory, if his historical visibility seems to bear little relation to his historical influence, this, I'd suggest, is the very point of his aesthetic positions and the reason he has been the inspiring muse of many German directors. Perhaps more than any other films being made today in Germany, Schroeter's films respond to history but only in proclaiming for his audiences individual possibilities and realities beyond the historical predicament; they work within the structure of narrative but only to expose the brilliant edges around those structures; they enounce themselves but only to say they and the potentialities of their spectator exceed any historical place or enunciation. For Schroeter and his films, their articulations of history are always consciously less than the possibilities and passions that inform those articulations and that they address. Not too surprisingly, it is Michel Foucault who, as an almost paradigmatic interlocutor and audience for Schroeter, inadvertently describes this historical edge on which Schroeter and his films always balance: whereas the art of self has in many ways become the main commodity of the German auteurs of the seventies, Schroeter's films, in Foucault's words, made "an art of the self which would be the complete contrary of self," expressing him and his films as a passion "which is always mobile but which does not move toward any given point," which "at its limit seeks to maintain itself only to disappear."[13] In this odd encounter between these two archaeologists of history's edges, Schroeter then responds, somewhat later, quoting part of the concluding paragraph of Foucault's *Order of Things* as an unwitting summary of the historical moment that his films continually perform, a moment when the composed face of the subject balances fragilely on the edge of the sea that surrounds history, an instant of history when "one can certainly wager that man would be erased like a face drawn in sand at the edge of the sea."[14]

"Breakdowns, other countries, and new directions"
(*Paris, Texas*). © 1984 Twentieth Century Fox Film
Corporation.

CONCLUSION

Other Courses in Time

Cultural and aesthetic history is an exchange, a dialogue moving forward and backward in time, just as artistic creation and production of any kind responds dialectically to its public reception. While a filmmaker like Wenders demonstrates more explicitly than many of his peers the passive attraction of Hollywood and its aesthetic fields of the past, Syberberg becomes an extreme instance of how that attraction can reverse its direction and so take the form of an active effect on those same fields. Whereas *Kings of the Road* dismantles the projection at its source, *Hitler* sets up a counterprojection as a source of fascination in its own right. The actual mark that a German director (like Syberberg, for instance) can in fact make on an industry like Hollywood (or even one on its fringes in San Francisco) is of course very questionable; and, in the wake of Wenders's painful *Hammett* project, his movements between Germany (*Wings of Desire*) and the rest of the world (*Paris, Texas, Till the End of the World*) suggest that the state of things is anything but consistent and stable.

Yet, the precedents are there. As one German critic pointed out, "a close tie has always linked Hollywood and the German film. Without the Germans in Hollywood, American cinema would be unthinkable."[1] For the time being, directors like Wenders, Schlöndorff, or Syberberg (not to mention the Hollywood presence of the cameras of Michael Ballhaus and Robbie Müller) appear as quite distinct and different versions of the same motif of cultural cross-insemination; although the individual reasons for their participation in the American film industry and the structures of that industry obviously differ from those of Lang, Lubitsch, or Sirk, their positions as reflective, critical perspectives outside a mainstream tradition do not. Naturally, this guarantees nothing: whether the conflicts and negotiations that West German films dramatized in the seventies resurface as new directions and expanded boundaries for commercial cinema in the future remains to be seen and remains to be fully evaluated in a larger historical light. That the singular visions of a Herzog, Kluge, or Fassbinder can appreciably alter the expectations of the ubiquitous Hollywood spectator (as, it might be argued, Lang and Sirk did)[2] is doubtless a great deal to hope for—even in light of international successes such as Fassbinder's *The Marriage of Maria Braun*, Percy Aldon's *Bagdad Cafe*, and Petersen's *Das Boot*.[3] What is certain, however, is that the original engagement with a postwar history and a Hollywood *vraisemblable* has been fully turned to the advantage of many contemporary German filmmakers, and the subsequent success of the seventies has brought with it the contingent problem that these filmmakers are now themselves a kind of establishment, a Hollywood abroad, against which German films of the eighties and nineties have had to work.

Hans Robert Jauss has clarified some of this historical and cultural movement by noting that "the new is not only an aesthetic category":

> It cannot be explained completely by the factors of innovation, surprise, surpassing, re-arrangement, and alienation, to which the formalist theory assigned utmost importance. The new becomes an historical category when diachronic analysis is forced to face the questions of which historical forces really make the . . . work new, to what degree this newness is recognizable in the historical moment of its appearance, what distance, route, or circumlocution of understanding were required for its full realization, and whether the moment of this realization was so effective that it could change the perspective of the old.[4]

A film's dialogic status within a culture, in other words, is by definition not a static affair: not only does the special history of an art form necessarily change the value of specific works that at one time appeared as innovations on the horizon, but the changing needs of a culture's social realities equally redefine the value of particular artistic works. Whereas the films examined in this study potentially widen "the limited range of social behavior by new wishes, demands, and goals, and thereby open avenues for future experience,"[5] these films and often the filmmakers have not necessarily kept pace with a historical perspective that it was their original aim to broaden, the significance of these works changing accordingly. The boundaries of a filmic *vraisemblable* are measured both by a cinematic tradition and by actual sociohistorical exigencies. What at one time challenges these borders as the new inevitably becomes an equally confining extension of these borders, so that whether or not a filmmaker actually enlists with the old patriarchy—as Wenders and Fassbinder sometimes seem to have done[6]—she or he nonetheless becomes an established horizon in his or her own right, against which new psychosocial realities must be introduced and against which other works (not perforce historically recent works) arise in turn as challenges to those borders.

Quite literally, therefore, the Filmverlag der Autoren, as the foundation and focus for much of the New German Cinema, is not what it used to be. Laurens Straub, perhaps the principal force behind the founding of this organization, has summed up the difference of ten years this way: "are we a cooperative of filmmakers who look after distribution or a distribution company that looks after certain filmmakers?"[7] The reference here is to the controlling image of directors such as Fassbinder, Wenders, and other figures in this study. And Straub's decision in 1977 to quit the Filmverlag in order to establish, with Christian Friedel, an alternative distribution house, Filmwelt,[8] is not only coincidental with the appearance of the latest films examined here but emblematic of a concerted reaction among many German filmmakers against the commercial tyranny that the central directors of the New German Cinema have come to represent. Having successfully challenged and partially usurped the postwar hegemony in German cinema, the subsequently celebrated directors have become a hegemony themselves, significantly sanctioned by the American production and distribution companies. Like the old order they once engaged, these filmmakers, inadvertently in most cases, have arrested audience expectations at the borders of their own films and have in many ways closed the channels of an ongoing dialogue with pertinent social issues, a dialogue that the competitive structure of the former system may have been better suited to monitor. One of the new executives in the Filmverlag, Joachim Hamman, seems, for example, to luxuriate in the notion that the New German Cinema of the sixties and seventies "is the whole of the German cinema and should control 100% of the industry."[9] And, sounding like a new manifesto against these fruits of Oberhausen, Straub has responded accordingly by noting that the consequence of this situation is that in 1980 "there is no direct relation between the public and those who make the films, all is mediated to an extreme. . . . A filmmaker has no concrete audience to refer to and his project thus becomes oddly the object of an abstract debate between all sorts of people who each have an idea about what should be the cultural aim, who should be the cinema and the public." Certain filmmakers like Herzog, Wenders, and Reinhard Hauff

> have been able to acquire an enormous political-cultural power and thus truly to control the market, outside of any direct relationship with the public. The incredible early success of the Filmverlag has further reinforced the problem. It has allowed some directors for several years to produce films outside the commercial system but as effectively as that system. Several of them have consequently succeeded in creating a particular image for themselves and acquiring a position of power. The actual result is disastrous. Because on the official market today there is no more room for a film as difficult as the first films of Herzog or Wenders. In a return of history, the efforts undertaken by filmmakers to obtain a better structure for the cinema have been so successful that they have destroyed the advantages of the old structures. These filmmakers have, from now on, become the figurative enemies of the German cinema.[10]

Indeed, in large part, *Germany in Autumn* is a pastiche of self-criticism, which several of these filmmakers turned on themselves as representatives of the position Straub describes. Moreover, despite the fact that many of the New German directors are now, in Straub's words, "no different from the famous, old producers" of the fifties and early sixties,[11] a number of this same generation have devoted time and money to talented filmmakers who represent various generations and who were passed over in the commercialization of the New German Cinema: the Bioskop Film company of Schlöndorff and Hauff has produced a film by the extraordinary and eccentric Herbert Achternbusch; Franz Seitz, a producer associated with the old conservatism but who was also responsible for *Young Törless*, has worked with Jean-Marie Straub, a filmmaker persistently on the radical fringe; Wenders has financially backed a film by his former editor Peter Przygodda. Similarly, while continuing to insist that a film be commercially viable and responsive to its audiences, Kluge has regularly fought politically and economically for more marginal experimenters like Werner Schroeter, Vlado Kristl, and Werner Nekes. He argues in 1976: "It is very difficult to assist these filmmakers; it is the same with literature: poetry has the least drawing power. Yet we are attempting to come to their aid. . . . We don't consider the cause lost. . . . I am sure that the powers of Nekes, Straub, Kristl,

"Rosa von Praunheim: lost voices and new visibilities" (*Anita—Dances of Vice*).

Schroeter, and Rosa von Praunheim is decisive. For me, their capacity is more important than all that is made as so-called quality cinema."[12]

Nonetheless, as the preceding generation of German filmmakers learned before them, both the youngest and more experimental filmmakers of today face a stubborn resistance as they in their turn confront a production/distribution system that is content to limit alternatives and that tightly controls even an expectation horizon in the process of making advances. Hans-Peter Cloos, a young and rather conventional director whose first film was appropriately a sequence in *Germany in Autumn*, remarks on the problem with the ingenuousness of a young Wenders recognizing the real power of the American cinema and preparing to counter it at its economic base: "The distributors do not give advances, not even the Filmverlag, because they are having troubles. They are wrong to want to be everywhere and to compete with the American majors. They would do much better to concern themselves with the young filmmakers." In spite of the progress made for the new cinema in Germany over the last ten years, Cloos continues, the situation is not necessarily progressive in itself: "our best known directors interest the Americans; and it's difficult to say what will happen. In any case, it is time that we, the young filmmakers, make our films . . . that we put all our resources together to produce these films and distribute them."[13] Like their predecessors, in short, filmmakers now making their appearance in Germany must tactically organize themselves for a confrontation with an economic and aesthetic structure already in place, an aesthetic confrontation whose economics demand compromises with the established machinery, politics, and filmic codes secured by that political machinery. (That West German directors have, since 1979, formed several effective special-interest groups and collectives—such as the *Bundesvereinigung des deutschen Films* [The Federal Association of German Films]—indicates some of the lessons that have been learned.) Hence, while members of the third generation, such as Rodl, often have strikingly original styles and subjects that answer social needs and reach audiences outside the cities (particularly Munich, Berlin, and Hamburg) and outside the auteur strategies of the previous generations, their films return at the same time to more traditional narrative structures and eagerly use the production equipment of the establishment. (Winkelmann, for instance, has used the television networks, perhaps even more aggressively than filmmakers before him, to produce his films.) Even more indicative as a historical index is that Straub, a figurehead for the old new wave of German filmmakers, has brought his business experience with alternative cinema to the aid of the new new wave: "the apparatus is too small," he explains once again in 1980, "to do what it should do: to produce the films of young directors who have not had our experience in production. . . . I don't see a short-term solution. It will be necessary, without doubt, to form again our small production organization, that is, to play again the economic game and to become true businesses."[14]

Straub has not, of course, stood behind just young filmmakers but filmmakers from a wide range of backgrounds and issues representing, above all else, alternative perceptions. Rosa von Praunheim, Elfi Mikesh, Hellmuth Costard, and Hans Noever are all part of the alternative force that Straub represents, and the variety of ages and concerns in that force is a testimony to Jauss's argument that the new has far less to do with a historical chronology of works than with the multiple determinations that decide the historical reception of those works. Regardless of its temporal origin or even its historical intention, a cultural production must intercept a historical expectation horizon; especially with the cinema, that action of interception requires certain concession and timings if alternative films are to be effective.

Despite parallels with the development of German cinema between 1962 and 1977, these concessions have also required revisions and renegotiations with significantly altered historical conditions. Thus, in September of 1979, sixty German filmmakers gathered for a film festival in Hamburg, where they produced the *Hamburger Erklärung* ("Hamburg Declaration"), a sort of historical reassessment and revision seventeen years after Oberhausen, made most notably in light of the augmenting power of television to accommodate (in every sense) film. This short document contains the usual romantic claims and complaints directed at a governmental and cultural support system that, through the seventies, became fraught with contradictions and corruptions. More importantly, it retains an abiding sense that its dialogic relationship with the changing definition of a film audience must determine the nature and direction of the movie: "We have learned that our only allies can be the spectators: that means the people who work, who have wishes, dreams, and desires, that means the people who go to the movies and who do not, and that also means people who can imagine a totally different kind of film." While the echoes of Oberhausen are unmistakable and absolutely necessary to seeing this document as a historical marker, Elsaesser rightly notes that it "has to be read not so much as a *volte face* with respect to the Oberhausen Manifesto, but as its logical extension into the changed historical situation. Whereas in 1962 aspiring filmmakers knew they had to turn to the government for assistance, by 1979 the appeal was to television. Yet because television represented both patron and consumer, the appeal could be ambiguously understood as an address directly to the public.''[15] If the economics and sociology of an industry's search for an audience have always played a fundamental role in the representations and engagements of the New German Cinema, the eighties would make television even more central to those filmmakers than it had been in the seventies. The burgeoning of that alignment, with more international and intra-European connections than ever before, would require crucial reconfigurations of audiences, economic packagings, and narrative forms.

In a sense, just as the Oberhausen Manifesto and *Germany in Autumn* reflect each other, the Hamburg Declaration might be seen as the companion piece to another event eight months earlier. With some obvious irony, this event and text—which, with the Hamburg declaration, may be the measure of the turn in German filmmaking from the late seventies into the eighties and nineties, is the German broadcast of the American television production *Holocaust* in January 1979. If throughout the seventies West German film struggled with and against a cultural hegemony typified by Hollywood as a way of claiming a particular film culture and an absent history, the advances and regressions of that decade were shaken severely by the controversy and debates that surrounded this showing of *Holocaust*. Despite Edgar Reitz's denunciation of the show for taking history out of the hands of the Germans, as Anton Kaes has explained, *Holocaust* in fact ''inspired renewed discussion about the various ways in which history should be presented on film. . . . The German Autumn of 1977 had evoked an 'excess motivation' (Kluge) among intellectuals and filmmakers to deal with German history, but only the broad reception of *Holocaust* allowed the numerous films about the recent German past to find an audience. *Germany in Autumn* presented impressions of a country on which the past weighs heavily; the German reaction to *Holocaust* showed how much still had to be done to master the past.''[16]

While the historical parameters of my study have been the years from Oberhausen to *Germany in Autumn* and more particularly films made between 1972 and 1977, *Holocaust* and the highly charged reactions to it become a media event that limns the still enormously important questions surrounding the power of present and future audiences who are more and more addressed through the institutions of television and who are capable of initiating and responding to the unresolved probings of those narrative images. Within the most dramatic (and politically nervous) moments in that next decade, this audience would appear capable of generating unimagined and seismic cultural changes, producing itself as a world television spectacle across the Berlin wall, exhibiting itself as the mythic beginning of another history. If, in the New German Cinema, a divided Germany frequently became a metaphor for a German identity divided by, in part, American culture, the recent unification of Germany might suggest that that identity, as it is addressed and developed by a new generation of filmmakers, will need to be reconfigured in a dialogue with a far different cultural grammar but with, hopefully, an equally trenchant

"Figures of the past crowding the future" (Fassbinder's
The Marriage of Maria Braun).

sense of its cultural memories. The historical issues and debates raised by the New
German Cinema have been perhaps only a transition into a more contested and varied dialogue with that cultural history.

As this particular period of contemporary German cinema unmistakably shows,
therefore, any new horizon can inevitably become part of a closed world and self-
serving circle through the turns of cultural history. The most important contribution
by the filmmakers and films studied here is consequently not that they have been
able to secure a place in the history and industry of cinema—as they succeeded in
altering that history—but that they may have established a pattern, in their work on
film and with its industry, of creative dislocations and imaginative detours through
which new presences and perspectives can usurp old absences. A dialogue and an
exchange, this pattern, through which images of history and identity are fashioned,
is the foundation for the continuation of any historically active and socially significant cinema in and beyond Germany. As Straub has optimistically envisioned: "the
others have opened the way; from now on it is easier: the industry is now prepared
for the arrival of a new generation of filmmakers."[17] That, of course, remains to be
seen.

Notes

INTRODUCTION

1. Although "German cinema" in this study means only West German films, East Germany of course had its own active film industry.

2. It is important to keep in mind that just as Oberhausen should not be read as a mythological genesis, neither can *Germany in Autumn* be seen as an actual closure of some kind. Both are critical markings which in actuality are not at all stable or definitive. See Miriam Hansen's "Cooperative Auteur Cinema and Oppositional Public Sphere: Alexander Kluge's Contribution to *Germany in Autumn*"; and Jan Dawson's "A Labyrinth of Subsidies: The Origins of the New German Cinema."

3. See, for example, Penelope Gilliatt's review of Herzog's *Aguirre, The Wrath of God*: "Gold." Even John Sandford's informative book *The New German Cinema* tends in this direction: "It is not a 'movement' or a 'school,' " he says, "nor is it a self-consciously 'underground' or 'alternative' cinema" (p. 6). For a more balanced account of the nature of this collective enterprise, see two essays by Eric Rentschler: "Critical Junctures since Oberhausen: West German Film in the Course of Time," *Quarterly Review of Film Studies*, vol. 5, no. 2 (Spring 1980), 141–156; and "American Friends and the New German Cinema."

4. How consciously coordinated this action has been is less important than that it has had the quality and quantity to be received as such. Compare, for instance, the fate of a filmmaker like Carlos Saura in this country or the recent efforts of Independent Filmmakers to organize as a single body.

5. See "Werner Schroeter's Operatic Cinema," *Discourse*, no. 3 (1981), 46–59.

6. The danger, which this book maps in its singular focus, is what Kluge argues as a kind of "Bonapartism": "In the New German Cinema there is, due to varying, individually well definable reasons, a tendency to want to conquer world-power in the cinema with a single film. It is a case of creeping Bonapartism: Syberberg's *Hitler*, Herzog's *Nosferatu*, Wenders' *The American Friend*" (Alexander Kluge [ed.], *Bestandsaufnahme: Utopie Film* [Frankfurt am Main: Zweitausendeins, 1983], p. 227).

7. Thomas Elsaesser, *New German Cinema: A History* (New Brunswick: Rutgers University Press, 1989), p. 303.

8. Directly related to these political events, Jürgen Habermas opened what has become known as "the Historians' Debate" in 1986 with the publication of an article in *Die Zeit* ("Eine Art Schadensabwicklung") attacking the recent apologist positions toward twentieth-century German history. The subsequent debates were heated and widespread. See Kaes, pp. 222–223 n. 70.

9. Of the numerous accounts of the New German Cinema that have appeared in the eighties and early nineties, some of the most important books (in English) are Thomas Elsaesser's *New German Cinema: A History*, Anton Kaes's *From Hitler to Heimat: The Return of History as Film*, Richard W. McCormick's *Politics of Self: Feminism and the Postmodern in West German Literature and Film*, Eric Rentschler's *West German Film in the Course of Time: Reflections on the Twenty Years since Oberhausen*, and Rentschler's collection of writings by German filmmakers, *West German Filmmakers on Film: Visions and Voices*.

10. Trinh T. Minh-Ha, *When the Moon Waxes Red: Representation, Gender, and Cultural Politics* (New York: Routledge, 1991), p. 199.

ONE. A HISTORY, A CINEMA

1. Jan Dawson (ed.), *Wim Wenders*, p. 7.

2. See Thomas Elsaesser's "Primary Identification and the Historical Subject: Fassbinder and Germany."

3. My survey of the historical development of the New German Cinema is indeed a sketch since much of this information is available elsewhere. For more detailed accounts, any of the following can be consulted: Eric Rentschler, *West German Film in the Course of Time*; Hans-Bernard Moeller, "New German Cinema and Its Precarious Subsidy and Finance System," *Quarterly Review of Film Studies*, vol. 5, no. 2 (Spring 1980), 157–168; Hans Gunther Pflaum and Hans Helmut Prinzler, *Film in der Bundesrepublik Deutschland*; Bernard Eisenschitz, "Le cinéma allemand aujourd'hui"; John Sandford, *The New German Cinema*; Thomas Elsaesser, "The Postwar German Cinema," in Tony Rayns (ed.), *Fassbinder*, pp. 1–17; and Sheila Johnston, "The Author as Public Institution: The 'New' Cinema in the Federal Republic of Germany."

4. See, for example, "Le cinéaste Wim Wenders," *Libération* (special edition): *L'Affaire Allemande* (no date), p. 88, where Wenders remarks that "we would have been able to produce some films but no one would have seen them."

5. "The Industry: German Weasels (Filmverlag Follies)." Wenders's temporary move to California, the problems and frustrations that were part of that experience with Hollywood and Coppola, and his recent return to Europe to film *The State of Things* indicate the tensions and confusion that are part of this marriage. See Walter Adler's interview with Wenders in *Filmkritik*, vol 22 (December 1978), 673–686; and "Wenders en Californie," *Cahiers du Cinéma*, no. 301 (June 1979), 54–64; and Lawrence Cohn's "Gray City Films as Wim Wenders N.Y. Distrib and Production Base," *Variety*, 30 September 1981, pp. 6, 38.

6. The nature and composition of these audiences is, of course, various: Hollywood was not necessarily the measure of all things, and the notion of a box-office hit was not so much an actual goal or achievement as it was an economic yardstick which had to be used or redefined.

7. Also important is the change of Jonathan's home from France to Germany (his birthplace in the film being Switzerland).

8. "Tranquenards," p. 28. I am generally indebted to this very rich article.

9. Much of the writing about Wenders concentrates on this level. See, for example, Michael Covino, "Wim Wenders: A Worldwide Homesickness"; and Karen Jaehne, "The American Fiend."

10. Jan Dawson, "Filming Highsmith," p. 36.

11. Christian Metz, "Le dire et le dit au cinéma: Vers le declin d'un Vraisemblable?," in *Essais sur la signification au cinéma*, vol. 1, p. 235.

12. Ibid., p. 238.

13. Again the sociohistory and the aesthetics unite here around the fact that *The American Friend* was the first German film shot with a newly developed American film stock, an element that Wenders clearly uses as a very special signifier.

14. Dawson, *Wim Wenders*, p. 13.

15. Covino, "Wim Wenders," p. 16.

16. Jan Dawson (ed.), *Alexander Kluge and the Female Slave*, p. 37.

17. "On the Notion of Cinematographic Language," p. 584.

18. Other versions of reception studies include empirical studies and historical studies of effect. In his polemic with Marxist theory and phenomenology, Jauss clearly refines and advances these positions considerably.

19. "Literary History as a Challenge to Literary Theory," in Ralph Cohen (ed.), *New Directions in Literary History*, p. 12. Recently this essay has been published as part of its original book-length study: Hans Robert Jauss, *Toward an Aesthetic Reception*, trans. Timothy Bahti.

20. For other examples, see Richard E. Amacher and Victor Lange (eds.), *New Perspectives in German Literary Criticism*.

21. Jauss, "Literary History," p. 12.

22. Ibid., p. 18.

23. Ibid., p. 27.

24. This problem of the plurality of a filmic text has been discussed notably in Raymond

Bellour, "The Unattainable Text"; and Umberto Eco, "Articulations of the Cinematic Code."

25. "*Deutschland im Vorherbst*: Literature Adaptation in West German Film," p. 11.

26. Rentschler has specified areas which come into play as part of this intertextuality in "Expanding Film Historical Discourse: Reception Theory's Use Value for Cinema Studies."

27. Rosalind Coward and John Ellis, *Language and Materialism: Developments in Semiology and the Theory of the Subject*, p. 135.

28. Rien T. Segers, "An Interview with Hans Robert Jauss," p. 86.

29. Probably the most debated effort in this direction has been the editors' "John Ford's *Young Mr. Lincoln*," *Screen*, vol. 13 (Autumn 1972). See also Daniel Dayan's "The Tutor-Code of Classical Cinema."

30. "Alexander Kluge, Cinema and the Public Sphere: The Construction Site of Counter-History," *Discourse* (forthcoming).

31. Rentschler, "Expanding Film Historical Discourse: Reception Theory's Use Value for Cinema Studies"; Elsaesser, "Primary Identification and the Historical Subject: Fassbinder and Germany" and "Myth as the Phantasmagoria of History: H. J. Syberberg, Cinema and Representation."

32. An obvious comparison can be made with *Far from Vietnam*, which, it seems to me, has a less dialogic structure: the French film is much more a counter-*statement*, far from its subject matter and undefined in terms of its audience. See Miriam Hansen's excellent examination of *Germany in Autumn*: "Cooperative Auteur Cinema and Oppositional Public Sphere: Alexander Kluge's Contribution to *Germany in Autumn*," *New German Critique*, nos. 24/25 (Fall/Winter 1981–82), 36–56.

33. In identifying the sections by the director, I am admittedly at odds with what the film attempts to accomplish with its mélange of styles and stories. This is, however, the only means of pinpointing and analyzing specific details in the film.

34. Recently, there have been several articles in English on the important but ambiguous role played by the television networks in the development of the New German Cinema. See, for example, Richard Collins and Vincent Porter, "Westdeutscher Rundfunk and the Arbeiter Film," *Quarterly Review of Film Studies*, vol. 5, no 2 (Spring 1980), 233–253.

35. "Le texte clos," *Semiotiké: Recherches pour une sémanalyse*, pp. 113–143.

36. See Hansen, "Cooperative Auteur Cinema and Oppositional Public Sphere."

TWO. WENDERS'S *KINGS OF THE ROAD*

1. "*That's Entertainment: Hitler*, A Polemic against J. C. Fest's Film *Hitler—A Career*."

2. The full text of *Kings of the Road* is available in English in a detailed shot breakdown: Fritz Müller-Scherz and Wim Wenders, *Kings of the Road*, trans. Christopher Doherty (Munich: Zweitausendeins/Filmverlag der Autoren, 1976).

3. See, for example, *Beyond the Pleasure Principle*, pp. 6–26.

4. *Le signifiant imaginaire*, p. 82; and "The Imaginary Signifier," trans. Ben Brewster, *Screen*, vol. 16 (Summer 1975), 59.

5. Ibid., p. 83/p. 60.

6. Ibid., p. 56/p. 45.

7. See ibid., p. 64/p. 48.

8. Ibid., p. 105/p. 74.

9. Ibid., p. 72/p. 53.

10. "Le défilement," in Dominique Noquez (ed.), *Cinéma: Theorie, lectures*, pp. 87–110; or "Le Défilement: A View in Close Up."

11. In his own work, Jauss uses this same circle metaphor and question-answer format (also very pominent in *Kings of the Road*). See "Literary History as a Challenge to Literary Theory," p. 12.

12. *Le signifiant imaginaire*, pp. 113–120.

13. Operating in a political context rather than a psychoanalytic one, Stanley Aronowitz

makes a similar point about conventional cinema: "it is only by deconstructing these films that the structure of desire can be revealed and the desiring machine, to borrow a phrase from Deleuze and Guattari, that 'records' and actually creates a mediated reality can be surpassed" ("Film—The Art Form of Late Capitalism," p. 110).

14. Metz, *Le signifiant imaginaire*, pp. 13–14/p. 5. Aronowitz makes a similar point: "film is that art form which requires no ideological justification other than its own production and no legitimation other than its reception" ("Film—The Art Form of Late Capitalism," p. 115).

THREE. TRANSFORMATIONS IN FASSBINDER'S *BITTER TEARS OF PETRA VON KANT*

1. "A Cinema of Vicious Circles," in Tony Rayns (ed.), *Fassbinder*, pp. 35–36. See also two essays by Sheila Johnston: "The Author as Public Institution: The 'New' Cinema in the Federal Republic of Germany" and "A Star Is Born: Fassbinder and the New German Cinema," *New German Critique*, nos. 24/25 (Fall/Winter 1981–82), 57–72.

2. See Richard Dyer (ed.), *Gays and Films*; Andrew Britton, "Foxed," *Jump Cut*, no. 16 (November 1977), 22; Bob Cant, "Fox and His Friends: Fassbinder's Fox," *Jump Cut*, no. 16 (November 1977), 22; Renny Harrigan, "Women Oppressed," *Jump Cut*, no. 15 (July 1977), 3–5; and Wolf Donner, "Der Boss und sein Team," *Die Zeit*, no 31 (1970).

3. "Reading Fassbinder's Sexual Politics," in *Fassbinder*, p. 58.

4. Ibid., p. 63.

5. Christian Braad Thomsen, "Interview with Fassbinder," in *Fassbinder*, p. 83.

6. "Fassbinder on Sirk," trans. Thomas Elsaesser, *Film Comment*, vol. 11 (November–December 1975), 23.

7. Tony Rayns explains that "this evaluation is characterized by its determination to meet Hollywood discourse, in all its 'affirmative' expansiveness and syntactic density, on its own terms" ("Fassbinder, Form and Syntax," in *Fassbinder*, p. 79). For more details regarding Fassbinder's early career, see: Ekkehard Pluta, "Die Sachen sind so, wie sie sind," *Fernsehen und Film*, vol 12 (1970); and several of the essays in *Fassbinder*, trans. Ruth McCormick.

8. Thomsen, "Interview," p. 101.

9. Ibid., p. 97.

10. Regarding Fassbinder's version of a Brechtian aesthetic, see John Hughes and Brooks Riley, "A New Realism: Fassbinder Interviewed," *Film Comment*, vol. 11 (November/December 1975), 14–17. Here Fassbinder remarks: "What's important to me and everyone else is the idea of alienation in Brecht, and my films have the character of the Brecht didactic pieces. But they are not so dry as the *Lehrstücke*. That's the thing that disturbs me about Brecht's *Lehrstücke*, the dryness; they have no sensuality." Also pertinent is Hans-Bernhard Moeller's "Brecht and 'Epic Medium': The Cinéaste Playwright, Film Theoretician and His Influence," *Wide Angle*, vol. 3, no. 4 (1980), 4–11. Despite the avowed differences, Fassbinder's whole aesthetic might be summarized in Brecht's comment that "one thinks feelings and one feels thoughtfully."

11. "Fassbinder and Spectatorship," *New German Critique*, no. 12 (Fall 1977), 65.

12. Wenders comments: "There's a capitalism that everybody recognizes. . . . But there's also a capitalism between people . . . between man and woman, as well as between father and son. Maybe that's why I can't breathe when I see American families in American films" (*Wim Wenders*, p. 10).

13. For more detail, see especially Elsaesser's "Primary Identification and the Historical Subject: Fassbinder and Germany"; and Sheila Johnston's "A Star Is Born: Fassbinder and the New German Cinema."

14. Elsaesser, "A Cinema of Vicious Circles," p. 29.

15. Mayne, "Fassbinder and Spectatorship," p. 72.

16. At one point, Petra dictates a letter to Joseph Mankiewicz, a Hollywood director who shares a great deal with Petra on this level.

17. See Stanley Cavell's *The World Viewed: Reflections on the Ontology of Film.*

18. Thomsen, "Interview," p. 55.

19. See Manuel Alvarado, "Eight Hours Are Not a Day," in *Fassbinder*, p. 40.

20. Thomsen, "Interview," p. 96.

21. Thomsen, "Interview," p. 83.

22. The distinction between seeing and reading is most rigorously used in the work of Jean-Louis Schefer. In regard to film specifically, refer to Daniel Dayan's "The Tutor-Code of Classical Cinema."

23. Prefiguring the pattern of the lovers, the father is dismissed because the company's concerns are "production and we haven't got room for people of your age."

24. Thomsen, "Interview," p. 94.

25. *Language and Materialism*, pp. 73–74.

26. Thomsen, "Interview," pp. 84–85.

27. Recently, Catherine Johnson has touched on some of these points in "The Imaginary and *The Bitter Tears of Petra Von Kant*," *Wide Angle*, vol. 3 (1980), 20–26.

28. Besides the work of these major theoreticians, there is a more specific examination of the filmic body (in Muybridge and Méliès) in Linda Williams, "Film Body: An Implantation of Perversions," *Ciné-Tracts*, no. 12 (Winter 1981), 19–36.

29. Michel Foucault, "Nietzsche, Genealogy, History," in *Language, Counter-Memory, Practice*, trans. Donald Bouchard and Sherry Simon, p. 148.

30. See, for instance, Thomsen, "Interview," p. 89.

31. "Difference," p. 54. There is also Laura Mulvey's important essay "Visual Pleasure and Narrative Cinema," *Screen*, vol. 16 (Autumn 1975), 6–18. More recently, Thomas Elsaesser has surveyed Fassbinder's films from a perspective much like mine here: "Primary Identification and the Historical Subject: Fassbinder and Germany."

32. Heath, "Difference," p. 100.

33. Ibid., p. 83.

34. Quoted in ibid., p. 92.

35. *La sexualité féminine* (Paris: Seuil, 1976), p. 137.

36. This is emphasized especially through the High German diction of Petra, the unmistakable sign of the stilted language of the father.

37. Heath, "Difference," pp. 107–108.

38. Quoted in "A Cinema of Vicious Circles," p. 33.

39. Thomsen, "Interview," p. 93.

FOUR. TYPES OF HISTORY

1. Note Schlöndorff's regular use of novels for his scripts, to which he remains relatively faithful.

2. "The Political Dimensions of *The Lost Honor of Katharina Blum*," p. 81.

3. Quoted in Barbara Bronnen and Corinna Brocher (eds.), *Die Filmemacher: Zur neuen deutschen Production nach Oberhausen 1962*, p. 86.

4. Dominique Bergouignan and Laurence Gavron, "Le cinéma d'auteur," p. 16.

5. Ibid., p. 16.

6. Quoted in *Libération* (special edition): *L'Affaire Allemande* (no date), p. 89.

7. Bergouignan and Gavron, "Le cinéma d' auteur," p. 19.

8. Ibid., p. 19.

9. See *Die Filmemacher*, pp. 82–89.

10. Rui Nogueira, *Melville*, p. 89.

11. Ibid., p. 28. See also Schlöndorff's "A Parisian-American in Paris," *Village Voice*, 6 July 1982, 44–45.

12. Nogueira, *Melville*, pp. 100 and 92.

13. *The World Viewed*, p. 33.

14. Ibid., pp. 34–35.

15. Lukács's position is most clearly worked out in *The Historical Novel*. Brecht's response to Lukács is most cogently stated in Bertolt Brecht, "Against George Lukács."

16. Quoted in Terry Eagleton, *Marxism and Literary Criticism*, p. 72.

17. In an introduction to the novel, Marguerite Yourcenar emphasizes the story's "classical nature"' noting that psychological truth "is bound up too much today with what is individual and specific to allow us . . . to remain ignorant of, or pass over, the external realities which govern a situation." She nonetheless claims that the novel is of "value as a human, not political, document" (*Coup de Grâce*, no page numbers).

18. *S/Z*, pp. 54–55.

19. *Marxism and Form: Twentieth-Century Dialectical Theories of Literature*, p. 196.

20. See Raymond Bellour, "The Obvious and the Code," pp. 7–17.

21. In this regard, Schlöndorff is clearly much more the romanticist of nature than someone like Wenders or Fassbinder, yet without the radical imagination of Herzog.

22. *Pour une critique de l'économie politique du signe*, pp. 30–31. See also *The Mirror of Production*, trans. Mark Poster, p. 128.

23. *"Die Blechtrommel": Tagebuch einer Verfilmung*, p. 50. Although this quotation refers to *The Tin Drum*, I believe it is applicable to most of Schlöndorff's films.

24. *Die Zeit*, 22 October 1976.

25. See particularly the work of Bellour on this notion of repetition and a reality effect. Also, chapter 2 in David Bordwell and Kristin Thompson, *Film Art*; and Bruce Kawin, *Telling It Again and Again: Repetition in Literature and Film*.

26. *Semiotics of Cinema*, trans. Mark E. Suino, p. 13.

FIVE. THE CHARGE OF TRANSLATION

1. Eric Rentschler, *West German Film in the Course of Time*, p. 129.

2. Quoted in Hans C. Blumenberg, "Das Jahr des Teufels," *Die Zeit*, 8 July 1977. This privileging of the immediacy of visual experience over language and literary discourse is discussed as part of the general cultural crisis in West Germany in the 1970s in Michael Rutschky's *Erfahrungshunger: Ein Essay über die siebziger Jahre*.

3. "The Backbone of German Cinema," *Kino: German Film*, no. 3 (Summer 1980), 25.

4. J. Hoberman, "She Vants to Be Alone," *Village Voice*, 7 April 1980.

5. A list of Handke's literary achievements includes *Kaspar* (1967), *The Goalie's Anxiety at the Penalty Kick* (1972), *Short Letter, Long Farewell* (1972), and *A Moment of True Feeling* (1975).

6. See Stanley Kauffmann, "Notes on Handke's Films," *The New Republic*, 8 March 1980.

7. Recently Handke and Wenders attempted another collaborative effort, a rendering of Handke's *The Slow Return Home* (*Die langsame Heimkehr*), but were unable to gain either government funding or television support.

8. Peter Handke, *The Left-Handed Woman*, trans. Ralph Manheim (New York: Farrar, Straus and Giroux, 1977), p. 25.

9. Richard McCormick, *Politics of the Self: Feminism and the Postmodern in West German Literature and Film* (Princeton: Princeton University Press, 1991), pp. 172–173.

10. Kauffman.

11. Given Handke's own social actions and his semiautobiographical writings, it is not difficult to see the author as a reflection of his protagonist. See Eric Rentschler, *West German Film in the Course of Time*, p. 169.

12. Noël Burch, *To the Distant Observer: Form and Meaning in the Japanese Cinema*, p. 161.

13. Ibid., p. 161

14. Handke, quoted in the press booklet prepared for the film by New Yorker Films.

15. Rentschler, p. 169.
16. The most celebrated versions of this position are Laura Mulvey, "Visual Pleasure and Narrative Cinema," *Screen*, vol. 16, no. 3 (Autumn 1975), 6–18; and Stephen Heath, "Difference," *Screen*, vol. 19, no. 3 (Autumn 1978), 51–112. See also Annette Kuhn, *Women's Pictures: Feminism and Cinema* (London: Routledge, 1982).
17. See Ruth Perlmutter, "Visible Narrative, Visible Woman," *Millennium Film Journal*, no. 6 (Spring 1980), 18–30.
18. Press booklet from New Yorker Films.
19. Ibid.
20. Peter Handke, *Iche bin ein Bewohner des Elfenbeint-urms* (Frankfurt am Main: Suhrkamp, 1972), p. 28.
21. Rentschler, p. 171.
22. In the novel the son to some extent parodies this utopian state when he reads a passage he had just written: "My idea of a better life: I would like the weather to be neither hot nor cold. There should always be a balmy breeze and once in a while a storm that makes people huddle on the ground. No more cars. All houses should be red. . . . I would know everything already, so I would not have to study. Everyone would live on islands. . . . Everything I don't know would disappear" (p. 4).
23. Rentschler, p. 173.

SIX. THE SEMANTICS OF SECURITY IN KLUGE'S *STRONGMAN FERDINAND*

1. Dominique Bergouignan and Laurence Gavron, "Le cinéma d'auteur," p. 21. Much has been written about Kluge; see, for instance: Rainer Lewandowski, *Die Filme von Alexander Kluge* and *Alexander Kluge*; the chapter on Kluge in Sandford's *The New German Cinema*; and Ulrich Gregor, interview with Kluge, in *Herzog/Kluge/Straub*, pp. 153–178.
2. For some of the details and complexities regarding Kluge's involvement with the Frankfurt School, see Miriam Hansen's "Alexander Kluge: Crossing between Film, Literature, Critical Theory."
3. Bernard Eisenschitz, 'Le cinéma allemand aujourd'hui," p. 110. See also Kluge's "On Film and the Public Sphere," *New German Critique*, nos. 24/25 (Fall/Winter 1981–82), 206–220.
4. Eisenschitz, "Le cinéma allemand," p. 97.
5. "Cooperative Auteur Cinema and Oppositional Public Sphere," p. 41. See also Johnston's "The Author as Public Institution."
6. Bergouignan and Gavron, "Le cinéma d'auteur," p. 27.
7. Jan Dawson (ed.), *Alexander Kluge and the Female Slave*, p. 27.
8. Eisenschitz, "Le cinéma allemand aujourd'hui," pp. 110–111.
9. See especially the very important 1972 study by Kluge and Oskar Negt, *Öffentlichkeit und Erfahrung: Zur Organisationsanalyse von bürgerlicher und proletarischer Öffentlichkeit*.
10. Eisenschitz, "Le cinéma allemand aujourd'hui," pp. 111–112.
11. Ibid., p. 89.
12. *Alexander Kluge and the Female Slave*, p. 31.
13. Ibid., pp. 31 and 34.
14. Michael Dost/Florian Hopf/Alexander Kluge, *Filmwirtschaft in der BRD und in Europa: Götterdämmerung in Raten*, p. 67.
15. *Alexander Kluge and the Female Slave*, p. 34.
16. Ibid., pp. 34–35.
17. The film is adapted from a Kluge short story, and Edgar Reitz had originally started the project before Kluge took over.
18. *Alexander Kluge*, p. 37.
19. Quoted in *Die Welt*, 14 September 1968.
20. *Alexander Kluge*, p. 19. Any quotation from *Occasional Work* comes from this text.

21. Heinz Schubert, who plays the lead, is a well-known television comic who played a German Archie Bunker in a popular series, a background which is obviously a key ingredient in the dialogue between the film and its audience.

22. *Alexander Kluge*, p. 39.

23. Ibid., p. 30.

24. This is from *Occasional Work*.

25. *Alexander Kluge*, p. 37.

26. Louis Althusser, quoted in Heath, *The Nouveau Roman*, p. 190.

27. Tom Milne (ed. and trans.), *Godard on Godard*, p. 182.

28. *Alexander Kluge*, p. 35.

29. *Öffentlichkeit und Erfahrung*, p. 140.

30. *Alexander Kluge*, p. 36.

31. *Alexander Kluge*, p. 48. Kluge happens to be referring to *Occasional Work* in this case, but the point is certainly applicable to many of his films. The original text is in *Gelegenheitsarbeit einer Sklavin: Zur realistischen Methode*.

32. *Alexander Kluge*, p. 38.

33. Ibid., p. 29.

SEVEN. SANDER'S *THE ALL ROUND REDUCED PERSONALITY—REDUPERS*

1. Judith Mayne, "Female Narration, Women's Cinema: Helke Sander's *The All-Round Reduced Personality/Redupers*," *New German Critique*, nos. 24–25 (Fall/Winter 1981–82), 164.

2. Helke Sander, "Men Are Responsible That Women Become Their Enemies: Tales of Rejection," in Eric Rentschler (ed.), *West German Filmmakers on Film: Visions and Voices*, p. 28.

3. Two very important accounts of the historical development of contemporary women's film in West Germany are Gudrun Lukasz-Aden and Christel Strobel, *Der Frauenfilm: Filme von und für Frauen*, and Renate Mohrmann, "Frauen erobern sich einen neuen Artikulationsort: den Film," in *Frauen Literatur Geschichte: Schreibende Frauen vom Mittelalter bis zur Gegenwart*, ed. Hiltrud Gnug and Renate Mohrmann (Stuttgart: Metzler, 1985). In English, there is Marc Silberman's "Cine-Feminists in West Berlin," *Quarterly Review of Film Studies* (Spring 1980), 217–232; Miriam Hansen's "Frauen und Film and Feminist Film Culture in West Germany," *Heresies*, no. 16 (1983); and two issues of *Jump Cut*, no. 27 (July 1982) and no. 29 (February 1984), with sections devoted to German women filmmakers. The larger issue of the women's movement in West Germany is covered from a variety of angles in a special issue of *New German Critique* (Winter 1978).

4. Anton Kaes, *From Hitler to Heimat: The Return of History as Film* (Cambridge: Harvard University Press, 1989), pp. 157, 158.

5. Thomas Elsaesser, *New German Cinema: A History* (New Brunswick: Rutgers University Press, 1989), p. 183.

6. Ibid.

7. Helke Sander, "Feminism and Film," in *West German Filmmakers on Film*, p. 80.

8. Ibid., p. 81.

9. Gertrud Koch, "Was ist und wozu wir eine feministische filmkritik?" *Frauen und Film*, no. 11 (March 1977), 15.

10. Where Kluge (of the earlier films at least) and Sander differ, writes Richard McCormick, "is with Sander's willingness to foreground her own position in structuring the film. Kluge does not foreground his own position as the authority who assembles the various elements that the spectator in turn must put into some kind of relationship" (*The Politics of the Self: Feminism and the Postmodern in West German Literature and Film*, p. 225). B. Ruby Rich describes the difference between Kluge and Sander this way: "The major break with Kluge's narrative model might be pinpointed in Sander's rejection of hegemony and authority

as narrative qualities. . . . Rather, the authoritarianism of narration is avoided in favor of a relationship that sounds at times more like a conversation than like any hierarchical ordering of narrative truth'' (''She Says, He Says: The Power of the Narrator in Modernist Film Politics,'' *Discourse*, no. 6 [1983], 40). These critical revisions of Kluge might, as importantly, be seen as an attempt to make that utopian notion of a more active spectator more concretely differentiated within the experience of a female viewer.

11. See especially Wolf's essays ''The Reader and the Writer'' and ''The Diary: An Aid to Work and Memory'' in *The Reader and the Writer: Essays, Sketches, Memories*, trans. Joan Becker (New York: International, 1977).

12. Mayne, ''Female Narration, Women's Cinema,'' p. 166.

13. Elsaesser, p. 61.

14. Kaja Silverman, ''Helke Sander and the Will to Change,'' *Discourse*, no. 6 (Fall 1983), 28.

15. Hans Günther Pflaum (ed.), *Jahrbuch Film 78/79* (Munich/Vienna, 1977), p. 115.

16. Helke Sander, ''Feminism and Film,'' pp. 81, 79.

17. Trinh T. Minh-Ha, *When the Moon Waxes Red: Representation, Gender, and Cultural Politics* (New York: Routledge, 1991), p. 27.

EIGHT. THE ORIGINAL TRADITION

1. Gene Walsh (ed.), *''Images at the Horizon,''* p. 33.

2. Ibid., p. 6.

3. Ibid., p. 7.

4. Ibid., p. 11.

5. Quoted in Vernon Young, ''Werner Herzog and Contemporary German Cinema,'' *Hudson Review*, vol. 30, no. 3 (1977), 409–414.

6. See Elizabeth Cleere's ''Three Films by Werner Herzog: Seen in the Light of the Grotesque,'' *Wide Angle*, vol. 3 (1980), 12–20.

7. *''Images,''* p. 25.

8. See *Was Ich Bin, Sind Meine Filme*, a film by Christian Weisenborn and Erwin Keusch.

9. Peter Handke, George Trakl, and Jacob Wassermann are only three who have adopted this character and tale.

10. See the nineteenth-century plates and drawings reproduced in Jacob Wassermann's *Caspar Hauser: The Enigma of a Century*, trans. Caroline Newton.

11. ''Werner Herzog's Ecran Absurde,'' *Literature/Film Quarterly*, vol. 7, no. 3 (1979), 223–234.

12. This is clearly a casual reference to a complex psychoanalytic notion, which strictly speaking, would entirely resist Herzog's idea of a nascent self-preceding language. Kaja Silverman has recently analyzed the film as anti-Oedipal, her argument being similar to mine in this section of the chapter: ''Kaspar Hauser's 'Terrible Fall' into Narrative,'' *New German Critique*, nos. 24/25 (Fall/Winter 1981–82), 73–93.

13. *''Images,''* p. 31.

14. In part, this use of the term *irony* derives from Wayne Booth's *The Rhetoric of Irony*. See also Thomas Elsaesser, ''The Cinema of Irony.''

15. *''Images,''* p. 9.

16. Herzog has remarked ''how extremely well memory works under hypnosis. One of the most fascinating things that I learned is the extent to which people can bring out something that is very deep inside'' (*''Images,''* p. 18).

17. I am thinking here of most of Bellour's work with Hitchcock, but the model turns up in many other films and a great deal of film theory.

18. *''Images,''* p. 19.

19. Klaus Wyborny is, in fact, responsible for the dream sequences.

20. Although I have underplayed the significant part music plays in this film, it is crucial

to note that the final aria is "This Image" from *The Magic Flute*. When it introduces the film the lyrics are:

> This image is enchantingly beautiful,
> like no eyes have ever seen.
> I feel the way this image of godliness
> with new excitement my heart fills.

Circling back, the film ends:

> This is something I cannot name,
> but I feel it like fire burning.
> Is this feeling love?
> Yes, it's love alone.

That distinct and ineffable image of Kaspar persists, in short, as the narrative returns on itself, a circular river of music.

21. This pressing desire to communicate may help explain the excessively commercial look of *Fitzcarraldo*.

22. "*Images*," p. 35.

23. Eisenschitz, "Le cinéma allemand aujourd'hui," p. 144.

24. "*Images*," p. 21.

NINE. THE EXORCISM OF THE IMAGE

1. *Der Spiegel*, 30 October 1978, p. 266.

2. *Frankfurter Rundschau*, 24 February 1979, p. 21.

3. *Hitler, Ein Film aus Deutschland*, p. 47; he refers to Wenders specifically. The slightly abridged English edition is *Hitler: A Film from Germany* (New York: Farrar, Straus and Giroux, 1982).

4. "Eye of the Storm," pp. 36–43. Two other major essays dealing with *Hitler* are: Fredric Jameson, " 'In the Destructive Element Immerse': Hans-Jürgen Syberberg and Cultural Revolution," *October*, no. 17 (Summer 1981), 99–118; and Thomas Elsaesser, "Myth as the Phantasmagoria of History." These two in some ways counterpoint each other, and both are to a certain extent controversial. Focusing on the problem of ideology and a political unconscious, the Jameson piece describes the film as modernist in a "classical, and what may now seem archaic, sense" (p. 112). Elsaesser, on the other hand, reads the film at the conjunction of history, myth, and psychoanalysis and responds more accurately, it seems to me, to the film's central argument with media and the crisis of media representation in Germany.

5. *Syberbergs Filmbuch*.

6. *Cahiers du Cinéma, Syberberg*, p. 84. This is an anthology of notes by Syberberg and about him (featuring Sirk, Coppola, and Foucault).

7. This does not mean, of course, that Syberberg rejects the notion of a political democracy.

8. *Filmbuch*, p. 80. Syberberg's *Sex-Business—Made in Pasing* (about the pornographic entrepreneur Alois Brummer) focuses specifically on this dimension of cinema.

9. *Filmbuch*, p. 12.

10. Ibid., p. 11.

11. Serge Daney, Yann Lardeau, and Bernard Sobel, "Entretien avec Hans-Jürgen Syberberg," p. 11. This entire issue has been a source for ideas and information.

12. See especially Jean-Louis Baudry's "Ideological Effects of the Basic Cinematographic Apparatus"; and his *L'effet cinéma*.

13. *Syberberg*, pp. 78–79. He has argued in various places about the contradiction of this system which produces films with public funds but which then forces these films to compete as commercial commodities.

14. Ibid., p. 83.

15. *Hitler* was, of course, intended as a studio film.

16. "L'état-Syberberg," p. 7.

17. "Entretien," p. 11.

18. The BBC, among others, was involved in the production.

19. *Syberberg*, p. 55.

20. Ibid., p. 61.

21. Ibid., p. 55.

22. Apropos of the American reception, even *Vogue* (May 1980) did not hesitate to laud this new find.

23. Syberberg notes: "In Frankfurt, during the six days of its showing, one hundred and fifty people in all saw *Hitler*. In San Francisco in three days alone more people saw it than all those who saw it in Frankfurt, Munich, and Hamburg combined. . . . The first showing of this film on German television took place without a discussion afterwards in order not to credit the film, and if discussion ever did occur, it was decided in every case that it would be without the director and without any discussion of the film itself. One can compare this with the full use of the media when *Holocaust* was shown on television, four times during four days, with discussion taking place directly in the studios and lasting as long as the program itself, with the participation of the spectators" (*Syberberg*, p. 78).

24. *Filmbuch*, p. 108.

25. *Syberberg*, p. 34.

26. See ibid., p. 34.

27. Syberberg describes this scandal as an attempt "to combine Brecht's theory of the epic theater with the musical aesthetic of Richard Wagner, to join in film the epic laws of a new myth" (*Hitler*, p. 28). The phrase "aesthetic scandal" comes from a headline that Syberberg noticed during the 1972 Edinburgh Festival.

28. *Hitler*, pp. 20–22.

29. *Filmbuch*, p. 108.

30. Interestingly, Ernst Bloch wrote an essay titled "Karl May, An Homage to Richard Wagner."

31. *Hitler*, p. 25.

32. All dialogue and script come from *Hitler*. Recently this book has been translated, with an abridged introduction, by Joachim Neugroschel: *Hitler, A Film from Germany* (New York: Farrar, Straus and Giroux). Quotations from the film here, however, are my own translations.

33. Preface to *Hitler, Un film d'Allemagne* (Paris: Laffont, 1978), pp. 5–6; "Myth as the Phantasmagoria of History," p. 136; and "Eye of the Storm," p. 43.

34. "Entretien," pp. 13–14.

35. See Jean-Louis Comolli and François Gere, "La real-fiction du pouvoir."

36. See Bruce Kawin's *Mindscreen: Bergman, Godard, and First-Person Film*. Here I'm using Kawin's term collectively, which is obviously very different from his use of it.

37. "Entretien," p. 10.

38. *Hitler*, p. 11.

39. "L'art du deuil," p. 18.

40. "Entretien," p. 11.

41. Again, the cinematic version of Lacanian models is behind my use of this term.

42. See chapter 1, and also Thierry Kuntzel's "Le Défilement."

43. See Elsaesser's "Myth as the Phantasmagoria of History."

44. *Le Monde*, February 1976. No doubt, this idea informs both Eisner's *The Haunted Screen* and Siegfried Kracauer's *From Caligari to Hitler*.

45. Fassbinder's *Petra von Kant* shares this operation.

46. See *Syberberg*, p. 53.

47. See *Hitler*, pp. 29–30.

48. Ibid., p. 27.

49. "Entretien," p. 13.

50. "L'art du deuil," p. 17.

51. "Entretien," p. 10.

204 / Notes to pages 164–86

52. Ibid., p. 13.

53. This problem of the *name* of Hitler is crucial to the film, for it is the exclusivity of its inscription that in part valorizes it. See Lardeau, "L'art du deuil," p. 21.

54. "Le rire de Déméter," pp. 308, 314–315, 320, 322.

55. This is Sontag's phrase.

56. *Hitler*, pp. 32, 27.

57. *Syberberg*, p. 62

58. See Lévi-Strauss's *L'homme nu*.

TEN. SCHROETER'S *WILLOW SPRINGS* AND THE EXCESSES OF HISTORY

1. Schroeter, "Propos Rompus."

2. Rosa von Prauheim's attack on *Kingdom of Naples*, "With Fond Greeting to Champagne-Schroeter," can be found in Eric Rentschler (ed.), *West German Filmmakers on Film: Visions and Voices*.

3. *Frankfurter Rundschau* (24 February 1979). The other important commentary on Schroeter is Gerard Courant's *Werner Schroeter*.

4. Serge Daney, "Schroeter et Naples," *Cahiers du Cinéma*, no. 307 (January 1980), 29.

5. Of the increasing attention paid to this notion of excess and the varying ways it can be mobilized, two very strong arguments are Kristin Thompson's "Cinematic Excess" in *Eisenstein's Ivan the Terrible* and Linda Williams's "Film Bodies: Gender, Genre, and Excess," *Film Quarterly*, vol. 44, no. 4 (Summer 1991).

6. Gary Indiana, "Scattered Pictures," *Artform* (March 1982), 48.

7. Daney, p. 28.

8. This is of course William Empson's phrase which Susan Sontag retrieved in her famous "Notes on 'Camp' " in *Against Interpretation* (New York: Dell, 1961). Of the many pertinent remarks in this essay, the following seems particularly appropriate: "The canon of Camp can change . . . Time may enhance what seems simply dogged or lacking in fantasy now because we are too close to it, because it resembles too closely our own everyday fantasies, the fantastic nature of which we don't perceive. We are better able to enjoy a fantasy as fantasy when it is not our own" (p. 286).

9. The position follows from Stephen Heath, *Questions of Cinema* (Bloomington: Indiana University Press, 1981).

10. I've explored this relation of opera and cinema more fully in "Werner Schroeter's Operatic Cinema," *Discourse*, no. 3 (Summer 1981). Central to my argument there is the work of Catherine Clement in *Opera, or the Undoing of Women*.

11. Lacan, *Le Seminaire livre XI* (Paris: Seuil, 1973), p. 60.

12. Heath, *Questions of Cinema*, p. 124.

13. In Gerard Courant, *Werner Schroeter* (Paris: Goethe Institut), pp. 45, 39.

14. *The Order of Things* (New York: Random House, 1970), p. 387.

CONCLUSION

1. Hans C. Blumbenberg, "Von Caligari bis Coppola: Junge deutsche Filmemacher in Hollywood auf den Spuren von Lubitsch, Murnau und Lang."

2. I have not actually seen this point argued, yet I am convinced it could be supported, particularly through close textual studies of films such as *Scarlet Street* and *The Woman in the Window*.

3. One could argue that particularly films like *Fitzcarraldo* and *Das Boot* represent more a coopting by Hollywood rather than of Hollywood.

4. "Literary History as a Challenge to Literary Theory," in Ralph Cohen (ed.), *New Directions in Literary History*, p. 31.

5. Jauss, "Literary History," p. 37.

6. Before his death, Fassbinder had begun to work with the epitome of the old order he once attacked, and Wenders completed *Hammett* for Coppola and supposedly signed another Hollywood contract. That Wenders filmed, in the interim, *Lightning over Water* (a kind of exorcism of his Hollywood nostalgia, about the death of Nick Ray) and then made a very successful film in Europe, *The State of Things*, indicates that he remains at least very ambivalent about his relationship with Hollywood.

7. Quoted in Dominique Bergouignan and Laurence Gavron, "Le cinéma d'auteur," p. 25.

8. That Filmwelt distributes in large part American B movies indicates that the problems and paradoxes don't disappear with new generations.

9. Bergouignan and Gavron, "Le cinéma d'auteur," p. 21.

10. Ibid., p. 23.

11. Ibid., p. 24.

12. Quoted in Bernard Eisenschitz, "Le cinéma allemand aujourd'hui," pp. 141–143.

13. Bergouignan and Gavron, "Le cinéma d'auteur," p. 24.

14. Ibid., p. 24.

15. Thomas Elsaesser, *New German Cinema*, p. 35.

16. Anton Kaes, *From Hitler to Heimat*, pp. 34–35. Compare Richard McCormick's formulation of this shift at the end of the seventies: "In the early 1970s there was a general disillusionment with politics in West Germany, and especially with dogmatic schemes of historical interpretation. By the late 1970s a need had emerged to confront German history again, but it was now examined through the perspective of (reconstructed) personal experience, rather than in terms of grand conceptual systems and teleologies. What resulted was a postmodernist examination of history and subjectivity" (*Politics of the Self*, p. 234).

17. Bergouignan and Gavron, "Le cinéma d'auteur," p. 25.

Filmography

Dates given indicate the year the film was completed. English titles may vary depending on the source, and in most cases I have followed the titles used by Sandford (*The New German Cinema*), Rentschler (*West German Film in the Course of Time*), or Elsaesser (*New German Cinema*).

These lists include only works that were directed by the individual.

RAINER WERNER FASSBINDER

1965	*The Urban Tramp (Der Stadtstreicher)*
1966	*The Little Chaos (Das kleine Chaos)*
1969	*Love is Colder Than Death (Liebe ist kälter als der Tod)*
1969	*Katzelmacher*
1969	*Gods of the Plague (Götter der Pest)*
1970	*Why Does Herr R. Run Amok? (Warum läuft Herr R. Amok?)*
1970	*Rio das Mortes*
1970	*The Cafe (Das Kaffeehaus)*
1970	*Whity*
1970	*The Niklashaus Journey (Die Niklashauser Fahrt)*
1970	*The American Soldier (Der amerikanische Soldat)*
1970	*Beware of a Holy Whore (Warnung vor einer heiligen Nutte)*
1971	*Pioneers in Ingolstadt (Pioniere in Ingolstadt)*
1971	*The Merchant of Four Seasons (Der Händler der vier Jahreszeiten)*
1972	*The Bitter Tears of Petra von Kant (Die bitteren Tränen der Petra von Kant)*
1972	*Jailbait (Wildwechsel)*
1972	*Eight Hours Don't Make a Day (Acht Stunden sind kein Tag)*
1972	*Bremen Freedom (Bremer Freiheit)*
1973	*World on a Wire (Welt am Draht)*
1973	*Nora Helmer*
1973	*Fear Eats the Soul (Angst essen Seele auf)*
1973	*Martha*
1974	*Effi Briest*
1974	*Fox and His Friends (Faustrecht der Freiheit)*
1975	*Mother Küster Goes to Heaven (Mutter Küsters' Fahrt zum Himmel)*
1975	*Fear of Fear (Angst vor der Angst)*
1976	*I Only Want You to Love Me (Ich will doch nur, dass ihr mich liebt)*
1976	*Satan's Brew (Satansbraten)*
1976	*Chinese Roulette (Chinesisches Roulette)*
1977	*Bolwieser*
1977	*Women in New York (Frauen in New York)*
1977	*Despair (Eine Reise ins Licht)*
1978	contribution to *Germany in Autumn (Deutschland im Herbst)*
1978	*The Marriage of Maria Braun (Die Ehe der Maria Braun)*
1978	*In a Year with 13 Moons (In einem Jahr mit 13 Monden)*
1979	*The Third Generation (Die dritte Generation)*
1980	*Berlin Alexanderplatz*
1981	*Lili Marleen*
1981	*Lola*
1982	*Veronika Voss*
1982	*Querelle*

PETER HANDKE

1977 The Left-Handed Woman (Die linkshändige Frau)
1986 Das Mal des Todes
1992 Die Abwesenheit

WERNER HERZOG

1962 Hercules (Herakles)
1964 Game in the Sand (Spiel im Sand)
1966 The Unparalleled Defense of the Fortress of Deutschkreutz (Die beispiellose Vertei-
digung der Festung Deutsch Kreutz)
1967 Signs of Life (Lebenszeichen)
1968 Last Words (Letzte Worte)
1968 Precautions against Fanatics (Massnahmen gegen Fanatiker)
1969 The Flying Doctors of East Africa (Die fliegenden Ärzte von Ostafrika)
1970 Fata Morgana
1970 Even Dwarfs Started Small (Auch Zwerge haben klein angefangen)
1970 Impeded Future (Behinderte Zukunft)
1971 Land of Silence and Darkness (Land des Schweigens und der Dunkelheit)
1972 Aguirre, The Wrath of God (Aguirre, der Zorn Gottes)
1974 The Great Ecstasy of the Sculptor Steiner (Die grosse Ekstase des Bildschnitzers
Steiner)
1974 The Mystery of Kaspar Hauser (Jeder für sich und Gott gegen alle)
1976 How Much Wood Would a Woodchuck Chuck
1976 No One Will Play with Me (Mit mir will keiner spielen)
1976 Heart of Glass (Herz aus Glas)
1976 La Soufrière
1977 Stroszek
1978 Nosferatu—The Vampyre (Nosferatu—Phantom der Nacht)
1978 Woyzeck
1982 Fitzcarraldo
1983 Where the Green Ants Dream (Wo die grünen Ameisen traümen)
1984 Ballad of the Little Soldier (Ballade vom kleinen Soldaten)
1985 Gasherbrumm der leuchtende Berg
1987 Cobra Verde
1988 Les Gaulois
1989 Wodaabe—Die Hirten der Sonne
1990 Echos aus einem düsteren Reich
1991 Jag Mandir
1991 Schrei aus Stein
1991 Lektionen in Finsternis

ALEXANDER KLUGE

1960 Brutality in Stone/Yesterday Goes on for Ever—co-directed by Peter Schamoni
(Brutalität in Stein/Die Ewigkeit von gestern)
1961 Race—co-directed by Paul Kruntorad (Rennen)
1963 Teachers in Transition—co-directed by Karen Kluge (Lehrer im Wandel)
1964 Portrait of an Accomplishment (Porträt einer Bewährung)
1966 Yesterday Girl (Abschied von gestern)
1967 Frau Blackburn, Born 5 Jan. 1872, Is Filmed (Frau Blackburn, geb 5. Jan., wird
gefilmt)

1967   *Artists under the Big Top: Perplexed (Die Artisten in der Zirkuskuppel: Ratlos)*
1968   *Fireman E. A. Winterstein (Feuerlöscher E. A. Winterstein)*
1969   *The Inimitable Leni Peickert (Die unbezähmbare Leni Peickert)*
1970   *The Big Mess (Der grosse Verhau)*
1970   *A Doctor from Halberstadt (Ein Arzt aus Halberstadt)*
1971   *We'll Blow 3x27 Billion Dollars on a Destroyer (Wir verbauen 3x27 Milla. Dollar in einen Angriffsschlachter)*
1971   *Willi Tobler and the Sinking Sixth Fleet (Willi Tobler und der Untergang der 6. Flotte)*
1973   *A Woman of Property, Born 1908 (Besitzbürgerin, Jahrgang 1908)*
1973   *Occasional Work of a Female Slave (Gelegenheitsarbeit einer Sklavin)*
1974   *The Middle of the Road Is a Very Dead End (In Gefahr und grösster Not bringt der Mittelweg den Tod)*
1975   *Strongman Ferdinand (Der starke Ferdinand)*
1977   *The People Who Are Preparing the Year of the Hohenstaufens (Die Menschen, die das Staufer-Jahr vorbereiten)*
1977   *In Such Trepidation I Creep Off Tonight to the Evil Battle (Zu böser Schlacht schleich ich ich heut nacht so bang)*
1978   Contribution to *Germany in Autumn (Deutschland im Herbst)*
1979   *The Patriot (Die Patriotin)*
1980   *The Candidate (Der Kandidat)*
1982   *Biermann—Film* (co-directed with Edgar Reitz)
1983   *War and Peace (Krieg und Frieden)*
1983   *Auf der Suche nach einer praktisch-realistischen Haltung*
1983   *The Power of Emotion (Die Macht der Gefühle)*
1985   *The Blind Director (Der Angriff der Gegenwart auf die übrige Zeit)*
1987   *Miscellaneous News (Vermischte Nachrichten)*

HELKE SANDER

1966   *Subjectivity (Subjektitude)*
1967   *Silvo*
1967   *Crush the Power of the Manipulators (Brecht die Macht der Manipulateure)*
1969   *What Now Nursery School Teacher? (Kindergärtnerin, was nun?)*
1970   *Children Aren't Cattle (Kinder sind keine Rinder)*
1971   *A Bonus for Irene (Eine Prämie für Irene)*
1972   *Does the Pill Liberate Women? (Macht die Pille frei?)*
1973   *Male Bonding (Männerbünde)*
1977   *The All Round Reduced Personality—Redupers (Die allseitige reduzierte Personlichkeit—Redupers)*
1980   *The Subjective Factor (Der subjektive Faktor)*
1984   *Love Is the Beginning of All Terrors (Der Beginn aller Schrecken ist Liebe)*
1984   *No. 1 Reports from the Surveillance Services (Nr. 1 Aus Berichten der Wach—und Patrouillendienste)*
1986   *Nr. 8 Reports from the Surveillance Services (Nr. 8 Aus Berichten der Wach—und Patrouillendienste)*
1986   *Nr. 5 Reports from the Surveillance Services (Nr. 5 Aus Berichten der Wach—und Patrouillendienste)*
1986   *Seven Women—Seven Sins (Sieben Frauen—Sieben Sünden)* (co-directed)
1987   *Felix* (co-directed)
1989   *Die Meisen von Frau S.*
1990   *The Germans and Their Men (Die Deutschen une ihre Männer)*
1991   *BeFreier und Befreite*

VOLKER SCHLÖNDORFF

1960   *Who Cares? (Wen Kümmert's)*
1966   *Young Törless (Der junge Törless)*
1967   *A Degree of Murder (Mord und Totschlag)*
1969   *Michael Kohlhaas (Michael Kohlhaas—der Rebell)*
1969   *Baal*
1970   *The Sudden Wealth of the Poor People of Kombach (Der plötzliche Reichtum der armen Leute von Kombach)*
1971   *The Morals of Ruth Halbfass (Die Moral der Ruth Halbfass)*
1972   *A Free Woman (Strohfeuer)*
1973   *Overnight Stay in the Tyrol (Übernachtung in Tirol)*
1974   *Georgina's Reasons (Georginas Gründe)*
1975   *The Lost Honor of Katharina Blum (Die verlorene Ehre der Katharina Blum)*
1976   *Coup de Grâce (Der Fangschuss)*
1977   *Just for Fun, Just for Play (Nur zum Spass—Nur zum Spiel. Kaleidoskop Valeska Gert)*
1978   contribution to *Germany in Autumn (Deutschland im Herbst)*
— 1979   *The Tin Drum (Die Blechtrommel)*
1981   *Circle of Deceit*
1983   *War and Peace (Krieg und Frieden,* co-directed with Kluge)
1983   *Swann in Love (Un amour de Swann/Eine Liebe von Swann)*
1985   *Death of a Salesman*
1989   *The Handmaid's Tale*
1990   *Voyager*

WERNER SCHROETER

1967   *Verona*
1968   *Callas Walking Lucia*
1968   *Callas Text mit Doppelbeleuchtung*
1968   *Maria Callas Porträt*
1968   *Mona Lisa*
1968   *Maria Callas singt 1957 Rezitativ und Arie der Elvira aus Ernani 1844 von Giuseppe Verdi*
1968   *Übungen mit Darstellern*
1968   *La morte d'Isotta*
1968   *Himmel Hoch*
1968   *Paula—"je reviens"*
1968   *Grotesk—Burlesk—Pittoresk* (co-directed with Rosa von Praunheim)
1968   *Faces*
1968   *Agressionen*
1968   *Neurasia*
1968   *Argila*
1968   *Virgin's Death*
1969   *Eika Katappa*
1969   *Nicaragua*
1970   *Bomber Pilot (Der Bomber-pilot)*
1970   *Anglia*
1971   *Salome*
1971   *Macbeth*
1971   *Funkausstellung 1971—Hitparade*
1972   *The Death of Maria Malibran (Der Tod der Maria Malibran)*

1973   *Willow Springs*
1974   *The Black Angel (Der Schwarze Engel)*
1975   *Johannas Traum*
1976   *Goldflakes (Flocons d'or/Goldflocken)*
1978   *Kingdom of Naples (Regno di Napoli/Neapolitanische Geschwister)*
1980   *Palermo or Wolfsburg (Palermo oder Wolfsburg)*
1980   *White Journey (Weisse Reisse)*
1980   *Dress Rehearsal (Die Generalprobe/La repetition generale)*
1982   *Day of Idiots (Der Tag der Idioten)*
1982   *Lovers' Council (Das Liebeskonzil)*
1983   *The Smiling Star (Der lachende Stern)*
1983–85 *About Argentina (De l'Argentina)*
1985   *Rose King (Der Rosenkönig)*
1985   *A la Recherche du Soleil*
1991   *Malina*

HANS-JÜRGEN SYBERBERG

1965   *Act Five, Scene Seven. Fritz Kortner Rehearses Kabale und Liebe (Fünfter Akt, Siebte Szene, Fritz Kortner probt Kabale und Liebe)*
1965   *Romy, Anatomy of a Face (Romy, Anatomie eines Gesichts)*
1966   *Fritz Kortner Recites Monologues for a Record (Fritz Kortner spricht Monologe für eine Schallplatte)*
1966   *Wilhelm von Kobell*
1967   *The Counts of Pocci—Some Chapters toward the History of a Family (Die grafen Pocci—Einige Kapitel zur Geschichte einer Familie)*
1968   *Scarabea—How Much Land Does a Man Need? (Scarabea—Wieviel Erde braucht der Mensch?)*
1969   *Sex-Business—Made in Pasing*
1970   *San Domingo*
1970   *After My Last Move (Nach meinem letzten Umzug)*
1972   *Ludwig—Requiem for a Virgin King (Ludwig—Requiem für einen jungfräulichen König)*
1972   *Ludwig's Cook (Theodor Hierneis oder: Wie man ehem. Hofkoch wird)*
1974   *Karl May*
1975   *The Confessions of Winifred Wagner (Winifred Wagner und die Geschichte des Hauses Wahnfried von 1914–1975)*
1977   *Hitler, A Film from Germany (Hitler, ein Film aus Deutschland)*
1982   *Parsifal*
1985   *The Night (Die Nacht)*
1985   *Edith Clever Reads Joyce*
1986   *Fräulein Else*
1987   *Penthesilea*
1990   *Die Marquise von O.*

WIM WENDERS

1967   *Scenes (Schauplätze)*
1967   *Same Player Shoots Again*
1968   *Silver City*
1968   *Victor I*
1969   *Alabama—2000 Light Years*
1969   *3 American LPs (3 Amerikanische LPs)*
1970   *Police Film (Polizeifilm)*

1970	*Summer in the City*
1971	*The Goalie's Anxiety at the Penalty Kick (Die Angst des Tormanns beim Elfmeter)*
1972	*The Scarlet Letter (Der scharlachrote Buchstabe)*
1973	*Alice in the Cities (Alice in den Städten)*
1974	*From the Family of the Crocodilia (Aus der Familie der Panzerechsen)*
1974	*The Island (Die Insel)*
1974	*Wrong Move (Falsche Bewegung)*
1976	*Kings of the Road (Im Lauf der Zeit)*
1977	*The American Friend (Der amerikanische Freund)*
1981	*Lightning over Water*
1981	*Reverse Angle*
1982	*Hammett*
1982	*The State of Things*
1982	*Reverse Angle*
1982	*Chambre 666*
1984	*Paris, Texas*
1985	*Tokyo-Ga*
1987	*Wings of Desire (Himmel über Berlin)*
1989	*Carnet de notes sur vêtements et villes*
1991	*Till the End of the World*

Bibliography

This is a partial and selected bibliography. Numerous reviews and articles have naturally appeared since the arrival of the New German Cinema, and in most cases these have not been included except when the essay has special importance to my study here. Journals which have devoted single issues to contemporary German cinema are listed here: *New German Critique* (24–25 [1981–82]), *Quarterly Review of Film Studies* (5, 2 [1980]), *Wide Angle* (3, 4 [1980]), and *Literature/Film Quarterly* (7, 3 [1979]). Each can be consulted for more extensive references.

Adler, Walter. "Wenders en Californie." *Cahiers du Cinéma*, 301 (June 1979), 54–64.
Adorno, T. W. *Negative Dialectics*. Trans. E. B. Ashton. London: Routledge and Kegan Paul, 1973.
Althusser, Louis. *Positions*. Paris: Editions Sociales, 1976.
_____. *Lire Le Capital*. Paris: Maspero, 1965.
Altman, Rick (ed.). *Cinema/Sound*. Yale French Studies, no. 60.
Amacher, Richard E., and Victor Lange (eds.). *New Perspectives in German Literary Criticism*. Princeton: Princeton University Press, 1979.
Arnheim, Rudolf. *Film as Art*. Berkeley: University of California Press, 1957.
_____. *Art and Visual Perception*. Berkeley: University of California Press, 1967.
Aronowitz, Stanley. "Film—The Art Form of Late Capitalism." *Social Text*, 1 (Winter 1979), 110–129.
Bachmann, Gideon. "The Man on the Volcano: A Portrait of Werner Herzog." *Film Quarterly*, 31 (Fall 1977), 2–10.
Bailbé, Claude, Michel Marie, and Marie-Claire Ropars. *Muriel*. Paris: Galilee, 1974.
Bakhtin, M. M. *The Dialogic Imagination*. Ed. Michael Holquist. Austin: University of Texas Press, 1981.
Balázs, Béla. *Theory of the Film: Character and Growth of a New Art*. Trans. Edith Bone. New York: Dover, 1970.
Barthes, Roland. *Writing Degree Zero and Elements of Semiology*. Trans. Annette Lavers and Colin Smith. Boston: Beacon Press, 1970.
_____. *S/Z*. Trans. Richard Miller. New York: Hill and Wang, 1974.
_____. *The Pleasure of the Text*. Trans. Richard Miller. New York: Hill and Wang, 1975.
_____. *Image-Music-Text*. Trans. Stephen Heath. New York: Hill and Wang, 1977. ⟶
Baudrillard, Jean. *Pour une critique de l'économie politique du signe*. Paris: Gallimard, 1972.
_____. *The Mirror of Production*. Trans. Mark Poster. St. Louis: Telos, 1975.
Baudry, Jean-Louis. "Ideological Effects of the Basic Cinematographic Apparatus." *Film Quarterly*, 28 (Winter 1974–75), 39–47.
_____. "The Apparatus." *Camera Obscura*, 2 (1977), 97–125.
_____. *L'effet cinéma*. Paris: Albatros, 1978.
Bazin, Andre. *What Is Cinema?* Trans. Hugh Gray. 2 vols. Berkeley: University of California Press, 1967, 1971.
_____. *Orson Welles*. Trans. Jonathan Rosenbaum. New York: Harper and Row, 1978.
Bellour, Raymond. "The Obvious and the Code." *Screen*, 15, 4 (Winter 1974–75), 7–17.
_____. "The Unattainable Text." *Screen*, 16, 3 (Autumn 1975), 19–27.
_____. "To Analyze, to Segment." *Quarterly Review of Film Studies*, 1, 3 (August 1976), 331–354.
_____, Thierry Kuntzel, and Christian Metz (eds.). "Psychanalyse et cinéma." *Communications 23*. Paris: Seuil, 1975.
Benjamin, Walter. *Illuminations*. Trans. Harry Zohn. New York: Schocken, 1969.

Berger, John. *Ways of Seeing*. London: Penguin, 1977.

Bergouignan, Dominique, and Laurence Gavron. "Le cinéma d'auteur." *Cahiers du Cinéma*, 308 (February 1980).

Blumenberg, Hans C. "Kampf mit der Welt. Handke verfilmt Handke." *Die Zeit*, 4 November 1977.

———. "Von Caligari bis Coppola: Junge deutsche Filmemacher in Hollywood auf den Spuren von Lubitsch, Murnau und Lang." *Die Zeit*, 22 February 1980.

Booth, Wayne. *The Rhetoric of Irony*. Chicago: University of Chicago Press, 1976.

Bordwell, David, and Kristin Thompson. *Film Art: An Introduction*. Reading, Mass.: Addison-Wesley, 1979.

Brecht, Bertolt. *On Theatre*. Trans. John Willet. New York: Hill and Wang, 1964.

———. "Against George Lukács." *New Left Review*, 84 (March/April 1974).

Bronnen, Barbara, and Corinna Brocher. *Die Filmemacher: Zur neuen deutschen Production nach Oberhausen 1962*. Munich: Bertelsmann, 1973.

Burch, Noël. *To the Distant Observer: Form and Meaning in the Japanese Cinema*. Berkeley and Los Angeles: University of California Press, 1979.

———. *Theory of Film Practice*. Princeton: Princeton University Press, 1981.

Cahiers du Cinéma. Syberberg. Hors-Serie, February 1980.

Canby, Vincent. "The German Renaissance—No Room for Laughter or Love." *New York Times*, 11 December 1977.

Cavell, Stanley. *The World Viewed: Reflections on the Ontology of Film*. Cambridge: Harvard University Press, 1979.

Chomsky, Noam. *Language and Mind*. New York: Harcourt Brace, 1968.

Clarke, Gerald. "Seeking Planets That Do Not Exist: The New German Cinema Is the Liveliest in Europe." *Time*, 20 March 1978.

Clement, Catherine. "Le rire de Déméter." *Critique*, 323 (April 1974), 306–325.

———. *Opera, or the Undoing of Women*. Trans. Betsy Wing. Minneapolis: University of Minnesota Press, 1988.

Cohn, Lawrence. "Gray City Films as Wim Wenders' N.Y. Distrib and Production Base." *Variety*, 30 (September 1981).

Comoli, Jean-Louis, and François Gere. "La réal-fiction du pouvoir." *Cahiers du Cinéma*, 292 (September 1978), 24–29.

Cook, David A. *A History of Narrative Film*. New York: W. W. Norton and Co., 1981.

Corrigan, Timothy. "Werner Schroeter's Operatic Cinema." *Discourse*, 3 (Summer 1981), 46–59.

Cott, Jonathan. "Signs of Life." *Rolling Stone*, 18 November 1976, 50.

Courant, Gerard. *Werner Schroeter*. Paris: Goethe Institut, 1982.

Covino, Michael. "Wim Wenders: A Worldwide Homesickness." *Film Quarterly*, 31 (Winter 1977–78), 9–19.

Coward, Rosalind, and John Ellis. *Language and Materialism: Developments in Semiology and the Theory of the Subject*. London: Routledge and Kegan Paul, 1977.

Daney, Serge. "L'état-Syberberg." *Cahiers du Cinéma*, 292 (September 1978), 5–7.

———. "Schroeter et Naples." *Cahiers du Cinéma*, 307 (January 1980), 28–30.

Daney, Serge, Yann Lardeau, and Bernard Sobel. "Entrétien avec Hans-Jürgen Syberberg." *Cahiers du Cinéma*, 292 (September 1978).

Dawson, Jan. *Wim Wenders*. New York: Zoetrope, 1976.

———. "The Industry: German Weasels (Filmverlag Follies)." *Film Comment*, 13, 3 (May/June 1977), 33–34.

———. "Filming Highsmith." *Sight and Sound*, 47, 1 (Winter 1977–78), 30–36.

———. "A Labyrinth of Subsidies: The Origins of the New German Cinema." *Sight and Sound*, 50, 1 (Winter 1980–81), 14–20.

———(ed.). *The Films of Hellmuth Costard*. London: Riverside Studios, 1979.

Dayan, Daniel. "The Tutor—Code of Classical Cinema." *Film Quarterly*, 28 (Fall 1975), 22–31.

de Lauretis, Teresa. *Technologies of Gender: Essays on Theory, Film, and Fiction*. Bloomington: Indiana University Press, 1987.

Deleuze, Gilles, and Felix Guattari. *Anti-Oedipus*. New York: Viking, 1976.

Derrida, Jacques. *L'écriture et la difference*. Paris: Seuil, 1967.

———. *Of Grammatology*. Trans. Gayatri Spivak. Baltimore: Johns Hopkins University Press, 1974.

———. *La verité en peinture*. Paris: Flammarion, 1978.

Dost, Michael, Florian Hopf, and Alexander Kluge. *Filmwirtschaft in der BRD und in Europa: Götterdämmerung in Raten*. Munich: Hanser, 1973.

Durzak, Manfred. *Peter Handke und die deutsche Gegenwartsliteratur*. Stuttgart: Kohlhammer, 1982.

Dyer, Richard (ed.). *Gays and Films*. London: BFI, 1977.

Eagleton, Terry. *Marxism and Literary Criticism*. Berkeley and Los Angeles: University of California Press, 1976.

Eco, Umberto. "Articulations of the Cinematic Code." *Cinematics*, 1 (January 1970), 6–11.

———. *A Theory of Semiotics*. Bloomington: Indiana University Press, 1979.

Eisenschitz, Bernard. "Le cinéma allemand aujourd'hui." *Documents: Revue des Questions Allemandes*, 31 (September 1976), 81–166.

Eisenstein, Sergei. *The Film Sense*. Trans. Jay Leyda. New York: Harcourt Brace, 1947.

———. *Film Form: Essays in Film Theory*. Trans. Jay Leyda. New York: Harcourt Brace, 1949.

Eisner, Lotte. *The Haunted Screen: Expressionism in the German Cinema and the Influence of Max Reinhardt*. Trans. Roger Greaves. Berkeley: University of California Press, 1969.

———. *Fritz Lang*. Trans. Gertrud Mander and ed. David Robinson. London: Oxford University Press, 1976.

Elsaesser, Thomas. "The Cinema of Irony." *Monogram*, 5 (1974), 1–7.

———. "Primary Identification and the Historical Subject: Fassbinder and Germany." *Cine-Tracts*, 11 (Fall 1980), 43–52.

———. "Myth as the Phantasmagoria of History: H. J. Syberberg, Cinema and Representation." *New German Critique*, 24–25 (Fall/Winter 1981–82), 108–154.

———. *New German Cinema: A History*. New Brunswick: Rutgers University Press, 1989.

Fassbinder, Rainer Werner. "Fassbinder on Sirk." Trans. Thomas Elsaesser. *Film Comment*, 11, 6 (November/December 1975), 22–24.

———. "Insects in a Glass Case: Random Thoughts on the Films of Claude Chabrol." Trans. Derek Prause. *Sight and Sound*, 45, 4 (Autumn 1976), 205–206, 252.

———. "Klimmzug, Handstand, Salto mortale—sicher gestanden. Über den Filmregisseur Werner Schroeter, dem gelang, was kaum jegelingt—anläßlich seiner *Neapolitanischen Geschwister*." *Frankfurter Rundschau*, 24 February 1979.

Feldmann, Sebastian, et al. *Werner Schroeter*. Munich: Hanser, 1980.

Foucault, Michel. *The Order of Things*. New York: Random House, 1970.

———. *Language, Counter-Memory, Practice*. Trans. Donald Bouchard and Sherry Simon. Ithaca: Cornell University Press, 1977.

Freud, Sigmund. *The Basic Writings*. New York: Random House, 1938.

———. *Beyond the Pleasure Principle*. Trans. James Strachey. New York: Norton, 1961.

Furstenau, Theo. *Wandlungen im Film: Junge deutsche Production*. West Berlin: Pullach, 1970.

Gadamer, Hans-Georg. *Truth and Method*. Trans. Sheed and Ward. New York: Seabury Press, 1975.

Gilliatt, Penelope. "Gold." *New Yorker*, 11 April 1977, 127–128.

Gmur, Leonhard (ed.). *Der junge deutsche Film*. Munich: Constatin, 1967.

Gombrich, E. H. *Art and Illusion: A Study in the Psychology of Pictorial Representation*. Princeton: Princeton University Press, 1961.

Gregor, Ulrich. *Geschichte des Films ab 1960*. Munich: Hanser, 1978.

———, et al. *Herzog/Kluge/Straub*. Munich: Hanser, 1976.

Halliday, Jon. *Sirk on Sirk*. New York: Viking, 1972.

Hansen, Miriam. "Cooperative Auteur Cinema and Oppositional Public Sphere: Alexander Kluge's Contribution to *Germany in Autumn*" *New German Critique*, 24/25 (Fall/Winter 1981–82), 36–56.

———. "Alexander Kluge: Crossing between Film, Literature, Critical Theory." The Thirteenth Amherst Colloquium on German Literature. In *Film und Literatur*. Bern: Francke, 1982.

———. "Frauen und Film and Feminist Film Culture in West Germany." *Heresies*, 16 (1983).

———(ed.). "Special Issue on Alexander Kluge." *New German Critique*, 49 (Winter 1990).

Heath, Stephen. "Narrative Space." *Screen*, 17, 3 (Autumn 1976), 68–112.

———. "Difference." *Screen*, 19, 3 (Autumn 1978), 51–112.

———. *Questions of Cinema*. Bloomington: Indiana University Press, 1981.

Henderson, Brian. *A Critique of Film Theory*. New York: E. P. Dutton, 1980.

Holloway, Ronald. "A German Breakthrough?" *Kino: German Film*, 1 (October 1979), 4–17.

Horak, Jan-Christopher. "Werner Herzog's Ecran Absurde." *Literature/Film Quarterly*, 7, 3 (1979), 223–234.

Indiana, Gary. "Scattered Pictures." *Artform* (March 1982), 46–51.

Jaehne, Karen. "The American Fiend." *Sight and Sound*, 47, 2 (Spring 1978), 101–103.

Jameson, Fredric. *Marxism and Form: Twentieth-Century Dialectical Theories of Literature*. Princeton: Princeton University Press, 1971.

———. *The Prison House of Language*. Princeton: Princeton University Press, 1972.

Jansen, Peter W., and Wolfram Schutte (eds.). *Herzog/Kluge/Straub*. Munich: Hanser, 1976.

———. *Rainer Werner Fassbinder*. Munich: Hanser, 1976.

———(eds.). *Film in der DDR*. Munich: Hanser, 1977.

Jauss, Hans Robert. *Literaturgeschichte als Provokation*. Frankfurt: Suhrkamp, 1970.

———. "Literary History as a Challenge to Literary Theory." In Ralph Cohen (ed.), *New Directions in Literary History*. Baltimore: Johns Hopkins University Press, 1974.

———. "Interview/Hans R. Jauss." *Diacritics*, 4 (Spring 1975), 53–61.

———. *Toward an Aesthetic of Reception*. Trans. Timothy Bahti. Minneapolis: University of Minnesota Press, 1982.

Johnston, Sheila. "The Author as Public Institution: The 'New' Cinema in the Federal Republic of Germany." *Screen Education*, 32/33 (Winter 1979–80), 67–78.

Kaes, Anton. *From Hitler to Heimat: The Return of History as Film*. Cambridge: Harvard University Press, 1989.

Kawin, Bruce. *Telling It Again and Again: Repetition in Literature and Film*. Ithaca: Cornell University Press, 1972.

———. *Mindscreen: Bergman, Godard, and First-Person Film*. Princeton: Princeton University Press, 1978.

Klinkowitz, Jerome, and James Knowlton. *Peter Handke and the Postmodern Transformation: The Goalie's Journey Home*. Columbia: University of Missouri Press, 1983.

Kluge, Alexander. *Lernprozesse mit todlichem Ausgang*. Frankfurt: Suhrkamp, 1973.

———. *Gelegenheitsarbeit einer Sklavin: Zur realistischen Methode*. Frankfurt: Suhrkamp, 1975.

———, and Oskar Negt. *Öffentlichkeit und Erfahrung: Zur Organisationsanalyse von bürgerlicher und proletarischer Öffentlichkeit*. Frankfurt: Suhrkamp, 1972.

Knight, Julia. *Women and the New German Cinema*. London: Verso, 1992.

Koch, Gertrud. "Was ist und wozu wir eine feministische filmkritik?" *Frauen und Film*, 11 (March 1977), 3–15.

Kolker, Robert Phillip. *The Altering Eye: Contemporary International Cinema*. New York: Oxford University Press, 1983.

Kracauer, Siegfried. *From Caligari to Hitler: A Psychological History of German Film*. Princeton: Princeton University Press, 1947.

_____. *Theory of Film: The Redemption of Physical Reality*. New York: Oxford University Press, 1960.
Kristeva, Julia. *Semiotikè: Recherches pour une sémanalyse*. Paris: Seuil, 1969.
_____. "The Semiotic Activity." *Signs of the Times*. Cambridge: Granta, 1971.
Kuleshov, Lev. *Kuleshov on Film*. Trans. and ed. Ronald Levaco. Berkeley: University of California Press, 1974.
Kuntzel, Thierry. "Le Défilement: A View in Close Up." *Camera Obscura*, 2 (1977), 51–65.
Lacan, Jacques. *Ecrits*. Paris: Seuil, 1966.
_____. *Le séminar: Les quatre concepts fondamentaux de la psychanalyse*. Paris: Seuil, 1973.
_____. *Le Seminaire livre XI*. Paris: Seuil, 1973.
Lardeau, Yann. "L'art du deuil." *Cahiers du Cinéma*, 292 (September 1978), 15–23.
Leiser, Erwin. *Nazi Cinema*. New York: Macmillan, 1975.
Lenssen, Claudia. "Die linkshändige Frau." *Frauen und Film*, 14 (December 1977), 42–44.
Lévi-Strauss, Claude. *L'homme nu*. Paris: Plon, 1971.
Lewandowsky, Rainer. *Die Filme von Alexander Kluge*. Hildesheim, N.Y.: Olms Presse, 1980.
_____. *Alexander Kluge*. Munich: C. H. Beck/Verlag Textkritik, 1980.
Liebman, Stuart (ed.). "Alexander Kluge: Theoretical Writings, Stories, and an Interview." *October* (special issue), 46 (Fall 1988).
Linville, Susan, and Kent Casper. "Reclaiming the Self: Handke's the Left-Handed Woman." *Literature/Film Quarterly*, 12, 1 (1984), 13–21.
Literature/Film Quarterly, 7, 3 (1979). Ed. Charles Eidsvik. (Special Issue: New German Cinema.)
Lloyd, Peter. "Objectivity as Irony: Werner Herzog's *Fata Morgana*." *Monogram*, 5 (1974), 8–9.
Lotman, Jurij. *Semiotics of Cinema*. Trans. Mark E. Suino. Ann Arbor: University of Michigan, 1976.
Lukács, George. *The Historical Novel*. London: Merlin Press, 1962.
Lyotard, Jean-François. *Des dispositifs pulsionnels*. Paris: 10/18, 1973.
Macbean, James Roy. *Film and Revolution*. Bloomington: Indiana University Press, 1975.
McCormick, Richard W. *Politics of the Self: Feminism and the Postmodern in West German Literature and Film*. Princeton: Princeton University Press, 1991.
McCormick, Ruth (trans. and ed.). *Fassbinder*. New York: Tanam, 1981.
Manvell, Roger, and Heinrich Fraenkel. *The German Cinema*. New York: Praeger, 1971.
Mayne, Judith. "Fassbinder and Spectatorship." *New German Critique*, 12 (Fall 1977), pp. 61–74.
_____. "Female Narration, Women's Cinema: Helke Sander's *The All-Round Reduced Personality/Redupers*." *New German Critique*, 24–25 (Fall/Winter 1981–82), 155–171.
Merleau-Ponty, Maurice. *Sense and Non-sense*. Trans. Hubert and Patricia Dreyfus. Evanston: Northwestern University Press, 1964.
Metz, Christian. *Langage et cinéma*. Paris: Larousse, 1971.
_____. *Essais sur la signification au cinéma*. 2 vols. Paris: Klincksieck, 1975, 1976.
_____. "On the Notion of Cinematographic Language." *Movies and Methods*. Ed. Bill Nichols. Berkeley: University of California Press, 1976.
_____. *Le signifiant imaginaire*. Paris: 10/18, 1977.
Meyn, Hermann. *Massenmedien in der Bundersrepublik Deutschland*. West Berlin, 1974.
Milne, Tom (trans. and ed.). *Godard on Godard*. New York: Viking, 1972.
Monaco, James. *The New Wave*. New York: Oxford University Press, 1976.
_____. *How to Read a Film*. New York: Oxford University Press, 1977.
Müller-Scherz, Fritz, and Wim Wenders. *Im Lauf der Zeit*. Munich: Filmverlag der Autoren, 1976.
Mulvey, Laura. "Visual Pleasure and Narrative Cinema." *Screen*, 16, 3 (Autumn 1975), 6–18.

Munsterberg, Hugo. *The Film: A Psychological Study.* New York: Dover, 1970.
Narboni, Jean. "Traquenards." *Cahiers du Cinéma,* 282 (November 1977), 26–29.
Nash, Mark. *Dreyer.* London: BFI, 1977.
New German Critique, 24–25 (Fall/Winter 1981–82). Ed. David Bathrick and Miriam Hansen. (Special Double Issue on New German Cinema.)
Nichols, Bill. *Ideology and the New Image.* Berkeley and Los Angeles: University of California Press, 1981.
Nogueira, Rui. *Melville.* New York: Viking, 1971.
Noquez, Dominique (ed.). *Cinéma: Théorie, lectures.* Paris: Klincksieck, 1973.
October, 21 (Summer 1982). Special issue devoted to Fassbinder.
Oudart, Jean-Pierre. "Cinema and Suture." *Screen,* 18, 4 (Winter 1977/78), 35–47.
Perlmutter, Ruth. "Visible Narrative, Visible Woman." *Millennium Film Journal,* 6 (Spring 1980), 18–30.
Pflaum, Hans Günther. *Germany on Film: Theme and Content in Cinema of the Federal Republic of Germany.* Trans. Helt Richter and Roland Richter. Detroit: Wayne State University Press, 1990.
_____(ed.). *Jahrbuch Film 78/79.* Munich/Vienna, 1977.
Pflaum, Hans Günther and Hans Helmut Prinzler. *Film in der Bundesrepublik Deutschland.* Munich: Hanser, 1979.
_____, and Rainer Werner Fassbinder. *Das bißchen Realität daß ich brauche.* Munich: DTV, 1979.
Phillips, Klaus (ed.). *New German Filmmakers: The First Generation.* New York: Ungar, 1983.
Prümm, Karl. "Das Buch nach dem Film." In *Fernsehforschung und Fernsehkritik.* Ed. Helmut Kreuzer. Göttingen: Vandenhoeck & Ruprecht, 1980, pp. 54–74.
Pütz, Peter. *Peter Handke.* Frankfurt am Main: Suhrkamp, 1982.
Quarterly Review of Film Studies, 5, 2 (Spring 1980). Ed. Eric Rentschler. (West German Film in the 1970s.)
Rayns, Tony (ed.). *Fassbinder.* London: BFI, 1976; 1979.
Rentschler, Eric. "*Deutschland im Vorherbst*: Literature Adaptation in West German Film." *Kino: German Film,* 3 (Summer 1980), 11–19.
_____. "Expanding Film Historical Discourse: Reception Theory's Use Value for Cinema Studies." *Ciné-Tracts,* 13 (Spring 1981), 57–68.
_____. "American Friends and the New German Cinema." *New German Critique,* 24–25 (Fall/Winter 1981–82), 7–35.
_____. *West German Film in the Course of Time: Reflections on the Twenty Years since Oberhausen.* South Salem, N.Y.: Redgrave, 1983.
_____. *West German Film in the Course of Time.* Bedford Hills: Redgrave, 1984.
_____(ed.). *German Film and Literature.* New York: Methuen, 1986.
_____(ed.). *West German Filmmakers on Film: Visions and Voices.* London: Holmes and Meier, 1988.
Rich, B. Ruby. "Concentrated Camp." *Chicago Reader* (14 March 1980), 12, 44–45.
_____. "She Says, He Says: The Power of the Narrator in Modernist Film Politics." *Discourse,* 6 (1983), 31–46.
Roeber, Georg, and Gerhard Jacoby. *Handbuch der filmwirtschaftlichen Medienbereiche.* West Berlin: Pullach, 1973.
Rothman, William. *Hitchcock—The Murderous Gaze.* Cambridge: Harvard University Press, 1982.
Roud, Richard. *Straub.* New York: Viking, 1972.
Rutschky, Michael. *Erfahrungshunger: Ein Essay über die siebziger Jahre.* Frankfurt: Fischer, 1982.
Safouan, Moustapha. *Sexualité féminine.* Paris: Seuil, 1976.
Sandford, John. *The New German Cinema.* Totowa: Barnes and Noble, 1980.
Schefer, Jean Louis. *Scénographie d'un tableau.* Paris: Seuil, 1969.

_____. *L'espèce de chose melancolie*. Paris: Flammarion, 1978.

Schlöndorff, Volker. *"Die Blechtrommel": Tagebuch einer Verfilmung*. Darmstadt/Neuwied: Luchter Hand, 1979.

_____. "A Parisian-American in Paris." *Village Voice*, 6 July 1982.

Schroeter, Werner. "Propos Rompus." *Cahiers du Cinéma*, 307 (January 1980), 30–31.

Segers, Rien T. "An Interview with Hans Robert Jauss." *New Literary History*, 11 (Winter 1979), 86–87.

Semiotexte: The German Issue, 4, 2 (1982). Ed. Sylvere Lotringer.

Silberman, Marc. "Cine-Feminists in West Berlin." *Quarterly Review of Film Studies* (Spring 1980), 217–232.

Silverman, Kaja. "Helke Sander and the Will to Change." *Discourse*, 6 (Fall 1983), 10–30. →

Sollers, Philippe. *L'écriture et l'experience des limites*. Paris: Seuil, 1968.

Sontag, Susan. *Against Interpretation*. New York: Dell, 1961.

_____. *On Photography*. New York: Delta, 1978.

_____. "Eye of the Storm." *New York Review of Books*, 21 February 1980.

Steiner, George. *In Bluebeard's Castle*. New Haven: Yale University Press, 1970.

Strick, Philip. "The Left-Handed Woman." *Sight & Sound* 48, 3 (Summer 1979), 195.

Syberberg, Hans-Jürgen. *Syberbergs Filmbuch*. Munich: Nymphenburger, 1976.

_____. *Hitler, Ein Film aus Deutschland*. Reinbek bei Hamburg: Rowohlt, 1978.

_____. *Hitler, A Film from Germany*. Trans. Joachim Neugroschel. New York: Farrar, Straus and Giroux, 1982.

Thompson, Kristin. *Eisenstein's Ivan the Terrible*. Princeton: Princeton University Press, 1981.

Thomsen, Christian Braad. *I Fassbinders Spejl*. Copenhagen: Fremads Fokusbøger, 1975.

Thomson, David. *America in the Dark: The Impact of Hollywood on American Culture*. New York: William Morrow, 1977.

Trinh, T. Minh-Ha. *When the Moon Waxes Red: Representation, Gender and Cultural Politics*. New York: Routledge, 1991.

Truffaut, François, and Helen Scott. *Hitchcock*. New York: Simon and Schuster, 1966.

Vogel, Amos. "A Nation Comes Out of Shell-Shock." *Village Voice*, 4 May 1972.

_____. *Film as a Subversive Art*. New York: Random House, 1974.

Walsh, Gene (ed.). *"Images at the Horizon."* Chicago: Facets Multimedia, 1979.

Wassermann, Jacob. *Caspar Hauser: The Enigma of a Century*. Trans. Caroline Newton. New York: Liveright, 1928. → ?

Weinberg, Herman. *Saint Cinema*. New York: Dover, 1973.

Wenders, Wim. *"That's Entertainment: Hitler*, A Polemic against J. C. Fest's Film *Hitler—A Career."* Die Zeit, 8 May 1977.

Wide Angle, 3, 4 (1980). Ed. Peter Lehman. (New German Cinema.)

Williams, Linda. "Film Body: An Implantation of Perversion." *Ciné-Tracts*, 12 (Winter 1981), 19–36.

_____. "Film Bodies: Gender, Genre, and Excess." *Film Quarterly* 44, 4 (Summer 1991).

Wolf, Christa. *The Reader and the Writer*. Trans. Joan Becker. New York: International, 1977.

Wollen, Peter. *Signs and Meaning in the Cinema*. Bloomington: Indiana University Press, 1972.

Young, Vernon. "Werner Herzog and Contemporary German Cinema." *Hudson Review*, 30, 3 (1977), 409–414. ↳ ?

Youngblood, Gene. *Expanded Cinema*. New York: Dutton, 1970.

Yourcenar, Marguerite. *Coup de Grâce*. New York: Farrar, Straus and Giroux, 1957.

Zipes, Jack. "The Political Dimensions of *The Lost Honor of Katharina Blum*." *New German Critique*, 12 (Fall 1977), 75–84.

Index

Achternbusch, Herbert, 187
Adler, Walter, 194n.5
Aguirre, The Wrath of God, 129, 131, 139
Akerman, Chantal, 49, 79
Aldon, Percy, 185
Alemann, Claudia, 112
Alice in the Cities, 20, 28
The All Round Reduced Personality—Redupers,
    111–24
Althusser, Louis, 104
Altman, Robert, 171
Amacher, Richard, and Victor Lange, 194n.20
The American Friend, 4–8, 17
Antigone, 14–15, 56–57, 76
Antonioni, Michelangelo, 86
Aronowitz, Stanley, 195n.13
Artists under the Big Top, 94
Ashby, Hal, 131
Astaire, Fred, 157
Augstein, Rudolf, xvi, 3
Autorenkino, 90, 113

Bagdad Cafe, 185
Bakhtin, M. M., 127
Balázs, Béla, 55
Ballhaus, Michael, 35, 185
Barthes, Roland, 64
Baudrillard, Jean, 68
Baudry, Jean-Louis, 12, 48, 202n.12
Bavarian cottage industry, 2
Bazin, André, 72
Being There, 131
Bellour, Raymond, 194n.24
Benjamin, Walter, 34, 181
Bergman, Ingmar, 79
Bergouignan, Dominique, and Laurence Gavron,
    199n.1
Berlin Alexanderplatz, 35, 87
Bertolucci, Bernardo, 173
Beware of a Holy Whore, 41, 171
The Big Sleep, 66
Bitburg, xvii
The Bitter Tears of Petra von Kant, 34–52, 60,
    72, 120–21, 172
Blake, William, 161
Blumenberg, Hans C., 198n.2
Böll, Heinrich, 14–15, 76
Bomber Pilot, 179
Booth, Wayne, 201n.14
Das Boot, 185, 204n.3
Bordwell, David, and Kristin Thompson,
    198n.25
Brauner, Arthur, 89
Brechtian aesthetics, 35, 59, 89, 149, 152, 164,
    181, 196n.10

Bresson, Robert, 86–87
Broadway Melody, 157
Brückner, Jutta, 113
Bundesvereinigung des deutschen Films, 189
Burch, Noël, 80–81

Callas, Maria, 171
Cant, Bob, 196n.2
Carmen, 180
Cavell, Stanley, 59–60, 65
Chaplin, Charlie, 164
Chinese Roulette, 42
The Chronicle of Current Events, 76
Circle of Deceit, 58
Citizen Kane, 48, 159, 167
Clement, Catherine, 164
Cloos, Hans-Peter, 188
Cocteau, Jean, 76
Cohn, Walter, 194n.5
Cold war policy, 2–4
Collins, Richard, and Vincent Porter, 195n.34
Coppola, Francis, 151
Corman, Roger, 131
Costard, Hellmuth, 51–52, 108, 189
Coup de Grâce, 55–73, 94, 105, 138
Courant, Gerald, 204n.3
Covino, Michael, 8, 194n.9
Coward, Rosalind, and John Ellis, 46

Daney, Serge, 150, 176
Dawson, Jan, 4, 193n.2
Dayan, Daniel, 195n.29, 197n.22
The Death of Maria Malibran, 169, 170, 182
Deleuze, Gilles, and Felix Guattari, 11
Donner, Wolf, 196n.2
Dore O., 112
Dürer, Albrecht, 161
Dyer, Richard, 34, 196n.2

Eco, Umberto, 194n.24
Edison, Thomas, 159, 167
Effi Briest, 87
Eika Katappa, 172
Eisner, Lotte, 129
Eisenschitz, Bernard, 194n.3
Eisenstein, Sergei, 76, 103
Elsaesser, Thomas, xvi, 12, 33, 113, 122–23,
    189, 193n.9, 194n.3, 195n.31, 197n.31,
    201n.14, 202n.4
Empson, William, 204n.8
Engels, Friedrich, 89
Even Dwarfs Started Small, 132, 172
Everyman for Himself and God against All. See
    The Mystery of Kaspar Hauser
The Executioner, 123

Export, Valie, 123

Far from Vietnam, 195n.32
Fassbinder, Rainer Werner, xvii, 3, 12, 13–14,
    34–52, 55, 57, 71, 87, 92, 93, 94, 98, 108,
    147, 169, 170, 172, 183, 185, 186
Fata Morgana, 129, 130, 142
Faye, Jean-Pierre, 154
Feminism and German filmmaking, 112–13
Film about a Woman Who . . ., 123
Filmverlag der Autoren, 2, 3, 186, 187, 188
Filmwelt, 186
Fitzcarraldo, 129, 130, 136, 172, 204n.3
Flaubert, Gustave, 83
The Flying Doctors of East Africa, 129
Ford, John, 7, 19
Foucault, Michel, 48, 169, 183
Frankfurt School, 90
Frauen und Film, 112
French New Wave, 35, 90, 112
Freud, Sigmund, 22, 23, 49, 79
Friedel, Christian, 186
Fritz, Roger, 3
Fritz Kortner, 152
Fuller, Samuel, 4, 5, 7

Gegeninformation, 12
General Rehearsal, 174, 182, 183
Germany in Autumn, xv–xvii, 2, 12, 13–17, 76,
    187, 189, 190
Germany Pale Mother, 113
Gilliatt, Penelope, 193n.3
Ginsburg, Mathias, 3
The Goalie's Anxiety at the Penalty Kick, 76, 77
Godard, Jean-Luc, 34, 90, 112, 171
Goethe, Johann Wolfgang von, 19, 160
The Grand Illusion, 66
The Great Dictator, 164
The Great Ecstasy of the Sculptor Steiner, 129
Gregor, Ulrich, 199n.1
Griffith, D. W., 103, 127–28, 141, 148

Habermas, Jürgen, 193n.8
Hamman, Joachim, 187
Hammett, 185, 205n.6
Hamburg Declaration, 189, 190
Handke, Peter, 7, 19, 75–87
Hansen, Miriam, 12, 90, 193n.2, 195nn.32, 36,
    199n.1, 200n.3
Harrigan, Renny, 196n.2
Hauff, Reinhard, 187
Heart of Glass, 132, 140, 142, 143
Heath, Stephen, 34, 49–50, 51, 177, 199n.16,
    204n.9
Heidegger, Martin, 19
Herzog, Werner, xvi, 108, 127–44, 148, 149,
    150, 172, 185, 187
Highsmith, Patricia, 4
Hitchcock, Alfred, 6–7
Hitler, A Film from Germany, 147–67, 185

Holloway, Ronald, 76
Hollywood and American Cinema, xvi–xviii,
    1–2, 4, 19, 30–31, 34, 36, 56–57, 59, 91,
    108, 128–29, 130, 147–50, 151–52, 169,
    185–86, 188–89, 190–91
Holocaust, 151–52, 190
Horak, Jan-Christopher, 132
Hughs, John, and Brooks Riley, 196n.10
Hunger Years, 113
Hutcheon, Linda, 111

I Am an Inhabitant of the Ivory Tower, 84
The Indian Tomb, 89
Indiana, Gary, 176
Ingarden, Roman, 10
Invisible Adversaries, 123
I Often Think of Hawaii, 113
Iser, Wolfgang, 9–10
Italian Neo-Realism, 69

Jaehne, Karen, 194n.9
Jailbait, 45
Jameson, Fredric, 65, 202n.4
Jauss, Hans Robert, 9–12, 14, 186, 189
Johnson, Catherine, 197n.27
Johnston, Sheila, 194n.3, 195nn.1,13

Kaes, Anton, 190, 193n.9
Karl May, 150, 152–53
Kauffmann, Stanley, 79, 198n.6
Kawin, Bruce, 198n.25, 203n.36
The Kingdom of Naples, 171, 172, 173, 176
Kings of the Road, 1–2, 4, 7, 19–31, 36, 78,
    154, 166, 185
Kinski, Klaus, 129
Kluge, Alexander, xvi, xvii, 8, 9, 12, 13, 15,
    57, 59, 89–108, 111, 123, 148, 149, 169,
    180, 185, 187, 190, 193n.2, 193n.6
Kluge, Alexander, and Oskar Negt, 199n.9
Kracauer, Siegfried, 72
Kristeva, Julia, 15
Kristl, Vlado, 87, 187
Kuhn, Annette, 199n.17
Kuntzel, Thierry, 26, 203n.42
Kuratorium Deutscher Film, 3

Lacan, Jacques, 23, 49
Land of Silence and Darkness, 129
Lang, Fritz, 30, 89, 141, 157, 185
Langlois, Henri, 171
Language and Materialism, 46
Lardeau, Yann, 156, 162
The Left-Handed Woman, 75–87, 120–21
Lemke, Klaus, 3
Lenz, 132
Lévi-Strauss, Claude, 204n.58
Lewandowski, Rainer, 199n.1
Lightning over Water, 205n.6
Lili Marleen, 207
Lindsay, Vachel, 76

Literature/film crisis, 75–77
Lola, 36
Lorre, Peter, 159
The Lost Honor of Katharina Blum, 55, 57, 58, 68, 72
Lotman, Jurij, 72
Love Is the Beginning of All Terror, 114
Lubitsch, Ernst, 164, 185
Ludwig—Requiem for a Virgin King, 148, 150, 152–53, 171
Lukács, Georg, 59, 65, 73
Lukasz-Aden, Gurdrun, and Christel Strobel, 200n.3

M, 159
McCormick, Richard, 78, 193n.9, 200n. 10, 205n.16
MacNeice, Louis, 75
Madame X, 113
The Magic Flute, 201–202n.20
Malraux, André, 76
The Marriage of Maria Braun, 35, 94, 185
Mayne, Judith, 35–36, 39
Mazursky, Paul, 79
Meetings with Anna, 79
Méliès, George, 148, 159
Melville, Jean-Pierre, 58–59
Le mépris, 90
Merleau-Ponty, Maurice, 19
Metz, Christian, 1, 5–6, 9, 11, 23, 24, 28, 30, 48, 50, 154
Mikesh, Elfi, 113, 189
Moeller, Hans-Bernard, 196n.10
Mohrmann, Renate, 200n.3
Monroe, Marilyn, 175, 176
Müller, Robby, 77, 80, 185
Mulvey, Laura, 197n.31, 199n.16
The Mystery of Kaspar Hauser, 127–44
Murnau, F. W., 128, 141, 163

Narboni, Jean, 5
Nekes, Werner, 187
New York Film Festival, 171
Nibelungen, 157
1900, 173
Noever, Hans, 189
Nosferatu (Herzog), 130, 131, 132, 139, 142
Nosferatu (Murnau), 163
La notte, 86

Oberhausen manifesto, xv–xvii, 2–3, 187, 189–90
Occasional Work of a Female Slave, 89, 93, 94, 97, 108
Öffentlichkeit, 91
Olympia, 157
One Sings, the Other Doesn't, 79
The Oppression of Women is Primarily Evident in the Behavior of Women Themselves, 51
The Order of Things, 183

Oshima, Nagisa, 171
Ottinger, Ulrike, 113
Ozu, Yasujiro, 80, 87

Palermo or Wolfsburg, 172
Paris, Texas, 185
Pasolini, Pier Paolo, 48
The Patriot, 93
Perlmutter, Ruth, 199n.17
Persona, 79
Petersen, Wolfgang, 185
Pflaum, Hans Gunther, and Hans Helmut Prinzler, 194n.3
Pluta, Ekkehard, 196n.7
Praunheim, Rosa von, 171, 188, 189, 204n.2
Przygodda, Peter, 77, 79, 187
Pynchon, Thomas, 147

Rainer, Yvonne, 123
Ray, Nicholas, 4, 5, 19
Rayns, Tony, 196n.7
Reception aesthetics, 9–12
Redupers. See *The All Round Reduced Personality—Redupers*
Reitz, Edgar, 190
Renoir, Jean, 58–59, 70
Rentschler, Eric, 12, 75, 81–82, 86, 193nn.3, 9, 194n.3, 195nn.26, 31, 198n.11, 204n.2
Reuter-Christiansen, Ursula, 123
Rich, B. Ruby, 169, 200n.10
Riefensthal, Leni, 157
Ripley's Game, 4, 7
Roud, Richard, 148
Runge, Erika, 112
Rutschky, Michael, 198n.2

Safouan, Moustapha, 50
Salome (film), 169
Salome (theater), 183
Samson and Dalila, 180
Sander, Helke, 111–24
Sanders, August, 159
Sanders-Brahms, Helma, 113
Sandford, John, 193n.3, 194n.3
San Domingo, 152
Saura, Carlos, 193n.4
Schefer, Jean-Louis, 197n.22
Schelling, Friedrich Wilhelm Joseph von, 164
Schilling, Nicholas, 76
Schlöndorff, Volker, 12, 13, 14–15, 55–73, 76, 92, 93, 169, 185
Schroeter, Werner, xvi, 108, 147, 169–83, 187
The Second Awakening of Christa Klages, 113
Seitz, Franz, 187
Semiotics of Cinema, 72
Shelley, Percy Bysshe, 127
Le signifiant imaginaire, 7, 23, 24
Signs of Life, 128
Silberman, Marc, 200n.3
Silverman, Kaja, 123–24

A Simple Heart, 83
Sirk, Douglas, 8, 34, 185
Sisters, or the Balance of Happiness, 113
Snow White, 157
Sollers, Philippe, 157
Sontag, Susan, 147, 204n.55, 204n.8
La Soufrière, 129
Der Spiegel, xvi
Spils, May, 112
The State of Things, 80, 183, 205n.6
Stöckl, Ula, 112
Strangers on a Train, 7
Straub, Laurens, 3, 186, 187, 189, 191
Straub, Jean-Marie, and Danièle Hulliet, xvii, 187
Stroheim, Erich von, 159
Strongman Ferdinand, 89–108, 162
Stroszek, 128–29
The Subjective Factor, 112, 114, 123–24
Subsidies, 2–4
The Sudden Wealth of the Poor People of Kombach, 72
Syberberg, Hans-Jürgen, 59, 147–67, 171, 172, 182, 185
Syberbergs Filmbuch, 148
S/Z, 64

The Third Generation, 98
The Third Man, 98
3 American LPs, 76
Three Women, 170
Ticket of No Return, 113
The Tiger from Eschnapur, 89
The Tin Drum, 55, 58, 65, 70, 72
To Be or Not to Be, 164
Tokyo Chorus, 81
Thompson, Kristin, 204n.5
Trakl, Georg, 63

Trinh, T. Minh-Ha, xviii, 124
The Trip, 131
Till the End of the World, 185
Tristan and Isolde, 167
Trotta, Margarethe von, 58, 113
Truffaut, François, 131
2 or 3 Things I Know about Her, 112
Types, 64–67

An Unmarried Woman, 79

Varda, Agnes, 79
Veronika Voss, 35
Vraisemblable, 5–7, 9, 17, 151, 185, 186

Wagner, Richard, 164, 165
Wassermann, 201n.10
Welles, Orson, 98
Wenders, Wim, 1–2, 3, 4–9, 16–17, 19–31, 36, 55, 76, 77, 80, 83, 108, 129, 158, 166, 169, 180, 183, 185, 186, 187, 188
Wicki, Bernhard, 86–87
Wiene, Robert, 163
The Wild Child, 131
Wilhelm Meister's Apprenticeship, 76, 78
Williams, Linda, 197n.28, 204n.5
Willow Springs, 169–83
Wings of Desire, 185
Wolf, Christa, 121, 122, 123
Wrong Move, 28, 76, 78
Wyborny, Klaus, 201n.19

Yesterday Girl, 94, 95
Young Mr. Lincoln, 179
Young Törless, 72, 187
Yourcenar, Marguerite, 71, 198n.17

Zipes, Jack, 55

TIMOTHY CORRIGAN is Professor of English and Film Studies at Temple University. He is the author of *A Cinema without Walls: Movies and Culture after Vietnam* and *Writing about Film* and contributing editor of *The Films of Werner Herzog*.